Sproutman's®
KITCHEN GARDEN
Cookbook

Sproutman's®

KITCHEN
GARDEN
Cookbook

by Steve Meyerowitz

illustrated by
Michael Parman

Newly Revised and Expanded
FIFTH EDITION
Copyright ©1999 by Steve Meyerowitz
illustrated by Michael Jon Parman, micjonparm@aol.com, edited by Beth
Robbins. Original Copyrights ©1983, 1984, 1989, 1990, 1994.

Printed in the United States of America.
ISBN 1-878736-86-8 Paperback

Publisher's Cataloging-in-Publication
(provided by Quality Books, Inc.)
Meyerowitz, Steve.
Sproutman's kitchen garden cookbook : sprout breads, cookies, soups, salads
& 250 other low fat, dairy free vegetarian recipes / Steve Meyerowitz. – 5th ed.
p. cm.
Includes bibliographical references and index.
Library of Congress Catalog Card Number : 99-90518
ISBN: 1-878736-86-8

1. Cookery (Sprouts) 2. Sprouts. I. Title.

TX801.M49 1999   641.6'5
                     QBI99-900712

The *Flax Sprout Bag* is a trademark name belonging to
The Sprout House and is used with permission.

Sproutman Publications
PO Box 1100, Great Barrington, Mass. 01230
413-528-5200. Fax 413-528-5201.
http://Sproutman.com   Email: Sproutman@Sproutman.com

Distributed by
Book Publishing Company
PO Box 99, Summertown, TN 38483
888-260-8458. 931-964-3571. Fax 931-964-3518
http://bookpubco.com e-mail: bookpubl@usit.net

TABLE OF CONTENTS

Introduction

The Art Of Making Sprout Bread & Other Grain Dishes

Milk—To Drink Or Not To Drink

Recipes From The Food Dehydrator

Salads & Salad Dressings

Soup, Juice, Soda Pop, Beverages

Raw Fruit & Vegetable Juices

Homemade Natural Sodas

Snacks & Other Fun Foods

Salt Alternatives

Low Cooking

Let's Go Shopping

Glossary Of Foods

Appendix

DEDICATION

This book of food ideas, philosophy, fun and feasts is dedicated to my children Gabrielle Victoria, Ari David and Noah Alexander Meyerowitz. Godspeed to them and the other members of the first generation of the second millennium, who will soon take over the stewardship of the earth.

Steve Meyerowitz, June, 1999

Sproutman

For Best Results Recite

THE SPROUT OATH

Each Day I Will...

- ★ Stand Up Straight and Tall
- ★ Always Follow the Sun
- ★ Think Green Thoughts
- ★ Drink Plenty Of Water
- ★ Bathe At Least Twice A Day
- ★ Listen To Classical Music
- ★ Keep My Head High
- ★ Stick To My Roots
- ★ Go To Bed At Dusk
- ★ Serve And Be Served
- ★ Be Sproutful And Multiply

A Good Sprout Is...

Loyal

   Friendly

      Courteous

         Kind

           Trustworthy

              Obedient

                Helpful

                  Clean

                    Brave

Be Good To Your Sprouts

AND THEY WILL BE TRUE TO YOU!

INTRODUCTORY RECIPE
Daily Recipe for Entering

The 21st Century

Ingredients

1 cup	Fresh squeezed juice in morning
3 deep	Breaths, fresh air
1 eyeful	Sunshine
5 minutes	Exercise, stirred
1	Massage, kneaded
1 large	Bath or swim, dipped
1 scoop	Gratitude, plain
1 slice	Funny story, to taste
1 raw	Good Deed Daily
1	Blessing before meals
1 tsp	Meditation
1 pinch	Prayer
1 dose	Freedom for all living things, spread
1 concentrated	Visualization of your dreams come true

Recipe For A Hug

Ingredients

2 people   a touch of love
4 arms   a pinch of humor
2 hearts   a spoonful of glee

Clear your mind. Extend arms and wrap around other person. Take a good look, then pull together and mix well. Serves two.

INTRODUCTION

Do We Eat to Live or Live to Eat?

The secret to healing ourselves is to tap into the inherent wisdom of the body. One of the best ways to do this is to manage what we put inside it.

Some years ago, one of this nation's largest chemical corporations created an advertising campaign for the purpose of promoting a positive public image about manufactured chemicals. The slogan of the day was: *"Better Living Through Chemistry."* Today, that same promotion would not work because so much of our government's time, taxpayer money and awareness is focused on the job of removing toxic chemicals that are harming our health and environment. Part of this chemical "pollution" involves food.

In the post World War II era, chemistry was seen as a way to improve our food—its shelf-life, appearance, taste and color. Ways were found to use chemicals on the farm to eliminate natural predators, speed growth and enlarge size. In the years since, we have come to accept as "normal" the presence of such chemicals as pesticides, preservatives, artificial colors and flavors, synthetic sweeteners and hormones in our food. In fact, it shocked us when, as a nation, we read the headlines telling us that DDT, saccharin and red dye #2 were threatening our health. Was it not their purpose to improve it, we asked? Why would it be allowed if it were not good? These and other questions were asked and a consumer revolution was launched to create responsibility among manufacturers and government to protect public health.

Because of this history, there are those of us who remain vigilant about our food quality and wholesomeness. New threats are emerging such as irradiation, bio-genetic engineering and altering the hormones of cows to produce more milk. Many simply pledge their allegiance to the status-quo. But ignorance, or more specifically, the unwillingness to educate ourselves about such basic elements as the food we eat, is a luxury that is fast becoming obsolete. Even manufacturers can no longer ignore these issues. There is an undercurrent in the mainstream food industry toward "natural" and it is a welcome trend. But they are not doing it for our health. They are responding to consumer buying trends that indicate an increase in health motivated purchases. It is our preferences and the power we wield with our wallets that is causing these changes.

A S.A.D. Diet

The "Standard American Diet" suits its acronym, S.A.D. It is synonymous with unhealthy eating habits and lifestyle. It is founded on what looks, smells and tastes good. True, our society has made great strides in identifying and measuring nutrients in foods, but it focuses exclusively on those quantities and ignores the intrinsic qualities of food including its energy or "chi" as it is known in Eastern cultures. Instead, we have turned food into a commodity. We are most concerned with its presentation and convenient availability. We freeze it, can it, preserve it, artificially flavor it, color it and otherwise separate it into parts and reassemble it in different ways to pique our interest and pry open our pocket books. Advances in technology serve mostly to improve production and distribution. We have largely ignored the multitude of ways that food influences our health. America's most popular foods are steak, hamburgers, hot dogs, chicken, poultry, cold cuts and canned tuna. We are also dairy and refined wheat addicts. We consume excessive amounts of hard cheeses like Swiss, cheddar, American, and provolone. We drink milk well beyond our ability to digest it and consume mountains of ice cream. In regard to wheat, we have taken an important grain and over indulged it. Our bodies respond to this excess with all kinds of alarms and signals: chest coughing, nose blowing, sinus dripping, palate itching, skin breaking out and pimpling. What does it take to get our attention? Allergies are the self-induced plague of civilized society. Breads, cookies, crackers, cakes, pretzels, pastries, bagels and pizza are not poison. But their ubiquitous presence and the daily intake of such low quality wheat products takes its toll. Bread companies proclaim the virtues of their brand by the number of synthetic nutrients they add. What irony that we remove natural vitamins and then seek praise for replacing them with synthetic substitutes. Breakfast cereals also make the same claim. America literally wakes up and launches the day with a cup of coffee and a bowlful of sugar and refined flour in designer shapes. Then, at dinnertime we pat ourselves on the back for eating a meatless meal in which we again consume refined flour, this time in curls, squiggles and pillows with excess salt instead of sugar. It never dawns on us that pasta, pizza, pretzels, crackers, cookies, breads and cereals are different forms of the same food.

Now for the real food. In the vegetable department, we eat tomatoes, potatoes, carrots, lettuce, green beans, cucumbers, peas, celery, corn and spinach. Unfortunately, the percentage of these vegetables in our diet relative to refined wheat, dairy products, sugar and fat is extremely low. Furthermore, many of these vegetables are consumed as canned and frozen foods. When you think about the great variety of vegetables that are available to us, this is a very limited selection. As a further insult, vegetables are considered a side-dish, not a main dish.

Dessert draws a bigger spotlight than vegetables. It is fair to say that America has a sweet tooth. We consume many refined sugar products in the form of desserts, candies, gum, soft drinks, bottled juices and sugar direct from sugar packets. With all of these refined sugars exhausting our energy quickly, it is no wonder that we take in so many stimulants such as coffee, tea, colas, chocolate, cigarettes and sweet juices. We also consume many artificial and synthetic foods like margarine, whipped toppings, coffee whiteners, MSG, saccharine and nutrasweet, and diet foods with artificial sweeteners.

When you break this all down, the typical American diet consists of 42% fat, 12% protein and 46% made up of carbohydrates of which more than half comes from sugar. So, two-thirds of our diet comes from fat and sugar. No wonder that as a nation, we suffer from obesity, exhaustion, heart disease, cancer, immune system deficiencies and other chronic diseases. What is missing? Whole grains and beans such as rice, millet, quinoa, spelt, amaranth, buckwheat, limas, peas, navy, lentils, soy and garbanzos; fresh and organic fruits and vegetables such as sea vegetables, sprouts, kale, swiss chard, collard greens, and more fresh fruits instead of fruit juice; and fresh juices such as carrot, celery, spinach and sprouts. Even fresh squeezed citrus juices such as orange and grapefruit are better than their pasteurized counterparts. We need to choose more whole foods such as rice instead of bread, and buckwheat instead of pasta.

Getting Support For Your Alternative Diet

Those of us who are choosing to eat differently have lots of challenges. Let's face it. You can't just go out to the corner restaurant and ask for a sprout and tofu sandwich. Our culture simply does not support vegetarianism or any other non-traditional diet. Our national diet is one of milk shakes, doughnuts, burgers, hot dogs, pizza, breads and cakes. If you eat vegetables, salads, grains and beans, you will have to seek out special restaurants, special food stores and special friends who understand you. Such are the challenges for those who seek to walk a different path. You will raise eyebrows amongst old friends, worry and bewilder family members and become controversial, all because you dare to be different. But you do not have a choice. What you put into your body, day in and day out, three times per day, year in and year out, will catch up with you. It is undeniable. Food is either your medicine or your poison.

Staying on a health diet in a society that does not eat like you is demanding. It forces you to make changes in your lifestyle in order to adapt. You may, for example, stay home more often in order to prepare a proper meal. When you go out, there are innumerable dietary temptations. Your will power and conviction will routinely be tested. Your old friends may intimidate or cajole you. You may be faced with the most difficult of choices: Eat junk or eat nothing. It is even harder when you are hungry! You thought you were just changing your diet but now you are faced with other challenges like will power, discipline and commitment. You need support!

Support Groups

The attraction of a diet like Macrobiotics is its built-in support. Such a diet is institutionalized and offers numerous opportunities to join with others, ask questions, share meals and discuss health issues. Macrobiotic restaurants, conventions and retreat centers exist all over. It is a microcosm—a sub-society within our larger society. It is a wonderful alternative. But if you opt to go with another alternative diet, you may be on your own. You will need to seek out like-minded friends, take classes, share dinners and maintain the strength and discipline to stick to your convictions. And you will need recipes.

Book Support

Bookstores are filled with recipe books that still recommend sugar, salt, alcohol, fried foods and other ingredients that are unacceptable to the health-minded. The recipes in this book are alternatives with which you can build a varied and healthful diet.

In addition to avoiding chemicals and all artificial ingredients, this book limits its recipes to the vegetarian world of plant foods. All the ingredients herein, originate in the soil, not in an animal. While some recipes may be described as eccentric, they are not elitist. You do not have to be a vegetarian to like them.

Many recipes use sprouted nuts, grains, beans, vegetables and seeds. This book demonstrates that sprouts not only can be salads, but can be used to make breads, soups, dressings, burgers, snacks and more. Sprouts are emphasized because they are high quality organically grown foods, rich in vitamins and enzymes that are affordable and accessible to everyone. These days, good foods, not to mention fresh organic foods, are hard to find year-round. Sprouted foods do not have a season or a geographical limitation. They are available twelve months per year, from Alaska to Florida and you don't have to have a green thumb to grow them.

Sprouts to the Rescue

Vitamin for vitamin, sprouts are a bargain. Sunflower lettuce, for example, a deep leafy green hearty sprout, costs about 35 cents per pound. What about your time? And space? The fact is, sprouts takes very little time and space. The real issue is the amount of mental energy it takes to develop and maintain an indoor garden. Like many things, it soon becomes a simple routine. It takes time and energy to own and care for a pet. It takes time and energy to own a car or care for house plants. But in each case, you get something back. In this case, it is a year round supply of high quality, low cost foods. Besides, the sprouts do all the hard work. All they ask is for a little water. When you come right down to it, it takes less time to care for your garden of sprouts than to stand on line at the supermarket.

There was a time when "health food" was thought to be boring—a pristine diet filled with vitamins, but void of flavor. Today, we can enjoy a wide selection of foods under the "health food" umbrella—ice creams, frozen yoghurts, cookies, breads, dairyless cheeses, soy burgers, tofu franks, coffee substitutes, egg substitutes, chocolate substitutes, natural sweeteners, natural sodas, even pizza—and supermarkets carry many of the popular health brands. If there is any guarantee this book can offer, it is that these dishes can be just as satisfying as conventional foods and even more so because they are truly nourishing.

This is a book of alternative recipes. Please use it as a launching pad to invent your own healthful alternatives to conventional dishes. And while you're at it, please share your ideas. We are all explorers on our personal dietary adventures. In a way, "health food" is merely a rebirth of old fashioned eating when chemicals in agriculture and modern food processing did not exist. Welcome to the club of "born again healthy eaters." Grab your sprouting seeds and head for the kitchen and don't forget to invite your friends over for the first harvest from your sproutful kitchen garden.

Bags in Bloom
Left to right: Sprouted wheat, red peas, Alaskan green peas,
baby lentils growing in Sproutman designed fabric bags
made from mold resistant flax.

The Art Of Making
SPROUT BREAD
& Other Baked Goods

What It Is And What It Isn't

Sprout bread is simply a loaf of bread made from ground up sprouts. Bread is commonly made from grains and sprout bread is made from sprouted grains. There is no flour, no salt, no yeast nor any leavening agent used in making sprout bread. In fact, basic sprout bread is made from one ingredient —Sprouts!

What Is Wrong With Regular Bread?

Flour is what is wrong with regular bread. Grain, possibly grown a thousand miles away from your home on artificially fertilized soil, is stripped of its germ and bran and then pulverized. What remains is a colorless, nutritionally void powder that is ultimately bleached white. Now it is perfectly pure—pure nothing! Since the onset of the health movement in this country, commercial bakeries and flour companies have started to provide unbleached white flour alongside the traditional bleached variety. Unfortunately, this does little for your health. There was nothing there before, now you get un-bleached nothing. The germ is removed because it contains all the live nutrients that spoil. The devitalized bread has a longer shelf life. But, at what cost? Surely there must be a better way.

PRESERVE HUMAN LIFE
NOT SHELF LIFE

Whole wheat is the whole grain berry, including the germ and bran, which is fractionated into flour. Bakers do not like whole wheat because it is coarse and difficult to work with. It contains bran and wheat germ and vitamins that detract from the purity of the gluten. Gluten is the gluey protein found in grain and abundant in wheat. Bakers love gluten because it makes bread dough stick together. The less gluten, the harder it is to shape the loaves. No other grain—not rye, oats or barley—has as much gluten as wheat. The purified flour makes the best dough. Health enthusiasts, on the other hand, prefer whole wheat because it includes the wheat germ with all its B-vitamins, essential oils and protein, and because it is naturally rich in fiber. Unfortunately, it is not a simple case of whole wheat being better than white. Whole wheat is subject to the spoilage and storage problems that the white flour industry originally set out to avoid one hundred years ago. Many diligent food store owners refrigerate the packaged whole wheat flour as soon as it arrives. This courageous effort is unfortunately futile. The germ of the wheat, with all its live protein, vitamins E, B-complex and essential fats, is most likely spoiled already. Most B-vitamins and fats are sensitive to heat, light and air. Once exposed, unprotected and left at room temperature, the germ has a brief lifetime and turns rancid in as little as 24–48 hours. Rancidity is the process whereby fatty acids deteriorate into peroxides and aldehydes. These products are known intestinal tract irritants and have been accused of causing bowel and other cancers. Fresh wheat germ, on the other hand, is sweet. Rancid wheat germ leaves an acrid aftertaste in the back of your mouth. Unfortunately, we rarely have an opportunity to taste fresh wheat germ because it is so perishable. New methods of packaging with nitrogen (in the absence of oxygen) are very exciting but more expensive and not fool proof. The most economical, efficient and nutritious way to get fresh wheat germ is from sprouted wheat.

Read Labels

If you think that buying whole wheat bread is the answer—Buyer Beware! Manufacturers frequently misrepresent whole wheat on their labels with terms such as "wheat," "wheat flour" and "unbleached wheat." They are all white flour! Even labels that read "whole wheat" frequently have "wheat flour" added. The most dependable wording would read "whole wheat flour" or even better, "Stone Ground Organic Whole Wheat Flour."

Unfortunately, the use of stone ground whole wheat is uncommon. Follow this itinerary to see why. First, the farmer harvests his wheat and grinds it into whole wheat flour on a high speed commercial mill that creates heat and friction. Then, he packages it in 50 and 100 pound bags and stores it in a warehouse. Already more than 24 hours have passed, but that is just the beginning. How long does it stay in the warehouse?—sometimes several weeks. It depends on how fast the farmer can sell his/her goods. Assuming it is sold, the flour then travels to another warehouse where it remains until purchased by grain brokers. The brokers sell it to distributors whose customers are natural food stores. How fast or slow the flour moves from point to point is anyone's guess. One thing is for certain, it is longer than 24 hours. No matter how we improve the system, it is unlikely that consumers will ever get any commercial flour product, whole wheat or white, that is "fresh."

Our grandparents did not have this problem. Their solution was to grind their own. This is the perfect solution—bread made from home-ground flour. Unfortunately, few of us have grain mills and even fewer are willing to take the time to use one. Electric mills are expensive and often create heat and friction that destroy fragile vitamins and nutrients. In addition, the art of baking bread at home is "old-fashioned" and not widespread.

Allergies

Wheat is also one of the most allergy-producing foods in our culture. This is caused, in part, by its omnipresence. Americans are becoming a race of glutenarians. Wheat and flour products make up nearly 30% of our diet. There is no grocery store in America without cookies, cakes, crackers, croutons, pretzels, pies, pastas, breads and bagels. Gluten is the primary allergic factor in wheat. It is an albuminous, elastic protein chiefly made up of gliadin and glutenin. These two components are responsible for a bread's cohesiveness. Although that is good for dough, it is bad for digestion. Undigested proteins irritate and cause allergic reactions. Gluten is so sticky that it is even a major ingredient in wall paper paste. Two glutenous grains, spelt and kamut, may be consumed by many allergically sensitive people because they are comprised of different proteins.

The Advantages of
SPROUT BREAD

Sprout bread is the answer to many of our bread problems. It is absolutely fresh, several times more nutritious than whole wheat, has old fashioned taste and texture, and is easy to make. Sprout bread requires no special skills to prepare and takes very little time. Just grow your sprouts, grind them, form a loaf and bake it. You need not knead! There is no yeasting nor rising and you do not need to buy a grain mill.

Sprout bread will not turn rancid. All the fragile vitamins and essential oils are there in perfect freshness. What could be more fresh than something that is alive? Sprouts are alive right up to the moment you grind them! There are no warehouses, distributors or middlemen. You are the grower, grinder, and of course, consumer.

Nutrition In Sprout Bread

Cancel those trips to the health food store for wheat germ and bran—it's all in the sprout bread! After only three days of sprouting, B-vitamins multiply up to 12 times (1200%) their value[7]. Riboflavin, vitamin B-2 for example, increases from 13 mg. in whole wheat bread to 54 mg. in sprout bread (per 100 grams). White bread has a riboflavin content of less than 1 mg! Wheat is also a rich source of fat soluble vitamins held within the germ. All essential fatty acids increase significantly during germination. One of these fat soluble nutrients is vitamin E. Sometimes called the "fertility vitamin," it multiplies 300% in only 3 days of sprouting[7]. What about protein? Sprouts are a protein factory. Nutritionist Dr. Jeffrey Bland tells us about sprouts and protein in his article on the *Nutrient Content of Germinating Seeds*[8].

> Sprouting leads to the synthesis of new protein from building blocks of starch, sugars and fats within the germinating seed. (Nandi)[17] has shown that seeds undergo an increase in all amino acids including the essential amino acids after germination. If, however, large amounts of dried sprouts were being used as flour, it would be possible to obtain the essential amino acid requirements solely from sprouts.

Gluten, the sticky, difficult–to–digest wheat protein, breaks down during germination. Other changes are the destruction of phytic and oxalic acids. These bind up minerals like phosphorus, calcium and zinc. Complex starches simplify into sugars producing, as a by-product, maltose, the grain sugar. Maltose gives sprout bread and sprouted grain its amazing natural sweetness. Enzyme levels elevate dramatically in the first few days of sprouting. Amylase initiates the breakdown of starches, protease the breakdown of protein, invertase of sugar and lipase of fats. This is the reason sprouts are easier to digest. You simply cannot buy bread or wheat germ as fresh or as nutritious as this. It makes one wonder how we ever survived on white bread! One thing for sure, if we keep it up, the species Glutenous Americanus is destined to turn to stone.

What about bran? No need to buy it in a bag. Sprout bread has 3–4 times the fiber of the most wholesome stone ground whole grain bread and is 400% higher in moisture. This means sprout bread does not stick around. Unlike white flour products that have little or no fiber and stick like glue to the intestinal walls, the combination of high moisture and high fiber keeps sprout bread moving through like an intestinal broom. Good housekeeping means good health!

The Amino Acid Content of Sprouts

Milligrams per 100 grams of sprouts

Amino Acid	Wheat 5th day	7th day	9th day	Oats 5th day	7th day	9th day
ARGININE	1.8	0.9	0.9	0.9	0.9	1.8
ASPARTIC ACID	1.5	2	3	2	0.5	1
GLUTAMIC ACID	0.8	0.6	0.5	0.4	0.5	1.6
LEUCINE	0.1	0.1	0.25	0.1	0.2	0.1
LYSINE	0	0	0	2	0	0
METHIONINE	0.3	0.35	0.2	0.2	0.3	0.2
THREONINE	0.2	0.4	0.2	0.45	0.3	1
TYROSINE	0	0.1	0.15	0.2	-.-	0.1
VALINE	0.7	0.07	0.06	0.07	0.07	0.07

This chart shows the protein development of wheat and oat sprouts between the fifth and ninth days of germination, in milligrams per 100 grams of sprouts [8].

Making Basic
SPROUT BREAD

Ingredients

2 cups   Hard Wheat Berries

Yield: 2 to 4 loaves

Quick Start

First, gather your ingredients. Here is a list of the things you won't need: No yeast, baking soda, baking powder, salt, leavening or flour. Here is what you will need: 2 cups of hard wheat berries—that's all! Here are the four easy steps to sprout bread ecstasy: Grow your sprouts; grind them into a paste; form a 2–3 inch round loaf and bake in an oven at 250°F. for approximately 3 hours.

Step 1   Sprouting The Wheat

First step is growing the sprouts. The best and easiest method for sprouting all grains and beans is the sprout bag. Soak your hard wheat berries in a jar for 12–15 hours, then sprout them for 2 days (48 hours). Dip the bag in water twice a day to rinse. That's it! *(See Appendix, Sprouting, p.287.)* After 2 days, examine the sprouts closely. You will see a few long, thin, white hair-like rootlets. These are the developing roots. Going in the other direction is a short, thick "shoot" that may be slightly green. This is the shoot. Ultimately, if planted, the shoot develops into a blade of grass. For the best sprout bread, the length of the shoot should be no longer than the length of the berry. This is the first critical factor in making a good sprout bread. If the shoot is too long, your bread will be chewy and sinewy and it will fall apart. If it is too short, it will be short on nutrition and too difficult to grind. Ready? Now let us grind the sprouts into dough.

THE LENGTH OF THE SHOOT, SHOULD BE
NO LONGER THAN THE LENGTH OF THE BERRY

Step 2   Grinding The Sprouts Into Dough

How do you turn sprouts into bread? Grind them up just as you would with regular wheat. Whereas regular bread grinds into flour and the flour is moistened to become dough, sprouts are already wet so once ground, you have instant sprout dough. At this point, unless you want to emulate our ancestors and grind your sprouts between two stones, the purchase of a suitable kitchen appliance (unless you have one) is necessary. There are four different kinds of kitchen equipment that will grind up your sprouts:

  a.   Food Processor
  b.   Champion Juicer
  c.   Wheatgrass Juicer
  d.   Meat Grinder

Unlike a grain mill that only makes flour, all the above appliances can be used for other chores. Food processors work very well for grinding sprouted wheat and they knead the bread at the same time. Use the stainless steel or "S" blade. Some food processors are better than others. Although they all do an equal job of making pretty slices and shapes, the real difference is in how they grind. The small model Cuisinart excels because it has a high blade-to-bowl impact ratio. Others may do equally well. When shopping, seek the models with small bowls and high rpm's. This creates tremendous force that finely decimates the grain. Meat grinders also work well.

Unfortunately, they require replacing the grain for a second cycle to achieve a smooth texture and a lot of elbow grease. They do the job if you don't mind a little sweat. Make sure to use the mincing blade —the one with small holes. Wheatgrass juicers, which squeeze juice out of full grown wheat grass blades, are similar to meat grinders in design. Their advantage is that they provide near 100% extraction of the juice without friction. They also make juice from leafy green sprouts, leafy green produce, herbs, and can make butter from nuts and seeds. But they too, require a lot of elbow grease. Of these, the ever versatile Champion juicer provides probably the smoothest grind of all. Other juicers, especially the common centrifugal type, do not work because they cannot function as grinders. The Champion is unique in that it is a multi-function appliance. Blenders do not work because they are liquifiers and need excessive water in order to function. Whatever grinder you choose, make sure the sprout "dough" is ground to a smooth—not chunky—paste. Strive for smoothness even if you have to run it through twice.

Using a Champion Juicer

This versatile machine makes vegetable juice, grates root vegetables, churns peanuts into butter and makes frozen desserts. In its "homogenizer" position, a blank door replaces the juicer screen. This is the position used for grinding peanuts and sprouted wheat. Although we can use this machine for grinding wheat sprouts, it was never designed to grind grain. The manufacturer provides a flour mill attachment for that purpose. Grinding sprouted grain, however, is different because the sprouts are moist and semi-soft. But please be careful. If you have not sufficiently soaked or sprouted your grain

(12 hours soaking and 2 days sprouting), the Champion will over-heat from the friction caused by your overly dry sprouts. Even though thousands of sprout breads have been made with the Champion, the manufacturer considers it an "unapproved" use and may void the warranty. Follow your sprouting instructions carefully. Push small amounts of sprouts down the spout, pausing until each batch has been processed before adding the next. If your Champion makes a clicking sound (overloading safety feature) and gets very hot, stop. Wet your sprouts and start again. If you see some steam, it is not electrical smoke, but the result of friction created by grinding the dry sprouts. Simply add a few tablespoons of water until they grind smoothly. It is also helpful to remove and rinse the juicing section in cold water. Always fill the juicer barrel only half way with sprouts and pump them through in two or three motions. Hold the pusher all the way down to clear the barrel. If your sprouts are not ground to a smooth paste, rerun them a second time. Grinding the grain is the greatest chore in making sprout bread. Don't get hot under the collar. Keep your juicer cool.

LET YOUR SPROUTS DRY 3–6 HOURS
BEFORE GRINDING THEM

Whatever your equipment, it is time to start grinding. First, make sure your sprouts have not been rinsed for the last 3–6 hours. Wet sprouts will run through the grinder too quickly and will not be properly ground. Excess moisture also adversely affects the bread's ability to hold its shape and stay together. Your dough will feel soft and soggy. On the other hand, if your sprouts are too dry, they will be too difficult to grind. With practice, you will learn the proper moisture level for the best bread.

THE CONSISTENCY OF THE SPROUT DOUGH
SHOULD BE THAT OF A SMOOTH PASTE

The result of your grinding is a "sprout dough." The consistency of the dough should be that of a smooth paste. This is the second critical factor in the making of sprout bread. Every grain should be fractionated into paste. If the dough is coarse or chunky it will contain little pieces of unfractionated wheat berries that give the unpleasant taste of little rocks in the finished bread. Also, coarsely ground dough does not provide as much gluten and the dough will not hold together as well.

Hard Wheat vs. Soft Wheat

Soft wheat is the softer brother of hard wheat. It is lighter in color and weight, has less protein and less gluten. Thus, it does not hold together as well. Bakers traditionally use soft wheat for pastries and hard wheat for breads. In fact, it is frequently labeled "pastry wheat." We will use it to make crackers and cookies. You also have a choice of hard wheats: Spring or Winter. The names refer to the season in which the wheat is harvested. Spring wheat has slightly more gluten than winter wheat, so it is the preferred choice for breadmaking. You could also use rye. Rye is a cousin of wheat with less gluten. Make rye bread the same way as you would make wheat.

Step 3 Making The Loaves

Wash your hands and roll up your sleeves. Here comes the fun! Sprout bread feels like nothing else you've ever stuck your hands into! It is impossible to be tense when your hands are in sprout dough. Next time you have a headache, don't take aspirin. Make sprout bread.

To knead or not to knead?—that is the question. Kneading is not mandatory for making sprout bread. If you are in a rush, just form a loaf and plop it onto the cookie sheet. However, there are advantages to kneading, and with sprout dough, it is simple to do. Take the dough and fold it into itself repeatedly. This action spreads the gluten that holds the bread together increasing the elasticity of the dough. The more you knead, the more cohesive your dough will be and the more it will rise. But don't expect too much. This bread has no yeast. The rising comes only from the enzymes present in the sprouts. While kneading, clean and wet your hands several times. If your hands get too sticky, it is hard to form a smooth looking loaf. As an alternative to water, you may use a good quality sesame oil.

Form a ball of dough about 3 inches in diameter and plop it onto a baking tray. Pad it down to a height of about 1½ inches and a diameter of 4–5 inches. You should get 2–4 patties from 2 cups of wheat.

Step 4 Baking Your Bread

Before baking, your first consideration is the type of tray. Flat pans or cookie sheets are best since sprout bread needs to get heat from all sides. Black steel is the recommended metal and can be found in good houseware or kitchen stores. Avoid using non-stick coated trays since many coatings can be scraped off and eventually consumed. Stoneware is ideal for baking, although hard to find. Avoid using aluminum pans. This soft metal can break down under certain conditions and the risk of aluminum contamination is serious.

Your next concern is to keep the bread from sticking to the pan. Here you have a few choices. The easiest and healthiest method is to use seeds such as sesame, poppy or flax. Spread your favorite seed evenly on the pan. Cornmeal or corn flour is an alternative to the seeds. These foods, though not ingredients, add texture and flavor to the bottom of the bread and, unlike oil, stand up well under high temperatures. As you know, oils can break down under heat and create compounds that are nearly impossible for the body to digest. However, if you prefer, use a couple of tablespoons of unrefined sesame oil, corn oil or peanut oil. These oils should hold up well under the low temperatures used for cooking sprout bread. A teaspoon of liquid lecithin mixed in with the oil improves its non-stick abilities. Sprout bread can be very sticky when it is cooking, but nothing sticks to liquid lecithin. *(See Glossary, p.* 269.)

Next, pre-heat your oven to 250°F. and put in your tray. The breads should be done in 2½ to 3½ hours, depending on their size. This low temperature, long-term cooking is the least destructive way to bake. You can cook many foods this way, potatoes, squashes, beans and rice, for example, and preserve their nutritional integrity. Unfortunately, you cannot speed up a sprout bread, even if you try. Sprout bread cooks slowly, from the outside in, because of its density and high moisture content. Normal bread baking temperature of 350°F., would result in a black bottom, a hard crust on top and a soggy center. Sprout bread won't be rushed!

When Is Your Bread Done?

Determining when a sprout bread is done is a matter of touch and taste. First is the finger (or spoon) test. Press the top of the bread. It should be firm, but not hard. If soft or mushy, it is not ready. You also may perform the same test on the bottom. Lifting the bread midway during the baking is also good because it ensures that the bread will not stick. The bread is ready according to the preferred moistness or dryness of the inside. This is a personal choice, but most prefer it after 2½ to 3½ hours of baking at 250°F. Smaller breads will be done sooner than larger ones. The usual test for a cake (using a fork), is not applicable here because a sprout bread never gets completely dry inside. Use caution with your oven. Each has its own personality. Two hundred fifty degrees on the dial may not be 250° inside. If your oven is fickle, use a thermometer. Lower temperatures simply require longer baking. Since this is a combination drying and baking process, 4–5 hours is not out of the question. If your loaf has a hard crust but is wet inside, lower your temperature. A stoneware cup filled with water and placed inside the oven may also help maintain a soft crust.

Storing Your Sprout Bread

Basic sprout bread can last for 2 weeks in the refrigerator and may be frozen for even longer storage. Old sprout bread is easily identified by the presence of mold spots just like regular bread. Since freezing is such a convenience, why not make twice as much and freeze half. It's almost the same work to make eight loaves of bread as it is to make four. Frozen sprout bread can be enjoyed warmed or toasted.

Variations

Congratulations! You have just made basic sprout bread. Taste it. It is sweet, chewy and filling. Do not eat a whole loaf. This is not regular bread. There is no air in this bread because there is no added yeast. Normal yeasted breads are almost half air. The combination of fiber, moisture and high nutrition, makes this bread very rich and satisfying. A little bite goes a long way. Unleash your creativity with sprout breads. Add new ingredients, take others away. You can't miss. Sprout bread always tastes great.

A Sweet Thing

You can enjoy the sweet flavor of these breads with a clear conscience because it is naturally sweet from the grain sugar maltose. Maltose is formed as the sprouting breaks down starch into sugar. If you would like your bread even sweeter, add some raisins and you have—Raisin Sprout Bread! Cinnamon spice is also nice and with the addition of a little ground sweet potato you can achieve Nirvana.

Raisin Sprout Bread

Ingredients

| 2 cups | Hard wheat berries |
| 1 cup | Raisins |

Yield: 3–5 loaves

Cinnamon Raisin Sprout Bread

Ingredients

2 cups	Hard wheat berries
1 cup	Raisins
2–3 Tbsp	Cinnamon, fresh ground

Yield: 3–5 loaves

No matter which of the above recipes you choose, your first step is to make the basic sprout bread. Sprout 2 cups of hard wheat berries for 2 days and then grind into sprout dough. Knead the dough, then add a cup of raisins and/or cinnamon. Mix everything together. Form 3 x 1 inch patties and bake at 250°F. for 2½ to 3½ hours. This yields 3–5 loaves. Baking instructions for all the breads are the same–250° for approximately 2½ to 3½ hours.

Sweet Potato Raisin Sprout Bread

Ingredients

2 cups	Sprouted Wheat Dough
I cup	Raw Sweet Potatoes, ground
¾ cup	Raisins
2 Tbsp	Cinnamon, fresh ground

Yield: 4 loaves

Here is a sweet and delicious sprout bread that is good for dinner or dessert and is wonderfully nutritious.

Begin with the basic recipe for making sprout bread *(see p.19)*. Sprout 2 cups of hard wheat berries for 2 days, then grind into dough. *(See Appendix, Sprouting, p. 287.)* Next, chop up 1 or 2 medium size uncooked sweet potatoes and place them in a food processor, a Champion juicer or a hand grinder. Grind to a paste. Take 1 cup of the ground sweet potato and add it to the sprouted wheat dough and mix. Knead the dough for a few minutes, then add the cinnamon powder and the raisins. Fresh ground spices are always preferred. Kneading is finished when the dough holds its shape. There should be enough dough to form about 4 loaves, each approximately 1 inch high and 3 to 4 inches in diameter.

Lay the loaves on a flat baking tray or cookie sheet. Prepare the tray with poppy seeds to prevent sticking. Place the breads in a preheated oven of 250°F. for approximately 3 hours.

Good luck.

Basic Rye Bread

Ingredients

2 cups   Sprouted Rye dough

Yield: 4 Loaves Rye

This *real* rye bread is made the same way as basic sprout bread *(see p.19)*. Start with 2 cups of organic rye berries and sprout them as usual for 2 days. *(See Appendix, Sprouting, p. 287.)* Grind and prepare the dough in the same manner described in the making of basic sprout bread. You should end up with approximately 2 cups of sprout dough. Knead it well.

Form loaves approximately 1 inch high and 3 inches round. Bake on a flat baking tray for approximately 2½ hours at 250°F. Prepare your tray with poppy seeds, flaxseeds or oil to prevent sticking. It is ready when crusty on the top and firm–to–hard on the bottom.

We call this bread "real rye" because it is made from 100% rye and nothing else. In commercial rye bread, wheat is added to increase the cohesiveness since rye is lower in gluten and won't hold its shape. This is great for bakers but a mine field for allergy sensitive folks who seek out rye bread as an alternative to wheat. We sprout bakers can do three things to compensate for rye's low level of gluten:

a. Knead the dough very well to increase the bread's elasticity.
b. Avoid wetting the sprouts before grinding. This makes a soggy dough. Make sure you rinse your sprouts several hours before grinding.
c. Make smaller patties that hold their shape better.

Sproutman's Onion Rye

Ingredients

2 cups	Sprouted Rye dough
I medium	Onion, chopped
2–3 cloves	Garlic
¼ cup	Miso, blonde
3 Tbsp	Caraway Seeds

Yield: 4–5 patties

Prepare according to the basic rye bread recipe. Gradually add and mix the additional ingredients into the dough.

About Miso

Miso is a salty paste prepared from cultured soybeans. In this recipe it replaces the salt normally used in baked goods and counters the natural sweetness of sprouted wheat. In addition, it adds its own unique flavor. Blonde or light mellow miso as it is sometimes known, is preferred over the common "hatcho" and dark misos because of its lower salt content, lighter color and delicate flavor. *(See Glossary, p. 269.)*

German Rye Crisps

Ingredients

2 cups   Sprouted Rye dough

Rye bread is great, but the Germans have a very popular rye cracker known as Zwieback or rye crisps. These tasty crisps are halfway between a bread and a cracker.

Just prepare your dough exactly as in the basic rye bread recipe *(previous page)*, but this time lay it out only ½ inch high and in 4–5 inch squares. Bake for 1½ to 2 hours at 250°F. Because crisps are so flat, they have no problem holding their shape and are chewier and crustier than their bigger bread brothers. You'll love 'em!

Not So Sweet!

Yes! You can avoid the natural sweetness of sprout breads. Use rye berries instead of wheat. Sprouted rye lacks the high malt content of wheat and is not nearly as sweet. However, it also has less gluten and thus requires more kneading. You also will need more time to grind the sprouts into dough because they are tougher than wheat. Keep grinding, repeat the same batch if necessary, until you achieve a smooth paste. Traditional rye bread often includes onions and caraway seeds. Once you add these ingredients any sweet taste is overcome. Other ingredients that offset the sweetness of these breads, either wheat or rye, are garlic, onion, miso paste, celery seeds, herbs such as thyme, oregano, sweet marjoram, basil and savory, to name a few. Herb breads are delicious without tasting sweet.

Herb Sprout Bread

Ingredients

2 cups	Hard Red Wheat Berries
1 Tbsp	Sweet Marjoram
1 Tbsp	Savory
1 Tbsp	Thyme
1 Tbsp	Basil

Yield: 3–4 loaves

Great Herb Sprout Bread

Ingredients

2 cups	Hard Red Wheat Berries
I onion	Diced or chopped
2 cloves	Garlic, diced
I Tbsp	Savory
I Tbsp	Sweet Marjoram
I Tbsp	Thyme
I Tbsp	Oregano
I pinch	African Paprika
I Tbsp	Sesame Seeds

Yield: 3–4 loaves

For those of you who wish to avoid the naturally sweet flavor of sprout bread, this is the bread for you. Just sprout, grind, knead and bake in the usual manner according to the basic sprout bread recipe *(see p. 19)*. Add the herbs listed above to the dough for a sensational bread. Use your favorite seeds on the bottom of the pan to keep the bread from sticking. The *Great Herb Bread* uses some seeds inside as well as some extra ingredients. Great!

Soybean Sprout Bread

Ingredients

2 cups	Soybean sprout meal
1/3 cup	Miso paste, blonde
2 Tbsp	Onion powder
1 tsp ea	Favorite herbs, optional:
	savory, thyme, sweet marjoram

Yield: 4–5 patties

Here is a completely wheat-free bread made from soybean sprouts. Start by sprouting the soybeans in a sprout bag for 2–3 days. The shoots should be at least as long as the length of the bean. Place the beans in a pot of pure water and bring to a boil. Let simmer on a low flame for about 1 hour or until soft. Drain and cool. Then, grind the sprouts to a meal or paste in a food processor or Champion juicer. Add the miso paste and onion powder. Add one, two or no herbs according to preference.

Mix and knead the dough until smooth. Form a patty about 1 inch high by 3 inches wide. Prepare a non-aluminum baking sheet with corn meal or oat flour and lay on the patties. Bake at 250°F. for approximately 1½–2 hours or until firm.

Baking vs. Sun Drying

Some people are uncomfortable with the baking of sprout bread, at any temperature. They point out that the original sprout bread, which dates back to biblical times, was dried in the sun. It is true that the Essenes, a religious sect who lived in the Middle East before the birth of Christ, made a bread from slightly germinated wheat. The sprouts were crushed and pounded into a wafer and baked dry in the hot Middle East sun. This wafer, cracker or matzoh, was mostly raw since the baking temperatures probably never rose above 125°F. But the Essene's would get a belly ache if they knew we were labeling our modern sprout bread "Essene." Our breads, and the breads that are commonly called "Essene" in natural food stores, are not "Essene" at all. Our sprout bread with its 1½ inch thickness and high moisture content would mold and sour before it dried. Today, we can replicate the "Essene" process by flattening our sprout dough and drying it in a dehydrator. A dehydrator dries the bread by removing its moisture. Dehydrators can usually be regulated between 90°F. and 145°F. You can achieve the equivalent of sun drying in a dehydrator and have the benefit of a controlled environment and the convenience of a kitchen. Actual sun drying can be a problem today with wind and air pollution not to even mention insects. If you do not have a dehydrator, you may simulate one by turning the temperature of your oven as low as possible and leaving the oven door ajar. Add a small battery operated fan to help circulate the air. It can take up to 24 hours to dry this "bread" and in that time, a slight souring may occur, giving it a sour-dough taste.

Cooked vs. Raw

Sprout bread is essentially raw sprouted grain. Raw grain is rarely consumed in any culture, unless of course, you happen to be a horse! True, sprouted grain is partially pre-digested during the germination process due to the breakdown of complex carbohydrates. The sweetness you taste in sprouted wheat, for example, is from complex starch being converted into maltose, the grain sugar. Soft white wheat is a more delicate version of hard wheat and thus easier to digest. The 3 day sprout makes a delightfully sweet snack especially when mixed with raisins. They are a great snack at parties and also the best way to obtain truly fresh, raw wheat germ. Wheat protein increases by 300% in the 3 day sprout as compared with regular (unsprouted) whole wheat. Nevertheless, as a raw grain sprout, it should be consumed in modest amounts because the 3 days of sprouting is not long enough to convert all the raw starch. Longer sprouting turns it into a grass which is not practical for snacking.

Modern sprout bread, baked in a low temperature oven, can be consumed in larger, dinner size portions since the cooked grain is easier to digest. However, sprout bread is dense. Yeast makes regular bread light and fluffy, but sprout bread has no added yeast. Consequently, a mouthful of sprout bread will be harder to digest than a mouthful of whole wheat bread because of the greater density.

About Enzymes

There is a common reluctance to bake sprout bread, because one is usually repulsed by the idea of cooking and thus killing sprouts. This is certainly the case for green leafy sprouts. One would oppose cooking these just as one would oppose cooking lettuce. However, the difference is that wheat is not a green. It is a grain. True, enzymes are destroyed when heated above 125°F. However, when making sprout bread only the temperature of the oven is 250°F. The actual temperature inside the bread is approximately 175°F. You can make this test yourself by sticking a thermometer into the center of the bread. Although this is still too hot for enzymes, it is considerably less destructive than conventional bread baking temperatures of 350°F.

Our diets often challenge us with tough decisions. One must have a clear goal and then decide the best approach to achieving it. A typical sprout dinner, including vegetable juices, sprout salad, fruits and nuts, is a prolific source of enzymes. Your question should be: Do I need to get every enzyme out of every mouthful from every part of the meal? There is such a thing as dietary whiplash.

Because the typical American diet is excessively cooked, denatured and generally devoid of enzymes, one can easily boomerang to the opposite extreme of getting enzymes in everything. In any event, despite the low temperatures, dehydrated and sun-dried breads cannot truly be considered "live" food. Real "live" foods are fresh fruits, vegetables and sprouts.

THE ESSENE BREAD SONG
to the tune of "Home On The Range"

Oh, give me a bread whose nutrition is not dead
Where the enzymes and the vitamins abound
Where Essene is the word and heating is absurd
And the bran and the wheat germ are found.

Bread, give me sprout bread
With the taste and the texture I love
The most wholesome that's known and organically grown
From little sprouts that grow happily all day.

Sourdough Sprout Bread

Ingredients

2 cups   Hard Red Wheat Berries

Yield: 2–3 loaves

"Oh Sour Mio"

Sourdough has been a popular "health" bread in Europe for generations. Its benefits are derived from enzymes and bacteria cultivated during the souring process. These "friendly" bacteria provide the same positive digestive effects as yoghurt. In traditional breads a culture is implanted to start the souring. Sprout bread, however, uses the abundant enzymes in the sprouts to initiate this process. If you wish to avoid the natural sweetness of sprout bread, sourdough is the bread for you.

Sourdough bread is prepared the same way as regular sprout bread *(see p.19)* with one big exception: it is aged. Prepare a plain sprout bread, knead well and set it in a warm place for 12–24 hours. A good spot is on top of or inside a warm stove. The warmer the spot, the quicker it will sour. You may also leave it on the counter at room temperature. It will simply take longer. Set it on a platter and cover it with a damp towel or place it on a greased cookie sheet. The souring has a drying and curing effect on the dough that reduces the baking time by 30–45 minutes. When done, bake in the normal manner at 250°F.

You will notice some cracking or separation in the bread as it ferments. This is the result of the friendly yoghurt-like bacteria that sour the bread and break down (digest) the starch and sugar, which is why it is no longer sweet. These beneficial lactic acid bacteria taste sour and provide lots of B-vitamins, including the elusive vitamin B-12. Sourdough is an alternative to the natural sweetness of basic sprout bread.

Your bread should smell sour and have a piquant flavor. But if it smells "bad" or tastes funny, please do not eat it. Only friendly bacteria will develop at room temperature within 24 hours. Temperatures may range from 75°F. to 110°F. but the fermenting time should be no longer than 24 hours. Too long a time may cause the development of unfriendly bacteria that can be recognized by their unappealing smell and/or visible mold. Higher temperatures require less time. At 110°F. your bread may be done in only 12–15 hours. Watch for signs of cracking and separation. This is the result of air bubbles forming within the bread from the activity of friendly bacteria. These friends are pre-digesting the bread for you and releasing harmless carbon dioxide gas in exchange. Your dough properly aged a few hours after the cracks first appear. Do not walk out on your sprouts! Set up the proper time and temperature for best results.

Sourdough Sprout Cracker

Ingredients

2 cups   Soft White Wheat Berries

Sprout, grind, knead and age your sprout dough for 24 hours as in the making of sour dough sprout bread. Using your hands or a moistened rolling pin, flatten into a wafer only 1/8 to ¼ inch thick. Dry in a dehydrator at 145°F. until dry (approximately 6–8 hours). If you do not have a dehydrator, heat it in your oven at the lowest temperature, 200°–250°F. Remove when firm and dry. If you want an absolutely raw or "Essene" cracker, you must use a dehydrator. An alternative would be to use your oven with the door slightly open. *(See Baking vs. Sun Drying, p. 34, and rejuvelac sprout bread, p. 171.)*

Sprout Matzoh!

You Don'T Have To Be Jewish To Love It!

Ingredients

2 cups   Soft White Wheat Berries

Yield: Approx. 1 lb of crackers

Matzoh is a traditional flat bread that is made from unleavened and unyeasted dough. This sprout cracker is like a matzoh because it is thin as a wafer and unyeasted.

It's easy. Just sprout and grind your wheat in the usual manner *(see p.19)* except this time use soft wheat berries. Knead the dough, then roll it out with a greased rolling pin or flatten it until it is ¼ inch thick. Wet your hands frequently to prevent the dough from sticking. Make sure your pan is prepared with a generous amount of sesame or poppy seeds, or, if you prefer oil, use sesame or peanut oil. Use 1–2 tablespoons of sesame oil and ½ teaspoon of liquid lecithin. Mix the two together and give the bottom of your non-aluminum baking tray or cookie sheet a thorough coating. This helps prevent sticking. *(See p.25)*.

Use a butter knife or spatula to carve squares or sections in your dough that will later help to lift off the finished bread. Place the crackers in the oven at 250°F. for approximately 1–1½ hours. Remove from the oven when firm and let cool until the desired brittleness is achieved. Definitely kosher.

Sprout Bagels

Ingredients

2 cups	Sprouted Wheat Dough
2 cloves	Garlic, crushed
1 medium	Onion, chopped or diced
3–4 Tbsp	Miso Paste, blonde
¼ cup	Seeds: Poppy, caraway or sesame

Yield: 8–10 Wholesome bagels

Not A Doughnut

Please do not confuse a bagel with a doughnut. Although related, bagels hail from a far more advanced species than their sugar coated cousins. This is evidenced by the voluminous hole in the center of the doughnut which indicates emptiness. The bagel, on the other hand, has a smaller, more distinguished opening pointing to its evolutionary link with the fully mature bread. Legend has it that donuts got their name because their intelligence was so limited, they could only respond "dono." We now know that their condition was probably a result of excessive sugar and empty calories producing malnutrition, malabsorption, hypo-glycemia and generally starved brain cells. Don't starve your cells! Choose sprout bagels...it's smart food.

Tired of health food recipes? Want to return to your roots? How about some sprout bagels! Sprout 2–3 cups of hard wheat berries for 2 days and make 2 cups of sprout dough according to the basic sprout bread recipe *(see p.19)*. Mix in garlic, miso and half the amount of seeds.

Tips in the Fine Art of Bagelry

The art of successful bagelry depends on the shape and strength of the dough. Knead your dough well before adding the ingredients in order for it to hold together best. The dough should be moist and firm. A soggy dough is usually the result of overly wet sprouts or too finely chopped onions. Soggy dough has floppier results looking more like a flat tire than a bagel. Roll the dough with wet hands into a small ball about the diameter of a half dollar. Run the ball over your choice of seeds and spread the center apart with your forefinger or thumb. Place the holy specimen on a cookie sheet covered with seeds. Try to get the shape as smooth and as round as possible before you lay it down.

Bake for 2–3 hours at 250°F. Remove from the oven when firm but still moist. Test the bottoms as well as the tops. Bagels should measure approximately 2½ to 3 inches wide by ¾ to an inch high. The hole should be about ½ inch. They will all end up a little different, but try to keep the thickness approximately the same or they won't bake at the same rate. Sprout bagels are smaller and thinner than their white flour counterparts. But what they lack in girth, they make up for in nutrition and taste.

Real bagel shops (most were born in Brooklyn) offer a variety of bagels such as plain, onion, garlic, sesame, poppy and salted. Sprout bagels give you much more than their branless brothers. You get the onion, garlic and seeds all in one. Why not? Then again, if you really want a plain bagel just leave out the onion and garlic when mixing the dough. Use your favorite seeds—sesame, poppy or caraway—for sprinkling on the tops and bottoms of the bagels. Also mix a small amount inside. Mmmm.

Sprout Bread Stix

Ingredients

2 cups	Hard Wheat Berries
3 Tbsp	Dried Onion
2 Tbsp	Dried Garlic
2 Tbsp	Miso Paste
To taste	Poppy or Sesame Seeds
Yield:	Approximately 36 stix

Start by making the basic sprout bread dough—sprouting the grain, grinding it into dough and kneading it—as in the basic sprout bread recipe *(see p. 19)*.

Now mix together all the above ingredients except the seeds. Take a large cutting board and coat it with unrefined sesame oil, or if you prefer, simply keep it clean and moist with water. Wet your hands, too. Now, grab a ball of dough the size of a silver dollar. Roll it into a snake on the cutting board. Divide the snake into 5 inch long pieces and roll each piece into a spread of either sesame or poppy seeds. Prepare your baking tray with seeds or oil and lecithin in a 3:1 combination *(see oil p.25)*. Lay down your stix. The thinner your stix, the faster they will bake. Sprout bread stix are thinner than the conventional kind, measuring only ½ inch in diameter. Bake at 250°F. for 1–1½ hours. Remove from the oven when firm. They harden as they cool.

Dehydrated onion and garlic granules are recommended here instead of fresh onion and garlic. The fresh pieces are too large and moist causing breaks in the smooth consistency of the dough and rendering it soggy. The dehydrated spices allow the stix to hold their shape better and roll more easily. For the best dehydrated onion and garlic or other herbs, make your own in your home dehydrator. It's really simple to do and the quality is superior to anything that is store-bought.

Sprout Croquettes

Ingredients

2 cups   Soft White Wheat Berries

This croquette is simple and sublime. Start by soaking 2 cups of soft white wheat for 8 hours and sprout for 2 days. *(See p.19)*. Grind the sprouts to a paste using a Champion juicer, meat grinder or food processor. Form into patties 3 inches wide by ½ inch high by hand or by using a dough mold *(see mini-pizza p.46)*. Lay on a cookie sheet prepared with a 3:1 ratio of sesame oil and liquid lecithin. *(See p.25)* Bake at 250°F. for 2 hours.

When done, croquettes should be golden brown on top and slighty moist inside. Sprout croquettes are naturally sweet because of maltose, the grain sugar, developed during germination. Store them in the refrigerator in a sealed plastic or glass container. They keep well for 7–10 days. Can be frozen. They are versatile. Enjoy them for dinner or just as a snack.

6 Ways To Eat Soft Sprouted Wheat

Crackers, cookies, croquettes...now here are some more ideas for using this versatile sprout. Sprout 1–2 cups of soft white wheat in a sprout bag for a maximum of 3 days. Then...

1. Serve your wheat sprouts raw as snacks plain or mixed with raisins.
2. Stir it in with cooked vegetables for added texture and flavor.
3. When kneading dough, add them for extra chewiness in your bread.
4. For a nutty snack, bake the sprouted wheat in the oven at 250 degrees until toasty (approximately one hour); serve plain or with raisins.
5. Grind baked sprouts into a powder with your blender or seed mill. Use the powder as a malt sweetener in breads and on cereals. If you have a food dehydrator, dry the sprouts instead of baking them. The powder is both sweet and rich in enzymes that promote rising (like yeast).
6. Use the two day old sprouts to make sprouted wheat cookies, crackers, breads, bagels, etc.

PIZZA WITHOUT SIN
Sprout Pizza Dough

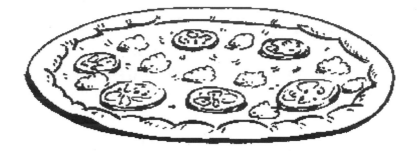

Ingredients

2 cups	Hard Wheat Berries
1 Onion	Large, chopped
4 cloves	Garlic, diced
2 Tbsp ea	Basil, Oregano
1 Tbsp	Savory
1 pinch	Cayenne Pepper

Yield: 1 medium size pizza

Our *Pizza Without Sin* is made in 3 stages: the dough, the sauce, and the topping.

Sprout, grind and knead the wheat as in the basic bread recipe, *(see p.19)*. Next, mix in the herbs, onion and garlic as listed above. Prepare your pan with the sesame oil and lecithin combination *(see p.25)*. Flatten out your patty to a typical 8 to 10 inch round size by ½ inch thick using your hands or a rolling pin. Prop up and thicken the edge just like the professionals do. Bake at 250°F. for approximately 2 hours. It is done when firm.

Raw Pizza Sauce
For Pizza Without Sin

Ingredients

4–5 medium	Tomatoes
¼ cup	Olive Oil
I or 2 Tbsp	Oregano
I or 2 Tbsp	Basil
1–2 Cloves	Garlic
I medium	Onion
2–3 Tbsp	Miso, blonde
Pinch	Cayenne Pepper
1	Lemon, juiced, optional

Yield: 1½ cups pizza sauce

Obtain the most aromatic olive oil and the ripest tomatoes available. Good tasting ingredients give good tasting results. Using a food processor or blender, blend the tomatoes and herbs, then add the rest of the ingredients. Add the juice of 1 small lemon, if desired. That's all! Use blonde miso instead of the dark miso's or tamari as they detract from the rich red color. You will be amazed at how simple and delicious this recipe is, and since it is a raw sauce, it is more nutritious than the boiled tomatoes used in jars and cans.

Pizza Topping
For Pizza Without Sin

Ingredients

2	Tomatoes
2 cakes	Tofu, firm
2 pinches	Sweet Paprika
2 pinches	Oregano or Basil

Pizza is half-bread, so now let's add the other half. Remove the pizza dough and add quarter inch thick slices of tomato all around the top. On top of the tomato add quarter inch slices of tofu. The tofu, in this case, functions as your vegetarian "mozzarella." Garnish the tofu with sweet red paprika and other Italian herbs such as oregano and basil. This time, return it to the broiler section of your oven for 20–30 minutes or until the tofu is browned.

In the first stage, we baked the pizza dough. In the second stage, we broiled the tomato and tofu topping. Now, it is time for the final stage—the pizza sauce. Pour on the pizza sauce and spread it all around the top. Place the pizza back in the broiler section and let the sauce get hot but do not cook. Mama mia!

Mini Pizzas

It's simple. Form 3 inch patties ½ inch high by hand or use a dough mold. Dough molds are available in kitchen or houseware stores in various sizes and shapes. We use one designed for forming hamburger patties. Add 1 tomato and 1 slice of tofu on top of each patty. The mini-pizzas cook faster, so the cooking of the dough will take less than 2 hours. The rest of this recipe is the same as the larger "Mother" pizza.

Sproutman's Famous
SPROUT COOKIE

Ingredients

2 cups	Soft wheat berries
1 cup	Raisins
1 cup	Coconut, shredded
2 tsp	Vanilla extract

Yield: 25–35 cookies

Walk into any grocery store in America and dare to find a cookie made without sugar and flour. It's nearly impossible! True, if you shop at a natural foods store, you can purchase cookies and desserts sweetened with honey, maple syrup, molasses, rice syrup, barley malt and fruit juice concentrate. It is a delight to behold. But the sprout cookie does not use any added sweeteners, nor any flour! How could this be? Is it truly a cookie? Perhaps it is a sprout bread masquerading as a macaroon? Or, maybe we call it a cookie, but it tastes like cardboard. No! No! A thousand No's.

So, What's the Secret?

All right, enough suspense. The secret is in the sprouts! As the tiny soft wheat berries germinate, they diligently break down and simplify their starches into grain sugar—maltose. They make their own sugar! To this, one may discreetly add a few raisins or other dried fruits to enhance the natural sweetness, but never any added sugar or sweeteners.

What, No Flour?

One more mystery solved. How can you have a cookie without having flour? Perhaps, we ought to be reminded of what flour is. It is grain—wheat, rye, oats, barley—that is ground into a powder. This powder is then manipulated in different ways by wetting it, kneading it, adding yeast and raising it, molding it, etc. But not the sprout cookie. This little wonder has only grain sprouts. Were we to plant this grain, it would grow into fields of grass. Here, soft wheat is germinated for just 2 days and the sprouts are then ground into a paste. In that paste are many things you cannot find in Wonderbread—wheat germ, bran, fiber from the roots and plenty of B-vitamins and protein.

Form the sprout dough paste into cookie size shapes, add your raisins or dried fruit and it's ready to go into the oven. That's all. No kneading, no yeasting...nothing. Here's the process, step by step.

Sprout 2 cups of soft white wheat berries for 2 days and grind them to a smooth paste following the procedure for making *Basic Sprout Bread (see p.19.)* Form the dough and mix it with the raisins, coconut and vanilla. With clean, wet hands, shape the dough into little 1 inch balls. Rinsing your hands periodically helps keep your hands clean of the pasty dough. Lay the balls on a cookie sheet that is matted with poppy or sesame seeds. These cookies do not rise, so if space is tight, they can be placed side by side, almost touching. Sprouts like it that way. Their shape resembles macaroons. Bake at 250°F. for 1½ to 2 hours. They are done when firm but still moist.

No Need to Knead

It's true, you don't need to, but it doesn't hurt either! Gluten is the gluey stuff that enables bread dough to stick together. Granted, there is less gluten in sprout dough than unsprouted dough because the germination process breaks the gluten down. Nonetheless, the more you exercise your sprout dough, the more cohesive and smoother your cookies will be. To knead, just fold and turn in the sprout dough until it thickens. Think of it as giving a sprout massage. They are very grateful.

THE SPROUT COOKIE

Interview With Sproutman

Transcribed from a live radio interview with Sproutman

ANNOUNCER: Folks, it isn't made with flour. It isn't made with sugar. It isn't made with eggs, milk, shortening, baking soda or chocolate. But believe it or not, it's a cookie! *The Sprout Cookie!* This delicious natural treat, invented by our guest, is made from an amazing blend of sprouts and natural fruit—that's all! And it actually tastes good! It's hard to believe, but something tastes good and is also good for you. We know it's true because it comes from the *Sproutman* himself. *Sproutman*, tell us, how do you make this?

SPROUTMAN: Well, the ingredients are soft wheat berries, raisins and coconut. You sprout the soft wheat berries for 2 days then grind them into a smooth paste. Mix in the raisins and coconut and shape into 1 inch balls. Lay the balls on a cookie sheet that has been sprinkled with sesame seeds. Bake at 250° for 1½ to 2 hours. They are done when firm but still moist.

ANNOUNCER: Thank you, Sproutman, that sounds absolutely delicious. Let's try one. Mmmm...mmm. Tell me, how did you dream this thing up?

SPROUTMAN: Well, it was a cold night in February when I suddenly felt that the sprouts were asking for some dessert.

ANNOUNCER: Really, Sproutman? Do they talk to you?

SPROUTMAN: Well yes...no. Not in the usual way, that is. Have you read the book *The Secret Life of Plants*?

ANNOUNCER: No. But I've heard of it.

SPROUTMAN: Well, plants are very cultural. They enjoy classical music, light discourse and good fertilizer.

ANNOUNCER: They don't sing do they?

SPROUTMAN: Yes, they do. But their key is above the human audible range. They sing often, as long as they are happy which is most of the time.

ANNOUNCER: Why would a sprout be unhappy?

SPROUTMAN: Drought. A basic water insufficiency is the main cause. But in this case, it was lack of dessert.

ANNOUNCER: Well, that's terrific, so instead of listening to the sprouts cry, you created the sprout cookie!

SPROUTMAN: Yes and I was also wanting a healthy dessert.

ANNOUNCER: Haa! I'll bet you've got a million of them...

SPROUTMAN: I've got a million sprouts.

More SPROUT COOKIES

Banana Sprout Cookie

2 cups	Soft wheat berries
2	Bananas, whipped
1 cup	Raisins
1 cup	Shredded coconut
½ cup	Sesame tahini
2 tsp	Vanilla
2 Tbsp	Liquid lecithin
1 Tbsp	Cinnamon, fresh

Yield: 25 small cookies

Cashew–Apple Nuggets

2 cups	Soft wheat berries
2 cups	Cashews, ground
1 medium	Apple, cored
1 cup	Raisins or currants
2 tsp	Vanilla
2 Tbsp	Liquid lecithin
1 tsp	Nutmeg or allspice

Yield: 25 small cookies

Sprout soft wheat for 2 days, then grind into dough. Knead the dough and mix in the other ingredients. Bananas, apples and cashews should all be whipped or ground. A food processor works best. Leave small chunks of cashews and apples for texture. You can shape the cookies into balls, flatten them or use a cookie mold. Your choice. Bake at 250°F. for approximately 2 hours. Remove when slightly moist and let cool to harden.

Other Grains

The family of glutenous grains includes wheat, rye, oats, barley, triticale (a hybrid of wheat and rye), kamut (Egyptian wheat) and spelt. Wheat has hundreds of species such as durum, hard and soft, red and white and the Spring and Winter versions of each. All this matters more to the connoisseur and professional baker than to you. Most stores carry only one or two varieties. Any hard wheat will do for making bread and any soft wheat for crackers or cookies.

Kamut and spelt are old varieties of wheat that have been resurrected and popularized. Their value is in their high protein and type of gluten that is different from regular wheat and less likely to elicit an allergic response. Kamut sprout bread is made exactly the same way as basic sprout bread. But there is a definite difference in taste. Some think it is the best tasting sprout bread. Don't miss making kamut sprout bread. It is superb.

Oats and barley will not sprout in the form in which they are commercially available. Their germ is damaged in the process of de-hulling their heavy husks. Since we cannot consume them with the husks on and cannot sprout them with the husks off, all we can do is soak these grains overnight. This at least commences enzyme activity and small amounts of the softened grain can be added to regular sprout bread recipes. Oats are mild tasting, easy to grind and excellent in cookie recipes. Barley may be tough to grind and require minimal light cooking to soften. It has a meaty taste.

Rice, millet, buckwheat, corn and soy are all non-glutenous grains and, except for corn, are unlikely to cause an allergic response. Technically, buckwheat and soy are not grains at all, although they can be used as grain substitutes. Of this group, hulled buckwheat, corn and soy are fair sprouters. Unhulled millet is an excellent sprouter but it is rarely available and its hull is tough to eat. Corn is also a good sprouter but tough to eat. Soy is a fair sprouter. Rice and unhulled buckwheat are poor sprouters. Although these grains are wonderful, none of them are functional sprouters and should be considered experimental.

Sweet Rice Crackers

Ingredients

1 cup   Sweet Rice

Non—Allergenic

If you are allergic to wheat, this recipe takes the sneeze out of eating crackers. Sweet rice is a variety of short grain rice with a delightful naturally sweet taste. It is sometimes called glutenous rice because it has a gluten–like material that makes it sticky. But the type of protein in this gluten is different from wheat and its glutenous cousins—rye, barley and oats. It is safe for allergy sensitive people. Obtain some from your natural food store or oriental grocery.

Minimal Cooking Technique

The best method of cooking rice or any grain is to pre-soak it for 5–8 hours or, simply leave it overnight. This softens the grain and eliminates some of the cooking. Pre-soak 1 cup of sweet rice in 2 to 2½ cups of water. After the grain swells (5–8 hours), turn on the heat and bring the grains to a boil, then shut it down. Cover for 35–45 minutes. It is done when the grain is completely soft and all the water has been absorbed. In some cases, you may need to repeat this final step. This low temperature method allows for thorough cooking while preserving maximum nutritional value. In a hurry? Forgot to pre-soak? Simply start cooking with the heat on its lowest position. This will slow–cook the grain at a relatively gentle, non-destructive temperature.

Now for the crackers. Let the rice cool and drain, then grind it through your food processor or Champion juicer. Be careful not to overwork your equipment. Do not overload. This stuff is sticky! Grind small amounts at a time. The ground rice should have a gluey-pasty consistency. Pour it like a pancake batter onto an oiled cookie sheet. The patty should flop down to a 5 inch diameter and ¼ inch high. Use a 3:1 ratio of regular sesame oil and liquid lecithin to grease your pan. If you do not have sesame, use peanut or corn oil. Pre-heat the oven to 250°F. and bake your pancake-looking crackers for approximately 1½ hours. Remove when they are almost dry. They will harden as they cool.

Sweet Rice Breads

Ingredients

2 cups   Sweet Brown Rice

What's the difference between a cracker and a bread? For the most part, it is size and moisture. If your rice batter is firm enough to hold its shape, plop a patty onto your baking sheet. It should settle to approximately 3 inches wide by ½ to 1 inch high. Baking will take 2 hours at the same temperature as always, 250°F. When done, it will be soft and moist inside and golden on top. Longer baking time makes for a chewier batch.

If your batter is too loose, it will not hold its shape. Use less water next time. To rescue an overly fluid batter, add arrowroot starch. Arrowroot is a white powder made from a non-glutenous starchy vegetable.

When completely dry, crackers can be stored out of the refrigerator in a sealed plastic bag and will survive for weeks. The breads or slightly moist crackers must be stored in the refrigerator where they will keep for at least a week.

Homemade Mochi

Ingredients

1 cup   Sweet Brown Rice

Mochi is a traditional Japanese dish made from a variety of rice known as "sweet rice." This is a short grain brown rice that is highly glutenous and sticky. Commercially, it is prepared by steaming the rice and mashing it into a dense flat cake. It has a chewy, moist flavor with a crisp crust that puffs up like a muffin as you bake. Mochi is known for promoting stamina.

Obtain sweet brown rice from your local natural food store. Not all stores carry this grain, although they may carry mochi. While the finished product is fine, it can cost as much as $3 for 12 ounces. Your homemade mochi costs about 35 cents for the same amount and is worth the effort. Choose between two methods, blender or food processor, depending on which appliance you have available. If you have both, processing is easier, although blending takes less time.

Blender Method

Grind 1 cup of sweet rice grains to a powder. The ideal appliance for this is, of course, a grain mill. Although there was a time when most homes had mills, this is no longer the case. Today, most homes have blenders and fortunately, this is one of the very few cases where a blender can substitute for a grain mill. Use the small 8 ounce blend and store containers for best results. If you do not already own these handy, inexpensive containers, now is a good time to get some. They have a thousand uses and add to the versatility of your blender. Thus, instead of a large 40 oz. glass container sitting atop your blender, there is a tiny 8 oz. container instead. The grain ricochets off the container walls only to be repeatedly cycled through the blades. The result is rice flour without a flour mill.

Bring 3 cups of water to a boil and add the rice flour slowly. Stir briskly and continuously. As the "porridge" thickens, add more water, about ½–1 cup until it has the consistency of thick oatmeal. Cooking takes approximately 15 minutes. Then, turn the heat off and let it sit. *(Skip to Baking.)*

Food Processor Method

Cook 1 cup of sweet rice in 2½ cups of water for approximately 40 minutes or until it softens and has the consistency of oatmeal. After it has begun to cool, pour half the contents into a Cuisinart or other food processor. Process until it achieves a mealy paste (about 1–2 minutes).

Baking

Preheat your oven to 375 °F. Grease a flat cookie sheet preferably with unrefined sesame or peanut oil. Or, better still, cover it with a layer of hulled sesame seeds. Pour the rice "porridge" onto the sheet and spread smoothly and evenly until ¼ inch thick. If using sesame, try not to dislodge the seeds. Bake approximately 1 hour until it is puffy and has browned. The center layer may remain moist while the top and edges are crispy. If you wish a drier center, lower the temperature to 350 degrees and wait another half hour. Store any leftovers in the refrigerator. Reheat small amounts in a toaster oven.

Not a Sandwich

Use these crackers and breads with salads, vegetable dishes, snacks or desserts. Rice breads and all sprouted breads, however, should not be thought of as sandwich breads. They are unyeasted patty breads that do not rise and are not sliceable. It is a wonderful bread, but it's no Wonderbread.

Sprout McBurgers

Ingredients

2 cups	Soybeans
½ cup	Tahini
½ cup	Sunflower seeds
5 Tbsp	Miso
2 cloves	Garlic, diced
1 small	Onion, Chopped
1 pinch	Cayenne Pepper
1 tsp	Favorite Herbs (optional)

Yield: 5–6 patties

Here's a hearty dish for those of you who want something to "stick to your ribs." Not only is it "meatless," it is "wheatless." Great for helping ease the transition to a vegetarian diet.

Start by soaking 2 cups of soybeans in pure water for 10 hours and sprouting them in a sprout bag or jar. *(See Appendix, Sprouting, p. 287.)* Rinse twice per day for 3 days. The sprouted tails should be at least the size of the bean, if not longer. Place the beans in a pot of pure water and bring to a boil. Let simmer on a low flame for about 1 hour or until soft. Drain and cool, then mash the bean sprouts to a paste. A food processor or a Champion juicer is ideal for this. Both of these leave you with a well whipped batch that makes for a pleasant texture. Add the garlic, miso, onion, sunflower seeds and tahini.

About the Ingredients

Miso and tahini. If you use a dark miso the result is more burger-like. If you use regular (toasted) tahini the batter will be softer and more fluid. Raw (untoasted) tahini—harder to find—is more firm. Regular tahini, however, has that nice toasted flavor. If you wish to revive the toasted tahini flavor to raw tahini, just add a tablespoon of dark sesame oil to it. *(See Glossary, p. 269.)*

Shape into patties 3 inches by ½ inch high or use a patty mold. Cover a flat non-aluminum cookie sheet with either corn meal, sesame seeds or a 3:1 ratio of regular sesame oil to liquid lecithin. Lay the patties down and bake for approximately 1 hour at 250°F. They should be firm and brown when done. Store what you cannot eat in the refrigerator. They should last for up to 6 days.

If your burgers are too wet, it is probably because there was too much moisture carried over from the cooked sprouts. Be mindful of draining all the cook-water off. If you find yourself with soggy soys, compensate by adding a teaspoon each of your favorite herbs: savory, oregano, sweet marjoram or parsley. You can also use granulated garlic *(1 tsp)* and onion *(3 Tbsp)* to absorb some of the water. Use raw tahini, eliminate any dark oil and lay on a corn meal covered cookie sheet.

Don't Go Nuts

Because this recipe has sunflower seeds, we think of this as a nut-burger. However, if you don't want nuts, use instead ½ cup of lentils, adzukis or China red peas. Sprout these beans along with the soybeans in the same bag. Proceed with the recipe as before but this time leave out the sunflower seeds.

Multi Bean Sprout Loaf

Ingredients

2 cups	Soybeans
1/3 cup	Lima Beans
1/3 cup	Green Pea
1/3 cup	Black Beans
2 Tbsp	Raw Tahini
1/3 cup	Light Miso Paste
4–5 cloves	Garlic, diced
4 stalks	Scallions, chopped
1 cup	Celery, diced
1–2 Tbsp	Kelp Powder or Flakes
2 tsp	African Paprika
1 pinch	Cayenne Pepper
Optional:	1–2 Tbsp Curry, Sweet
	Marjoram or Savory

Yield: Serves 5

Sprouting and Cooking Beans

Soak all beans in pure water for 10–12 hours. Sprout the soybeans in one sprout bag and the green peas in another. Rinse twice or more daily for 3 to 5 days. (See *Appendix, Sprouting, p. 287.*) Lima and black beans are traditionally poor germinators. After soaking for 12 hours, sprout them together for only 24 hours. Check all sprouts for bad odors and rotten, broken or discolored beans. Thorough rinsings plus short term sprouting eliminates potential problems. If you do not have black beans, you may substitute with northern, navy, pinto or kidney beans. Cook all the beans together until soft, approximately 30–45 minutes, over low heat. *(See technique for low cooking p. 236.)* Large beans must be thoroughly cooked.

Drain, cool and grind them to a coarse blend using a food processor, Champion juicer or manual meat grinder. Add the miso, tahini, garlic, scallions, celery, kelp and your choice of herbs. Ladle the mixture into a casserole or bake-proof oven dish. Cover the bottom generously with yellow corn meal. Bake for 1 hour at 250°F. Remove and garnish with sprouts such as alfalfa or buckwheat. Serve hot or cold. It makes a great centerpiece for your salad and a hearty dish for your tummy.

Grain & Bean Sprout Bread

Ingredients

2 cups	Hard Wheat berries
½ cup	Lentil
¼ cup	Green peas
3 Tbsp	Miso
½ small	Onion, chopped
3 Tbsp	Nutritional yeast or vegetable powder
½ cup	Poppy seeds

Sprout the wheat berries for 2 days in one sprout bag and the lentils and green peas for 3 days in another. *(See making basic sprout bread p. 19.)* Drain, cool and grind them to a coarse blend using a food processor, Champion juicer or manual meat grinder. Add the miso, chopped onion and nutritional yeast. Vegetable powder is a mix of powdered vegetables and spices that makes a great instant soup base or a quick herbal flavoring agent. Form patties 3–5 inches in diameter and 1–1½ inches high. Place on a cookie sheet generously covered with poppy seeds. Bake for 3 hours at 250°F. Center should be moist but not wet.

Mighty Millet Bread

Ingredients

¾ cup	Millet
¾ cup	Rice, short grain
5 Tbsp	Miso Paste, blonde
1 tsp	Garlic Granules

Yield: 3–4 loaves

Here's a non-glutenous loaf that's great for those allergic to wheat and those wanting a more interesting way to enjoy millet and rice.

Start by soaking both grains in a covered pot overnight or for approximately 6–8 hours in 3½–4 cups of pure water. Then, bring the water to a boil, turn off the heat, cover and let sit for 35–45 minutes. During this time, the water should be absorbed and the grains soft enough to eat. If not, repeat the last step—boil, shut down and steep. *(See Sweet Rice Crackers, p.54.)*

When done, drain and let cool, then grind using a meat grinder, food processor or Champion juicer. Careful not to overwork your appliance if your grains are too dry. *(Champion juicer owners see p.21.)* Grind to a smooth paste, then mix in the miso and garlic by hand or add them with the grain if using a food processor. Wet your hands and form patties 3 inches wide by 1 inch high. Lay them on a non-aluminum cookie sheet covered with sesame seeds, flax seeds or with a 3:1 spread of sesame oil and liquid lecithin. Preheat the oven to 250°F. and bake for 1½–2 hours. Ready when partially moist in the center and golden brown on top.

Serve with salads and vegetable dishes. Millet is an excellent source of B-vitamins and minerals and is the most alkaline of all grains. Take advantage of millet.

Buckwheat & Millet Loaf

Ingredients

1 cup	Buckwheat, hulled (Kasha)
1 cup	Millet
3 Tbsp	Miso Paste, blonde
1 ¼ cup	Raw tahini
2 tsp	African Paprika
1 Tbsp	Savory
1 Tbsp	Thyme
1 cup	Sunflower Sprouts

Yield: 6–8 servings from 1 loaf

Here's a vegetarian dish fit to show off to your non-vegetarian friends. Guaranteed to stick to the ribs!

Soak buckwheat and millet together in approximately 4 cups of water and cook according to the instructions for the millet or *Sweet Rice Crackers (p.54)*. Using a food processor, meat grinder or Champion juicer, chop the grains to a coarse grind. Mix in the herbs, miso, sunflower sprouts and tahini, and pour all into a ceramic (preferred) casserole dish. Bake in a pre-heated oven at 250°F. for 2 hours. It should be golden brown on top when done.

Sprout your silver (hulled) sunflowers for 2 days in a sprout bag. *(See Appendix, Sprouting, p. 287.)* To serve, sprinkle some sunflower parmesan cheese *(see p. 162.)* on top and garnish with shredded carrots and your favorite green sprouts. As an alternative to sunflower sprouts, use about a 2/3 cup of broccoli tips. Serve hot or cold.

Buckwheat is a superbly nutritious herb that is terribly neglected. The use of the term "herb" here is botanically accurate because technically it is neither a grain nor a wheat. Buckwheat is actually a herbacious plant that is a distant cousin of rhubarb. It is high in rutin, choline and inositol, as well as minerals such as phosphorus, and is very popular with honey bees. Use the right kind of buckwheat. For cooking, use buckwheat groats. Raw groats are light green in color or brown when toasted. Toasted groats are called kasha. Both are suitable for cooking. Black buckwheat still has its shell or hull and is the kind we use for sprouting buckwheat salad greens.

Soybean Sprout Croquettes

Ingredients

2 cups	Soybeans, dry
¼ cup	Peanuts
1 small	Onion, chopped
1–2 cloves	Garlic, pressed
3 Tbsp	Miso paste, white or blonde
2 Tbsp	Optional herbs. Choose one: thyme, oregano, sweet marjoram

Sprout 2 cups of soybeans in a sprout bag or jar for 3–4 days. *(See Appendix, Sprouting, p. 287.)* Grind the bean sprouts in a food processor or other grinder into a smooth paste. Grind the peanuts as well. Use standard roasted peanuts and grind to a coarse texture. No peanuts? Yes, you can use 2 Tbsp of peanut butter, instead. Add in chopped onion, garlic and miso and let the food processor mix all together or mix by hand. Form into patties that are approximately 3 x ½ inches. Bake at 250°F. for 1½ hours.

Sprout Tortilla

Ingredients

2 cups	Corn sprouts
3 Tbsp	Corn Oil or Butter
1 Clove	Garlic, medium size
2 pinches	Cayenne Pepper

If you enjoy eating Mexican, now you can try your hand at the sprouted version of this famous corn pancake. Roll up your sleeves; this recipe is for advanced sprouters and bread makers only. Sprouting and grinding corn is a tough job. First of all, only popcorn sprouts successfully. Secondly, corn is the hardest of all grains to grind. Many flour mills are not even rated for grinding corn. The combination of sprouting and cooking makes the corn soft enough to grind, but it still takes elbow grease!

Sprout popcorn for 4–5 days, then cook for 50 minutes or until soft. *(See Appendix, Sprouting, p. 287.)* Pour off the water, but save 1 cupful. At this point, you have two options in grinding the corn:

1) Grind small amounts of cooked, sprouted corn in the Champion juicer, food processor or meat grinder. Add the saved cook water if necessary to help lubricate the grinding process. The key to making a successful tortilla is in achieving a smoothly ground paste. This may require two run-throughs in your grinding machine. Take your corn paste/dough and add the spices. Flatten onto a cookie sheet greased with either the corn oil or the butter (not both) and bake in the oven at 250°F. You may also dehydrate this batter in your food dehydrator,until dry and crisp.

2) Dry the corn sprouts in a low oven (200°F.) or food dehydrator. When they are completely dry, grind them to a fine flour in your nut/seed grinder, food processor or flour mill. Make sure the flour is finely ground. Add the spices, butter or oil and a small amount of water as necessary to form a paste. Flatten onto a greased cookie sheet. Bake at 250°F. until toasty. Muy sabrosa!

Quinoa Sprout Bread

Ingredients

2 cups	Hard Wheat Berries
¾ cup	Quinoa grain

Yield: 2–4 loaves

Quinoa, pronounced "keen-wa," is the world's richest source of grain protein. Both quinoa and other newly re-discovered grains, amaranth, spelt and kamut, have been around for centuries. Quinoa has been cherished by native tribes throughout the Andes in Central and South America and North American Indians in Colorado and along the Rockies. As a grain, it has more protein than wheat, rye or even amaranth. When it is sprouted, the degree of assimilable protein is increased.

Quinoa is cooked and eaten much like rice, although it is closer in size to millet. Like millet, it takes only 20 minutes to cook. The sproutable form of the seed contains a saponin that protects the seeds but tastes bitter. The grain, with this sheath still on it, is hard to find, but it sprouts easily. Germinate quinoa for only 2 days. If sprouted longer, quinoa develops a pink shoot that is mildly bitter and unsuitable for making bread.

Sprout both the wheat and quinoa separately for 2 days. You may grind the quinoa along with the sprouted wheat and proceed to make dough and bake as with the basic recipe (see p.19). Use sesame seeds to cover the tray. They stick to the bottom of your bread. Quinoa adds a delicious taste and complementary proteins to the basic sprout bread.

Quinoa Crunch

It's simple. Just sprout the quinoa for the 2 days, then dry the sprouts in a dehydrator or a low oven (200°F). That's all! Pop them in your mouth as you would eat rice crispies. Quinoa is much smaller, more delicate and easier to digest. Add them to breakfast cereals, too.

Quinoa Cracker

Grind the 2 day-old sprouts into a paste. They are very easy to grind. Flatten the quinoa paste onto a greased cookie sheet and dry in the oven or dehydrator. They are very delicate and tend to fall apart but are delicious. Use them like crackers or add to cereals.

Sprout Nuts, Sprout Flour, Sprout Pie Crust

Sprout nuts really are not nuts at all but actually dried or baked wheat sprouts. Sprout soft wheat berries for 3–4 days. Spread the sprouts on a cookie sheet in your oven on low, approximately 200°F., and bake until thoroughly dry. Sprouted nuts are a real treat. They are crisp, nutty and sweet. Add raisins for a great mix. If you prefer not to bake, dry the sprouts in your dehydrator at 125°–145°F. or lower if you want an enzyme-safe temperature. The dehydrated sprouts have a less nutty, more raw flavor and are preferred for making sprout flour. Sprout nuts are perfect for kids' snacks or parties where pretzels and potato chips are served. They're a hit.

Sprout flour is made by grinding up sprouted wheat nuts. A blender or small seed mill is suitable for this. This flour is so sweet that it even smells like malt! Sprout flour can be used like wheat germ or yeast or in recipes that call for a sweetener. Grind it coarse like grits and use it in your breakfast cereal. Add some apple juice and liquid lecithin and you can make a pie crust.

Sprout Pie Crust

Ingredients

1 cup	Sprouted wheat flour
¼ cup	Apple juice
3 Tbsp	Lecithin granules

Grind your sprouted wheat nuts into flour using a blender or nut mill (see previous page). Blend or process the apple juice and lecithin together. Add 1 cup of sprout flour and mix. Apple juice serves as a sweetener. Lecithin replaces the role played by eggs to thicken the mixture and hold it together. Lacto-Vegetarians may use raw unpasteurized butter instead of lecithin if they wish to have a butter flavored crust. Stir until you form a thick paste, then pat it down on a non-aluminum pie pan. Handle with care, because with its low gluten content, this crust is fragile and crumbles easily. Although this crust is a dessert in itself, it is always good to have a pie go along with it!

Raw Banana Filbert Pie

Ingredients

2 cups	Filberts
2	Bananas
8oz.	Tofu cake, firm
1	Apple, cored
1 cup	Raisins
2 Tbsp	Vanilla extract
2 Tbsp	Liquid lecithin

Grind the filberts into a meal using a food processor or nut grinder. Whip the banana, tofu and apple together and add it to the filberts with the vanilla and lecithin. Once thoroughly whipped, add the raisins.

Lay the batter into your pie crust and smooth it out. Top with sliced bananas, strawberries and a few nuts. This is a raw pie. No cooking necessary.

Words Of Wisdom from the Food Guru

❀ SWAMI ❀
SPROUTANANDA

Today, people have rediscovered the soy bean. They are very impressed with it because it can make vegetarian burgers, hot dogs, soy milks, ice-creams and cheeses. For you, tofu has become a new mantra. You are so impressed with these modern recipes that you have forgotten the soybean itself!

The same thing has happened to wheat. We have become so accustomed to it that we have forgotten how versatile and nutritious it is. It makes breads, crackers, pretzels, pizza, bagels, cakes, cookies, etc. It is even more versatile than the soybean! But this does not mean we should forget the wheat berry. In my country we eat rice—the whole grain or berry. Why in America, the "bread basket" of the world, do you ignore the wheat berry? They can be prepared just like rice and sprouted wheat berries are by themselves a delicious snack. The less processing, the more nutrition. That is the natural way.

MILK

✿ TO DRINK OR NOT TO DRINK ✿

The Controversy Over Dairy

"Milk is a natural," so the American Dairy Council commercials say, and most of us have been brought up to agree. From birth to adulthood, milk follows us through life like a magic formula, adding a feeling of "nutritional security" to everything we eat. Undoubtedly the first food we eat, milk accompanies us on life's long journey through breads and chocolates, cereals and soups, cakes and cookies, ice creams and candy. You can have it hot or cold, fresh or dry, or with honey for a sore throat. You can curdle it, butter it, sour it, pasteurize it, homogenize it, evaporate it, condense it, skim it or take it raw. With so many applications, such a food is surely a miracle. Americans consume nearly 60 billion dollars worth of it every year; nearly one third of the average American's diet.

Unfortunately, not everyone is in complete agreement with the benefits of milk. Some experts allege that its overconsumption is responsible for many health problems including allergies, asthma, colds and indigestion. Others say it was never meant for human consumption, only for baby cows. People should use it only during childhood, if at all. Amongst vegetarians, the decision to take milk and milk products is even more important since their diet has already undergone the elimination of meat, poultry and fish.

🥛 PRO-MILK 🥛

Americans are not the only fans of milk. If you really want to find out why milk is so loved, just ask the Hindus. They worship the cow as a holy animal whose milk is viewed as a gift from God. The cow is treated with the utmost care and respect. According to Yogic philosophy, milk also calms the central nervous system, relaxes the mind and soothes the body.

In American society, we have no such sacramental respect for the cow. Yet, we worship milk by virtue of its ubiquitous presence in our diet and culture. It is fair to say that as a society, we would truly be at a loss without it. It has been called "the perfect food" because it:

a. Provides a complete protein
b. Contains an abundance of calcium and phosphorus in an ideal ratio for building strong bones and teeth
c. Provides a rich source of fat soluble vitamins A, D, E, K
d. Supplies B vitamins, especially Riboflavin (B2)

Indeed, milk is "good food" when compared with the plethora of "junk" foods we eat, including highly processed, frozen, canned, preserved, colored, denatured foods and the toxins in polluted foods like meat, fish and poultry. Americans count on it for their supply of vitamins, minerals and protein. And unlike some other "health foods," milk is available everywhere. Even in the smallest towns, where vegetarians and "health" eaters would find it impossible to manage, milk, yoghurt, cottage cheese, butter and hard cheeses are in abundant supply.

Milk is also an extremely versatile food. The fluid itself is available pasteurized for longer use, raw for more vitamins and enzymes, skimmed for fewer calories, dried for long term storage and travel, and creamed or evaporated as an additive to hot drinks and desserts. Through different processes of aging and preparing, milk is turned into butter and cheese. Cheese itself has been described as milk's leap to immortality. Hundreds of varieties exist and its heritage dates back to biblical times. All cheeses are forms of curdled milk and are classified as soft, semi-soft and hard. Most are curdled with rennet, which comes from the enzyme *rennin* found in the cow's stomach. Some are coagulated by a bacteria starter. The rennet or bacteria makes the milk form curds that are then pressed and drained. These curds can be eaten without much further processing as in Cottage Cheese, Pot Cheese, Ricotta and Farmer Cheese. These soft cheeses are easy to digest, contain 55% to 80% moisture, are low in calories, low in fat (4%), and contain almost 4 times more protein (16%) than regular milk. The hard cheeses such as Cheddar, Swiss and Parmesan require an involved ripening and aging process. They are much harder to digest because they are higher in fat (30%), lower in moisture (35%) and higher in protein (25%–35%).

Yoghurt, buttermilk, acidophilus milk and kefir represent still another family of milk products. These forms of milk have been cultured or fermented by the addition of special starter bacteria. The milk incubates for a while and then is cooled to stop the bacterial activity. Many cultures have verified the health benefits of fermented milk. In fact, America is really brand new to it, taking a back seat to the Russians, Eastern Europeans and Middle Easterners who have been eating it for thousands of years. The Bulgarians eat pounds of the stuff each day and boast that only their strain of bacteria, *bacillus bulgaricus*, provides the proper results. What are those results? A digestive system alive with "friendly" bacteria that synthesize B vitamins including B-12, helping in the digestion of foods and fighting off invading bacteria and disease. Fermented milks provide a low calorie, easily digestible (even for those with a lactose intolerance), protein food. Societies that make yoghurt a mainstay of their diet are known for their longevity and their ability to fight off disease. Americans must believe in it because we eat over 100 million cups of it a year.

Raw milk is one of the most healthful forms of milk and represents a return to the horse-drawn milk wagons of our great grandparents that carried "warm" milk (straight from the cow) and butter. Raw milk provides friendly lactic acid bacteria, active enzymes, a

larger amount of vitamins C and B and is easier to digest. Unfortunately, raw milk must be kept cold and drunk in a couple of days,
which makes it impractical for mass marketing. Raw milk dairies are
fighting for their economic existence against the power and competi-
tion of regular dairies and the stringent certification controls required for raw milk products. Raw milk is scrutinized carefully for
bacteria and freshness. The cost of raw milk is inevitably higher and
the availability lower, but the quality and nutrition is far superior to
pasteurized milk. In addition, raw milk dairies do not subscribe to
factory farming techniques. Their animals are thus healthier and so
are you.

On the other hand, we can thank pasteurization for removing the
specter of milk as a disease–carrying food, as it was less than 100
years ago. Salmonella, epidemics of diarrhea, scarlet fever and tuberculosis, were all milk carrying micro-organism diseases that are
now virtually a thing of the past. We cannot assume, however, that
milk is bacteria free. It is not. That is why milk is graded—grade A,
grade B, etc.—with grade A having the lowest bacteria count. The
longer you keep milk, the more bacteria will grow. In this respect,
the raw milk products are more reliable because of greater scrutini-
zation and effort to deliver the product fresh.

🥛 ANTI - MILK 🥛

"YOU NEVER OUTGROW YOUR NEED FOR MILK."

—*The American Dairy Council*

Spiritual Argument

Despite the American Dairy Council's promotional efforts to keep us drinking it forever, most animals suckle on mother's milk until old enough to take solid food. In addition, there is no evidence of one species cross–feeding from another's milk. One might assume, for example, that a kangaroo would be "out of synch" if it took its milk from a cow. Or, would human milk be suitable for a calf? Milk is, after all, the lymph secretion from the mammary glands of the female. Man is the only mammal who has decided to feed on "foreign" milk and, what's more, he is never weaned.

To be exact, human milk is decidedly different from that of a cow, and, fortunately for us, so is the resulting child. Cow's milk has 3 times the protein and calcium, 2 times the phosphorous, and is substantially higher in fat and sugar. Human milk, on the other hand, has 2 times the lecithin, 6 times the vitamin C, 3 times the iron, and more niacin, riboflavin and water. The comparison can go on for every nutrient, but the fact is, nature has provided every animal with a specific combination of nutrients necessary for its growth. The extra protein and calcium in cow milk is needed because cows develop their large bones and bodies early. Humans develop their brains and nerves, first. Doctors tell us that a child has a fully developed brain by the age of 5, but his physical development is much slower. The phosphorus–sulphur ratio in human milk is just right for this mental growth but out of balance in cow milk. Calves, on the other hand, are up and running a few days after birth and have children of their own in a few years. Humans take 1 to 2 years to build the strength in their legs just to walk and about 13 years before they can produce offspring. Calves grow quickly into 1500 pound adults, while humans take years to reach 150 lbs. Which milk is right for you?

Rennin, the digestive enzyme that digests the milk protein casein, diminishes after an infant's teeth are formed. Many of us also lack *lactase*, the enzyme for digesting *lactose* or milk sugar. Present in our intestines, lactase is responsible for splitting lactose into *glucose* and *galactose*, which can then be absorbed and metabolized. In all mammals except humans, lactase disappears after childhood. In some human populations that have a long tradition of using milk, lactase is still secreted presumably because of evolutionary change. Nevertheless, most non–Caucasian adults including Africans, Arabs, Asians and Native American Indians are 70 percent lactase deficient. In light of this, the dairy industry's advertising slogan, *"You never outgrow your need for milk,"* is far from accurate [1]. Another absurdity is society's attempt to compensate for our biological deficiency by providing us with lactase supplements so we can "readapt" to milk.

Ethical Argument—Animal Cruelty

Sadly, dairy cows are subject to many of the same injustices that befall beef cows. In commercial operations, they live very stressful lives crowded in tight windowless quarters with artificial lighting controlling the animals' sleeping and waking cycle for maximum growth. Permanent hot iron or freeze branding is done without anesthesia; steers are castrated with only physical restraint (no anesthesia) and calves are dehorned by clippers, saws and knives. Frequently, complications set in after these procedures, including hemorrhage, maggot infestations and infections [2].

Animal cruelty has struck a resonant chord in the hearts of many. Books like *Animal Liberation* by Peter Singer (Avon Books) and *Animal Factories* by Jim Mason (Crown) illustrate a horror the likes of which the world has not known since the concentration camps of Nazi Germany. Mark Mathew Braunstein, author of *Radical Vegetarianism,* eloquently relates his impressions after working on a farm with relatively "good" conditions.

> *A slave, she earns no sick pay or leaves of absence for maternal affairs. Forced to lactate at least eleven months a year, her body becomes diseased. But rather than give her a vacation, humans give a vaccination. And her milk becomes tubercular. But rather than put her out to*

*pasture, humans pasteurize her milk...They are prisoners,
able only to stand up and sit down for all but an hour of
Winter's day. The single bull, confined to a pen large
enough only to contain him, literally and constantly knocks
his head against the wall. While walking down each aisle
doling out their feed, I felt like a warden. Their moo's
sounded more like cries of pain. None were truly healthy,
which means none were truly happy...They must forever
be crying over their spilled milk* [3].

Young calves are taken from their mothers soon after birth and fed a diet deficient in iron to keep their veal white. Hormones are injected to make mothers produce more milk, reduce their sex drive and make them more docile. Grain feed is laden with heavy doses of antibiotics to avoid the spread of disease common in such crowded operations. By human standards, diseases are epidemic. Because of intensive animal husbandry, contagious disease has become the number one problem in commercial dairies. In 1978, 5½ million kilograms of antibiotics were used in animal feeds. That is 48% of the total antibiotic production in the United States that year and they didn't even work![4] Mastitis, a common inflammatory disease among dairy cows is even more common today (50%) than it was before antibiotics were introduced in 1945 (35%)[5]. Scientists from the Federal Centers for Disease Control in Atlanta reported tracing 18 cases of salmonella poisoning to a single South Dakota herd that had been raised on Tetracycline feed. The Food and Drug Administration claimed that the evidence justifies a ban on Tetracycline and Penicillin in feed. But their efforts have been stymied in Congress for years by farm–state legislators and the chemical and livestock industries, who challenge this and other studies as inconclusive [6].

Farm animal factories account for the greatest mass slaughter of sentient beings in history. Each day, over 15 million warm–blooded creatures—chickens, pigs, sheep, calves and cows—lose their lives, 96% of them in slaughterhouses where they die for our dietary preference [9].

Health Argument

The health risks involved in using commercial dairy products to-day include:

a. Allergic reactions, excessive mucous production
b. Antibiotics and hormones
c. Pesticides
d. Processing and additives
e. Pasteurization and homogenization
f. Fear hormones released prior to slaughter
g. Disease producing bacteria
h. Contamination of infant formulas
i. Contamination from detergents, disinfectants, wax
j. Radioisotope traces
k. Rancidity

What's In Milk? (But Not on the Label)

a. Hydrogen peroxide: a preservative and bacteria killer. On the FDA GRAS list (Generally Regarded As Safe).
b. Oat gum: a plant extract used as an antioxidant. Can cause occasional allergic reactions in some.
c. Propyl gallate: an antioxidant, on FDA list to be studied for mutagenic and reproductive effects.
d. Nordihydroguaiaretic acid or NDGA: an antioxidant, banned in Canada as an additive in 1967 after it was shown to cause cysts and kidney damage in rats. Removed from GRAS list in 1968 and prohibited in products over which FDA has control. Control over milk belongs to the Department of Agriculture.
e. Residual antibiotics.
f. Wax particles [3].

Antibiotics and Hormones

No one knows the full impact on human health of the infusion of antibiotics and hormones secondarily through dairy products. But it is commonly accepted that consistent low level feeding of antibiotics causes the development of resistant strains of bacteria. If humans become infected with resistant bacteria, normal treatment with anti-biotics may be ineffective. The two most widely used antibiotics in factory farming, Tetracycline and Penicillin, are also the most commonly used in humans. Several studies have recommended the restriction of these drugs. The Swann Committee in England, The FDA Environmental Impact Statement, The Office of Technology Assessment, The World Health Organization and a U.S. FDA task force have all supported the restriction. "Majorities of the individuals involved in these various studies recommended policies restricting the sub-therapeutic use of anti-microbials in animal feeds...[10]." The meat and dairy industry claim that after 30 years, no human illness has been traceable to feeds. However, the absence of traceable evidence is not proof that hazards do not exist. A complex chain of events occurs between the addition of antibiotics to feeds and the contraction of human disease. The various individual links in the chain have been demonstrated in different cases, but it is extremely difficult to conduct such a comprehensive study [11].

Penicillin is one of our least toxic antibiotics but also one of the most allergenic. For some, even the tiniest dose can cause swellings, fever, rash, asthma, stomach disorders, shock, and in severe cases, death. Yet, despite all your precautions, you may be getting it anyway—in your milk. That includes all milk–bearing foods: bread, cheese, cookies, soups, etc.. To make matters worse, many antibiotics and hormones are prepared in an oil base, which means that the cow will remain contaminated for a longer period of time. Symptoms in humans may not be easily noticeable because they are also delayed and subtle. In an incident in Puerto Rico, young girls 5 and 7 years old, began developing breasts in unusually high numbers. This was attributable to the high consumption of poultry on that island and the use of female hormones on the chickens to increase egg production. Puerto Rico is the largest per capita consumer of egg and poultry products. Unfortunately, pasteurization does not remove it and you cannot cook it out. You can count on antibiotics and hormones being there because literally tons of it are used in animal feed each year.

Pesticides

*"No milk available on the market today, in any part
of the U.S., is 100 percent free of pesticide residues."*
— United States Dairy Association

Pesticide residues are another major problem. Most of them are
chlorinated hydrocarbons that have long been known to be fat soluble and are thus concentrated in cream, butter and cheese, and in
the fats of animals who ingest these products. In humans they are
stored in our liver. If the food chain extends through many animals,
all who have fat tissue, the pesticide level in the final animal is many
times greater. If milk contains 3 parts per million of DDT, butter
from this milk will contain 65 parts per million. Milk from cows eating DDT-contaminated hay will have 3 to 4 times the amount in the
hay. This concentrating effect is exemplified by a bull in Clear Lake,
California who was immortalized for having 2,500 parts per million
of a chlorinated hydrocarbon in his body as a result of the spray
used in the lake he drank from [12]. Before DDT was prohibited for
use on edible crops, "three–fourths of milk tested in California in
1961 showed traces of contamination with chlorinated hydrocarbons, but by using the legal test or the old method of testing only 28
dairies were actually suspended [12]." DDT laden milk consumed by
pregnant mothers was shown to have contaminated their babies
and was implicated in a wide range of birth deformities.

Morton S. Biskind, M.D., a distinguished physician now retired
but formerly in charge of the endocrine laboratory and the endocrine
clinic in the Beth Israel Hospital in New York, cited the case of a
pregnant woman directly exposed to DDT, who, following delivery,
produced milk containing 116 parts per million of DDT. *What happens* (Dr. Biskind asks) *to the growing child already born with DDT in
its body? This substance passes the placental barrier and he gradually stores the additional DDT from his diet. [12]*

Unfortunately, even though the use of DDT has been restricted, it
is still allowed on non-edible crops including cotton. Crop dusters,
which bomb the cotton, leave a cloud of dust that drifts to adjacent
hay fields where cows feed. By its own admission, the United States

Dairy Association says: "No milk available on the market today, in any part of the U.S., is 100 percent free of pesticide residues [13]." Dairy owners are supposed to withhold the sale of treated milk for 3 to 4 days after the administration of antibiotics, but this is extremely difficult to oversee and many owners simply do not comply. It is important to remember that limits for pesticide residues are not determined by what is safe for human consumption, but by what is practically achievable by the industry today. Pesticide tradesmen are not ready or willing to forego profits from spraying such major crops as alfalfa and cotton. As for you and me, if we consume high fat content dairy products like butter and cheese, we will be receiving higher dosages of pesticides and hormones. You cannot trim the fat off of a piece of cheese or glass of milk to get rid of these contaminants.

Other Contaminants

Traces of radioactive isotopes is yet another problem that plagues milk. Nuclear fallout, or "accidents" such as Three Mile Island, taint milk with strontium 90, among other isotopes. The cow picks it up from contaminated grain. Most of it is absorbed into his bones and only a small percentage makes its way into the milk. The theory is that calcium in the milk acts as an antagonist for the radioactive minerals and competes with it. If this is correct, then relatively little would be absorbed by our bones. We hope they're right.

Other contaminants that may end up in the milk are: wax carton particles, detergents and disinfectants that are used to clean milking machines. They can invade the milk if not entirely rinsed off. Some hydrocarbons, which are purported to be carcinogenic, are used to coat the wax milk containers. They may break off and mix with the milk. Use plastic or glass containers when possible.

Processing

Pasteurization is the short boiling process that destroys most disease forming bacteria. Before the advent of pasteurization, milk carried many diseases such as salmonella, tuberculosis, scarlet fever, diarrhea and other stomach disorders. But pasteurization also destroys enzymes, vitamin C and many B vitamins, and it does not necessarily kill 100% of the bacteria. Milk is still perishable and capable of hosting micro-organisms if not stored properly and used within a few days.

Homogenization refers to the emulsification of milk fat so that it is suspended throughout and does not settle as cream on the top. The process involves a high pressure machine that forces the milk through a fine screen breaking apart the fats into small segments.

Milk and milk products are highly processed foods and bear with them many of the questions and concerns involved with the safety and nutritional value of all processed foods. Yoghurt for example, can have in it sugar, non-fat dry milk, artificial color, artificial flavor, guar gum, xanthium gum, food starch, sugar sweetened preserves, emulsifiers, starter culture and a little milk. Ice cream may contain propylene glycol, glacial acetic acid, aldehyde C16 and up to 50% air. Cheese may have mold inhibitors, stabilizers for smooth texture, thickeners, artificial flavor, and artificial color. Some cheese is so processed that it can no longer be labeled "cheese." Leftover cheeses are in fact recycled, ground, heated, mixed and emulsified into a new blend called "processed cheese," "processed cheese spread," "processed cheese food" and even "imitation cheese!" Needless to say, these have their share of additives. The high heat and processing reduce the nutritional value, and the artificial flavors and colors cover up the old cheeses. Like herds of sheep, we assume the shepherd knows what is good for us and we buy it.

Infant formulas are sometimes made with non-fat dry milk. As if it was not bad enough to feed an infant milk that is overly concentrated and out of synch with his nutritional needs, nutritionally inferior dry milk is used. Dry milk is low in essential fatty acids, high in milk sugar, high in synthetic "enriched" vitamins, and overall unbalanced in comparison to whole milk. It is often sold to third world countries where, with polluted water supplies, mothers reconstitute it and serve their babies this sub-nutritious product made with contaminated water.

Allergies

If infectious diseases are the major health problem of Third World countries, then milk allergies are the plague of affluent societies. The most common complaint is congestion of the nasal passages, chest and mucous membranes, tiredness, rashes and acne. This is due, at least in part, to the indigestibility of milk protein, which acts as an irritant, inflaming the mucous membranes and causing excessive secretions. Inability to digest milk sugar (lactose intolerance) and the high concentration of fat may also contribute to allergies. Goat's milk, which is lower in protein, sugar and fat—much closer to the content of mother's milk—is almost free of these mucous forming factors.

Other allergic symptoms are asthma, skin rashes, acne, gas and headache. Once again, reactions may occur not just to dairy products, but to other foods such as breads, chocolate and cookies that have milk as one of their ingredients.

ALTERNATIVES TO MILK

Reasons for becoming a Vegetarian

Necessity is the mother of invention. If you cannot eat dairy products, you will most certainly find other things to eat. The nature of those foods depends somewhat on your motivation and your talents. If you are ordered not to eat dairy by your doctor, then you are most likely to look for substitutes. Unfortunately, this kind of non-dairy diet is not self-motivated and is thus generally less satisfying. The "forced Vegetarian" is forever striving for food replicas, and soy ice-cream and tofu franks compare poorly to the real thing. This person would eat dairy if he could. If, however, your dairyless diet is ethically motivated, all the alternatives are fine. In fact, with a little imagination, you will discover a whole world of new foods and enjoy the challenge of exploring new tastes and textures. What's more, you'll boast about the abundant variety and unlimited combinations. Motivation is half the battle.

Vegetarianism Vs. Veganism

The other half is talent. Vegetarians as a group are forced to be more creative. There is little support for vegetarianism in our culture. As you walk past the fast food shops, the groceries, the vending machines and most restaurants, there are few if any places a hungry vegetarian can alight. The non-dairy vegetarian has it worse. He can't even be sustained by a Dannon yoghurt or some cheese. While the vegetarian eats no animal, the non-dairy vegetarian or vegan (pronounced vee-gan), eats no animal products. For decades, the U.S. Department of Agriculture's infamous 4 food groups officially recommended that 50% of the American diet be meat and dairy. Although its new food pyramid has increased the prominence of fruits and vegetables, it will take years for our dietary infrastructure (restaurants, groceries, vending machines) to change. A vegan must be a talented person, willing to experiment and study, be handy in the kitchen and have the grit to stick to it.

With a little talent, enthusiasm, well placed motivation, and help from your friends, you can turn beans into milk, seeds into cheese, nuts into yoghurt and fruits into ice-cream.

Some Dairy Substitutes

MILKS
Soy Milk
Almond Milk
Sunflower Milk
Sesame Seed Milk
Cashew Milk
Cashew Egg Cream
Fruit Smoothies
Coconut Milk

ICE CREAMS
Banana
Carob Banana
Banana Strawberry
Cashew
Vanilla
Coffee
Carob

CHEESES
Sunflower
Sesame
Parmesan
Hot n' Spicy
Cheese n' Chips
Tofu

YOGHURTS
Cashew
Sunflower
Sesame
Pignolia
OTHER
Rejuvelac Wines

The above food substitutes are just some of the possibilities. As with all creative endeavors, the possibilities are limitless. But before you cross the bridge into this new world, you should make sure that in leaving milk behind, you are not saying good-bye to good nutrition.

Nutrition In Milk Vs. Non–Dairy Foods

Food values in mg/100 grams except IU's (Int'l units)[14]

NUTRIENTS IN WHOLE MILK vs. NON-DAIRY FOODS			
NUTRIENT	**MILK**	**DAIRY**	**NON-DAIRY**
VIT D	40 IU		Sunflower seeds 90 IU. Mushrooms 40 IU
VIT K	3	Butter 30	Turnip Greens 650. Broccoli 200
CHOLINE	15		Lecithin 2200. Wheatgerm 406
INOSITOL	13		Lecithin 220. Wheatgerm 770
CALCIUM	118	Swiss Cheese 925	Kelp 1093. Dulse 296. Carob 352
MAGNESIUM	13		Kelp 760. Wheat germ 336. Almonds 270
PHOSPHORUS	93		Yeast 1753. Pumpkin seeds 1144
POTASSIUM	144		Kelp 5273. Dulse 8060. Sunflower 920
CHROMIUM	11		Yeast 112. Potatoes 24
IODINE	7		Kelp 150,000. Lettuce 10

The above chart shows the nutrition in milk relative to other foods. Milk is no match for many vegetables, seeds and grains. It is even a lower performer in comparison to vegetarian "superfoods" such as sprouts, Spirulina, Yeast, Bee Pollen, Wheatgrass or even good ol' Spinach and Swiss Chard. Milk is short on Vitamin C, iron and most B vitamins. Vegetables and seeds, for example, provide more Vitamin A and D than milk, which has built a reputation for providing these nutrients.

NON-DAIRY MILKS

& BEVERAGES

This kind of milk really is "a natural" because it is made from natural foods—nuts, seeds, fruits and beans. It can be used wherever you would use the "other" milk: on cereals, as a drink, or as an ingredient in a variety of dishes.

Soy Milk

Soy milks are rising in popularity and improving in taste. Once upon a time they tasted just like watered down beans, which is basically what they are. The soy beans are cooked, mashed and strained. The resulting water is cooled, honey or carob is added for flavor and voilà—soy milk! More industrialized manufacturing techniques are now common. Soy milk is pasteurized and homogenized like regular milk to give it a smooth consistency. Modern dairy processing machines evenly distribute the small amount of added safflower or corn oil as well as the sweeteners—honey, barley malt, carob, etc. This processing is the reason behind the success of the new "brick pack" soy milks. A lot of nutrients are lost in the processing. Nevertheless, the finished product is high in calcium, iron, phosphorus, thiamine, riboflavin and Vitamin C, and contains 2.6 grams of protein per 100 grams.

Coconut Milk

Coconut milk is commercially available as a canned or frozen drink. It is milky white and often mixed with fruit juices as a sweetener. One popular drink, called "Pina-Colada," mixes coconut milk with pineapple juice.

Coconut milk involves quite a workout if you are going to make it at home. First you must open the coconut. That's enough to knock most people out even if you are not hit on the head by one. Then, you must rip the "meat" out of the shell. Next, chop the meat into small pieces, scrape it or grate it in the food processor. Add fruit juice such as white grape juice, apple juice, pear juice, lime or pine-apple juice. Or just use water and add honey. Strain and serve. As with other milks, keep your fresh coconut milk refrigerated.

Nut Milks

If you want a milk that is easy to prepare, does not need to be cooked and is alive with enzymes, try some nut milk. The theory be-hind nut milk is simple. Just blend your nuts with water or juice, then strain. The ratio of fluid to nuts is usually 3 or 4 to 1. The hard nuts, like almonds, should be softened first by soaking. Strain with a fine sieve, refrigerate and drink within a couple of days.

Sesame and Other Seeds

Sesame milk is prepared just like sunflower. Because the seed is so small, no soaking is necessary. The milk is very satisfying. Additionally, you may experiment with other exotic tastes like pumpkin seeds, walnuts or pecans.

Nutrition

Almonds and sunflower seeds are an exceptional addition to your daily nourishment. Almonds are a superb source of all the major minerals: calcium, magnesium, phosphorus, potassium, iron, man-ganese and zinc, and have a good amount of vitamin E. Sunflower seeds are also high in vitamin E and are one of the few vegetable sources of Vitamin D.

Comparison Chart Nuts & Seeds & Soy Vs. Whole Milk

Food Values in Milligrams per 100 gram Amounts[14]

	Almond	Sun-flower	Soy	Sesame	Cashew	Milk
Protein	18.6	24	34.1	18.2	17.3	3.7
Vit A	-.-	50	80	30	100	143.4
Vit E	48	90	-.-	-.-	-.-	-.-
Vit D	-.-	90	-.-	-.-	-.-	40
B-1	0.24	1.96	1.1	-.-	-.-	0.03
B-2	0.92	0.23	0.31	0.13	0.25	0.27
Calcium	234	120	226	110	38	118
Magnesium	270	38	265	-.-	267	13
Phosphorus	504	837	554	592	373	93
Sodium	30	-.-	60	-.-	50	-.-
Potassium	773	920	1,677	-.-	-.-	44
Iron	4.7	7.1	8.4	2.4	3.8	-.-
Manganese	2.5	-.-	-.-	-.-	-.-	0.02
Zinc	3.1	-.-	-.-	-.-	-.-	0.4
Niacin	3.5	5.3	2.2	5.3	-.-	-.-
Panta Acid	-.-	1.4	1.7	-.-	1.3	-.-
Choline	-.-	-.-	340	-.-	-.-	15
Inositol	-.-	-.-	200	-.-	-.-	13

The figures in the above chart relate to the seed, not the milk, since nut milks have not been charted by the U.S. Department of Agriculture, which charts all major food lines. Similarly, the figures for soy, use dry beans, not soy milk. Nevertheless, there is enough information to draw your own conclusions as to which is the right "milk" for you.

BASIC NUT MILK

Almond Milk

Ingredients

1 cup	Almonds
2 cups	Pure Water
1 cup	Apple juice

Yield: 4 cups

Here is a recipe for basic nut milk, using almonds. Other nuts may be substituted in place of almonds, although as in the sunflower milk below, the ratio of nuts to water will vary.

Soak your almonds overnight or for at least 6 hours. Almonds are the hardest nut we use for nut milk and take the longest to soften. Thoroughly blend them with water and pass the mixture through a fine sieve or strainer. Now add the apple juice, stir and drink—that's all. You'll be surprised at how creamy and sweet it is.

Sunflower Nut Milk

Follow the basic nut milk recipe above. However, with sunflower, it is not necessary to soak the seeds. Because of their small size and softness, you may use them as is, or if you prefer, soak them for only 2 hours. Just put the raw, shelled (silver) sunflowers in a blender and start whipping. If you like your milk thick, don't strain it. However, straining gives you the smoothness of a milk while not straining leaves you with the thickness of a milk shake. You may also achieve the desired consistency by increasing or decreasing the amount of water.

Cashew Milk

Ingredients

1 cup	Cashews
4 cups	Pure Water
2 Tbsp	Maple Syrup

Yield: 4 cups

One of the most seductive members of the nut kingdom is the ever sensual and provocative cashew. Grown in exotic far–away lands like Mozambique and Brazil, this succulent ambrosia is no nut, but rather the seed of the cashew apple. While growing, it hangs in the sun from the bottom of the cashew fruit and is protected (of course) by a poisonous shell that must be removed and discarded before it can be enjoyed. Though equipped with a healthy amount of phosphorus, magnesium and B vitamins, it is not the nutrients that we desire so much as it is the smooth white color, texture and taste.

Nut milk made from cashews looks like the real thing. Blend it with 3 to 4 parts water, add a tablespoon of maple syrup or honey and you're off on a journey to dairyless heaven.

Like sunflowers, cashews do not require a pre-soaking stage. Prepare it just like sunflower and almond milk with one exception: this milk does not need to be strained. In fact, because the cashew has such soft fiber, it cannot be strained. When you drink cashew milk, you are drinking a blend of cashews and water. This is in contrast to almond milk in which the almond pulp is removed and only the water extract is drunk. Nevertheless, it is creamy, smooth, white and delicious.

Vanilla Malted

Ingredients

I cup	Cashews
4 cups	Water
2 Tbsp	Maple Syrup
1 stick	Vanilla, fresh
2 Tbsp	Lecithin

Yield: Serves 2

Once you make a cashew vanilla malted, you won't want to have any other kind.

Blend the cashews with water, then add maple syrup, vanilla and lecithin. For vanilla, you can use a fresh vanilla bean or the liquid extract. For the extract, use 1 Tbsp. If you are using the fresh bean, just chop up half a bean into ¼ inch pieces and blend. *(See vanilla in Glossary, p. 269.)* Increase or decrease the water to achieve desired thickness.

Cashew Egg Nog

Ingredients

I cup	Cashews
4 cups	Water
2 Tbsp	Maple Syrup
1 stick	Vanilla, fresh
1	Golden delicious apple, cored
2 Tbsp	Lecithin
3–4 grains	Cinnamon
3–4 grains	Cardamon
3–4 grains	Nutmeg

Yield: Serves 2

When holiday time comes, why not nog it up with your cashew sweetheart.

Proceed as you would for preparing the vanilla malted only this time blend in the cored golden apple and the spicy ingredients. The apple serves to give the recipe body just like heavy cream. A golden delicious apple is chosen for its light color and sweetness.

Whenever possible, buy your spices whole and grind them at home. If you only grind what you need, you will be rewarded with the freshest spice and a sensational taste. It is also helpful to grind the 3 spices separately, then blend them with the milk. No, it's not alcoholic, but it certainly has a festive flavor. Happy holidays.

Juiceless Nut Milk

Ingredients

3 cups	Water
1 cup	Nuts
1 Tbsp	Maple syrup or Honey

Yield: 4 cups milk

About Sweeteners

Apple juice is often used in the nut milk and beverage recipes as both the liquid medium and a sweetener. If you prefer, you may substitute 1 cup of water instead of the juice. If you prefer, of course, you need not sweeten nut milks at all. However, a tablespoon of maple syrup or raw honey makes these drinks more delectable. Such is the recipe on this page. Dee-licious!

The Family Of

FERMENTED FOODS

Dairy

The idea of something being "fermented" may sound unsavory to us, but it has been the mainstay of many cultures for hundreds of years. Fermentation involves the aging or culturing of foods and it is not limited to milk. In Europe, the Germans are proud of their pickles and sauerkraut, the Slavs their sour bread, the Russians their Kefir, the Swiss their sour cream. And everybody eats yoghurt—Europeans, Greeks, Middle Easterners and Indians. In the Orient, the Japanese pride themselves on fermented soy foods like miso, tamari and tempeh. Among the cultured and aged milk products that we are familiar with are:

Cultured And Aged Milk Products

Yoghurt	Sour Cream
Kefir	Cottage Cheese
Buttermilk	Farmer Cheese
Clabber milk	Ricotta Cheese
Acidophilus Milk	

Even popular American hard cheeses like Cheddar and Swiss are aged from 6 months to 2 years, allowing bacteria to ripen them. In fact, it is the active bacteria that form the famous Swiss cheese holes!

Non–Dairy Fermented Foods
Commercially Available

Sour Dough Bread	Amazake Rice Drink
Miso Paste	Sauerkraut
Tamari (Soy Sauce)	Beetkraut
Tempeh	Sour Pickles
Mochi Rice	Sour Beet
Umeboshi Plum	Koji Rice

Fermented foods are defined as those aged for short (12–96 hours) periods, under controlled conditions, that begin to break down (self–digest) due to the action of living organisms. These "friendly" bacteria provide many benefits *(next page)*, but are mainly known for their beneficial effect on the digestive system. As you can see, fermented foods like yoghurt need not be made only with milk. Although yoghurt is synonymous with milk, it is only because of common usage. If you are sensitive to milk, it is nice to know that other mediums will support the growth of "good" bacteria. Some nuts, seeds and grains do this very well and open up a whole new arena of substitute, non–dairy yoghurts, cheeses and drinks.

Fermented Foods Substitutes
For Common Dairy Foods

Cashew Yoghurt	Rejuvelac Wheat Drink
Rejuvelac Wine	Cashew Cottage Cheese
Sunflower Yoghurt	Sunflower Parmesan Cheese
Sunflower Sun Cheese	Sprout Sunflower Yoghurt

Benefits Of

FERMENTED FOODS

To fully understand the benefits of these foods, one is obliged to look more at tradition than textbooks. Documentation on the fermentation of foods in this country concerns itself mostly with the manufacture of beer and wine. In Germany, on the other hand, there is much literature on the fermentation of grains and vegetables, some of it going back hundreds of years. However, if you do not read German, one only has to look at the different populations that traditionally consume these foods to understand its benefits. The Hunzas (Himalayas), the Georgians (Caucasus Mountains, Russia), and the Equadorians (Andes) all consume pounds of yoghurt daily along with sauerkraut, sour bread and fermented vegetables. These people are known for their longevity, health and good digestion.

Digestive Aid

During the process of controlled fermentation, living organisms propagate and ingest complex proteins, simplifying them in the process. The same is true for starches that are saccharified into sugars and fats that are decomposed into essential fatty acids. The result is a partially digested food that is able to be assimilated with less digestive effort. Dr. Johannes Kuhl, a German physician and researcher who has done extensive work with the fermentation of wheat berries, explains the advantages of fermentation as follows:

The natural lactic acid and fermentive enzymes,
which are produced during fermentation processes, have
beneficial effects on the metabolism and a curative one on
disease. Lactic acid destroys harmful intestinal bacteria
and contributes to better digestion and assimilation of nutri-
ents. Fermented foods, being in an already pre-digested
state, are easily absorbed and assimilated, especially by
persons with weak digestive organs. Fermented foods im-
prove the intestinal tract and provide a proper environment
for the body's own vitamin production within the bowels,
being especially beneficial to persons with constipation, di-
arrhea and cancer problems [16].

The natural enzymes, held dormant within the nuts, seeds and grains come alive and help friendly bacteria such as lactobacillus fidus, bulgaricus and acidophilus to grow. They, in turn, give off lactic acid, a natural astringent, which helps manufacture vitamins and checks the proliferation of disease–producing bacteria. Fermented foods thus have many benefits:

Digestion: They act as a digestive aid by the partial or pre-digestion of food.

Nutrition: They provide nutrition through the production of vitamins including vitamin B–12.

Fight Disease: They maintain good health and long life by providing almost "anti-biotic" action against disease producing intestinal bacteria.

Enzymes: They supply much needed enzymes that are critical to the body's operations of building up and breaking down.

Enzymes have a reputation for being unrespected, trivialized nutrients, when in fact, they are vital co-constituents of almost all biological activities. Ann Wigmore talks about the benefits she has experienced because of enzymes.

In a healthy person, the enzymes are manufac-
tured by the body. However, when the glands, nerves,
muscles and even blood of an elderly person become over-
drawn, the body becomes weaker and weaker. The skin

wrinkles, the hair thins and turns gray. During my many years with sick folks, I had the great privilege to observe what enzymes can do in health building. I was born sickly and had poor digestion all my life. Yet, I can keep healthy and full of energy, applying the catalyst enzymes in extra form by drinking Rejuvelac, the fermented soak water of wheat. I drink six glasses every day [16].

Rejuvelac is one of the most active and easiest to digest of the fermented foods. Unlike nut yoghurt and cheese, which are relatively concentrated because they are made from nuts, Rejuvelac is mostly water and thus easy to digest, even for people with weak digestion. According to Dr. Ann Wigmore, Rejuvelac contains the following living organisms:

a. Molds (Rhisopus, Mucor, Penicillium and Aspergillus)
b. Yeasts
c. Lactic Acid Bacteria
d. Ferments
e. Vitamins — B complex
f. Hormones
g. Aromatics
h. Natural Antibiotics

In a letter to Dr. Ann Wigmore, food research chemist, Dr. Harvey Lisle, reported his results on the testing of Rejuvelac:

You have opened up a Pandora's Box with that Rejuvelac. Its potentials are tremendous. That Rejuvelac sounded like a nutty idea to me and I didn't even want to get into it but you kept hounding me on it so I figured I had better see what gave...I used a 2:1 ratio of water to wheat as you recommended and kept it on the top of my hot water heater where the temperature maintained an even 70 degrees. Each day I poured off the Rejuvelac and ran a series of tests on it. After the second day, there was a slight sour odor that I couldn't quite identify. But after the third day, the odor was unmistakable. It is similar to the odor of milk turning into yoghurt (lactobacilli) or the odor of beer (beer yeasts called Saccharomyces cerevisiae). I ran a bacteria culture on it and it was loaded with lactobacilli and yeasts...The Rejuvelac is undoubtedly rich in proteins, carbohydrates, dextrines, saccharines, phosphates, lactobacilli, saccharomyces and Aspergillus oryzae. Amylases are derived from aspergillus oryzae and they have the facility of breaking down large molecules of glucose, starch and glycogens. That is the reason the Rejuvelac is so beneficial to your digestion [16].

It may be a cliché, but it is not only good for you, it tastes good, too! This is a truly refreshing drink that leaves you feeling clean inside. The abundance of B complex vitamins including vitamin B–12 gives you a little "lift" to carry you through your day. Happy flying.

IF IT DOESN'T SMELL RIGHT OR
TASTE RIGHT, DON'T EAT IT.

Good and Bad Fermentation

The word "fermentation" has a bad reputation. Many equate it with spoilage. Spoilage is fermentation that is wild and uncontrolled. In all our recipes for yoghurt, cheese and Rejuvelac, we have taken special care to monitor the fermentation process for ideal environment, temperature, time, odor and taste. Spoilage has none of these controls and takes place over a longer stretch of time, perhaps days or weeks. With the exception of Rejuvelac, fermentation takes place in a matter of hours. The making of wine and cheese is also a fermentation process. And as everyone knows, that requires a fine art of sampling, monitoring and an ideal environment. If the temperature is wrong or too much time has elapsed, spoilage bacteria will propagate instead of lactic acid bacteria. In addition, different foods yield different results. We are working only with nuts, seeds and wheat. When fermented, these foods break down according to their nutrient personality. Protein changes into amino acids, fats into essential fatty acids and starches into sugars. However, if you ferment a fruit, its high sugar content will change to alcohol (like grapes to wine.). Apples ferment first to alcohol which, when acted upon by friendly bacteria, is oxidized into apple cider vinegar. Your best protection against bad fermentation is, again, your nose and your tongue.

Who Should Not Eat Fermented Foods

Certain people are just not made to eat fermented foods. These are very active foods that permeate the entire digestive tract. If you have a sensitive system, fermented foods may not be right for you. All fermented foods have a strong smell. This is their trade mark—like hard cheese. If you do not like the strong smell, then fermented foods are probably not for you. You could be allergic to them, they could make you tired after a meal, cause a headache, create a rash, gas or general gastric distress. Sometimes these symptoms represent an initial period of adjustment, but other times they remain. It may also be too acidic for you. Too many acid foods in the diet are not good for anyone. They overthrow the delicate acid–alkaline balance in the blood and cause a condition of acidosis. Often, enthusiastic vegetarians overeat these cheeses and yoghurts out of the thrill of having such foods again. They are forgetting that these foods are still concentrated because they are made from concentrated sources—nuts and seeds. Whether we like it or not, the best way to tell if fermented foods like Rejuvelac, etc. are good for you, is to try it. If you are allergic to these foods, take care to read labels as many of them, such as tamari and miso, are found as ingredients in other foods. Know your limits for the best results.

BASIC NUT &
SEED YOGHURT

Nut and seed yoghurts are completely dairyless desserts perfect for those who are sensitive to milk or want to cut down on their consumption of milk products. They can be made from sunflower seeds, cashews, almonds and sesame seeds to name a few. Yoghurt making is a bit of an art somewhat akin to making fine wine or cheese because it involves working with live cultures. In this respect, it may require more trial and error than other recipes to get the taste you want. If you are a beginner, we recommend you start with cashew yoghurt. *(Cashew yoghurt, p. 106.)*

Temperature Time and Place

The temperature you set for your yoghurt and the time it takes to mature are directly related to one another. The best temperature is 90°F. which takes approximately 8 hours for a 2 cup quantity (1 cup water, 1 cup nuts). As you raise the temperature, the yoghurt ferments faster, as you lower it, it takes longer. In either case, the temperature should never exceed 100°F. or fall below 70°F. in order for the proper bacterial action to take place. At the high temperature, yoghurt will be done in as little as 6 hours and at the low temperature, in as long as 24 hours. Temperatures or times beyond these limits will cause the wrong bacteria to propagate and the yoghurt may not be suitable for eating. Regularity of temperature is also important. For example, if you place your yoghurt on top of the radiator or in the sun, the temperatures will rise and fall. This will affect both texture and taste and ultimately the success of your batch.

If you have a gas stove, one of the best places to set your yoghurt is on top of the pilot light. This light can be adjusted with a screwdriver to raise or lower the flame so that it is just right. (Increasing or decreasing it will not affect the operation of your stove.) If you have a warm oven, you may place it inside, or you may use a yoghurt maker. If you set it inside a stove that has a pilot light that is always on, you should achieve a constant temperature and the best results. Yoghurt makers and food dryers (dehydrators) are okay. Dehydrators allow you to regulate the temperature. Yoghurt makers are usually preset at 75°–80°F., which is fine for dairy but on the low side for nut and seed yoghurt. Thus a longer fermenting time of perhaps 15 hours or more will be necessary. If you cannot find a special spot, you can still make yoghurt, it will simply take longer. Any warm spot in the house (houses are usually 70°) will do. Your batch will be ready in 15 to 24 hours. In summertime, it will be faster. Use the following guidelines to make sure it is done.

How To Tell When It Is Ready

Just like fine wine, it is taste that does the telling. Yoghurt is done when it has achieved a tart, sour or lemon–like flavor and the presence of air bubbles becomes visible. As the yoghurt sits, friendly bacteria proliferate and begin breaking it down (actually eating the yoghurt) and giving off carbon dioxide gas as a by–product. This is why yoghurt is considered a "pre–digested," or easy-to-digest, food. The gas makes the yoghurt rise just like yeast does in bread. For this reason, we do not cap the yoghurt but cover it with material that breathes. This is a very important sign. If your yoghurt does not rise or show gas bubbles, it is not right. You will also notice liquid on the bottom. This is the whey, which in the yoghurt making process, separates out from the curd. There should be approximately ½ inch of whey. You may drink it, discard it or mix some of it in according to your taste. It is commonly drained off. Use a knife or chopstick to create a path through the curds so the whey can drain. If there is no whey present, it indicates that more water should be added to the recipe.

How Much Water?

The amount of water required will vary depending on the size of the nuts. Cashews come in sizes such as jumbo, whole, splits, pieces and butts. The smaller the size, the more water you will need. For example, the same recipe with sunflower seed requires slightly more (1¼ cups) water, because of their smaller size. Since this will always vary slightly from seed to seed, simply aim to create the consistency of heavy cream. Add water to achieve the desired consistency while blending. Neither cashews nor sunflower seeds need to be soaked in order to prepare for this recipe because both are soft to begin with.

Other Nuts and Seeds

In addition to cashews and sunflowers, a variety of other nuts and seeds can be used, such as sesame seeds, almonds, pumpkin seeds, pecans, walnuts and filberts. Some ferment easier than others (sesame) and some have rather exotic flavors (pecans). The hard seeds, like almonds, require pre-soaking for at least 6 hours. The amount of water used should be between 1 and 2 cups. Again, use enough to achieve a consistency of thick cream. Sunflower and cashew are the easiest to make and the most popular. Start with them if this is your first time.

Sprouted Sunflower Yoghurt

If you like to experiment, try making sunflower yoghurt from sprouted sunflower seeds. Soak 1 cup of seeds for 8 hours and sprout them for 2 days maximum using a sprout bag. *(See Appendix, Sprouting, p. 287.)* Blend with water and warm as usual following the regular yoghurt recipe.

Storage

Seed yoghurt stores surprisingly well. Keep it refrigerated in a covered jar for a week. It can last longer. It keeps best if you pour off the whey and just save the yoghurt. Despite its long endurance, it is preferable to eat within a few days. Cashew yoghurt stores best of all the varieties and is the yoghurt of choice for beginners.

Create Your Own Culture

It sounds revolutionary! Marxist! Stalinesque! Not quite. The society you are propagating is bacteria! If you like the taste and texture of a particular batch, save it just like beer brewers do in order to make their own unique brand. Take a tablespoon of the good stuff and add it as a starter to your next batch. It should have the same taste and will mature faster, too. Try to start a new batch just before the old one is finished. In case you cannot, store the starter in a cold spot, but do not freeze it. Like a mad scientist mating the genes of one species with another, you will be saving your favorite bacterial strain so that it can "live" forever.

Here's another biological experiment that is designed to clone your personality. Ordinarily, enzymes in the nut or seed initiate the breakdown into yoghurt, and bacteria from the air join in to complete the process. This time you can replicate your own private batch of enzymes with your own personality blueprint to start the process. Just chew a small amount of nuts thoroughly and add it to the basic recipe. Blend it all together and proceed as usual. Your very own salivary enzymes will initiate the yoghurt process. Just don't tell anybody you did it!

What About Whey?

Whey is the liquid portion of seed yoghurt that separates from the solids or curds during the yoghurt process. This by–product is often discarded, although some is dried and sold commercially. It is added to cereals and used as a general digestive aid much the same as yoghurt. If you make your yoghurt correctly, ½–1 inch of whey will settle at the bottom of your jar with the "curds" floating on top. In dairy milk, whey is often referred to as buttermilk, the thin watery fluid that separates out after cream is churned into butter. Whey is rich in B vitamins, has lots of B–12 and easily digestible protein.

Cashew Yoghurt

Ingredients

1 cup	Cashews
1 cup	Pure Water

Yield: 2 cups

Blend a cup of cashews with a cup of pure water. Blend the mixture thoroughly until smooth. Keep adding water, until you have the consistency of heavy cream. Pour it into a pint jar and cover with a cheese cloth, towel, napkin or sprout bag. This affords the transfer of air and gases. Set your jar in a warm place where the yoghurt temperature can heat up to 90°–100°F. It will be ready in approximately 6 to 8 hours or when it tastes tart and sour.

La Cucumber Sandwich

Ingredients

1	Cucumber, large
1 cup	Almonds
1 cup	Water
1 Tbsp	Dulse, flakes
1 Handful	Alfalfa sprouts
1 Pinch	Garlic sprouts

A boat departing its berth isn't nearly as momentous as when your almond cream coated cucumber sandwich launches down your gullet into gastronomical heaven.

First make almond cream by soaking the almonds in water for 4 hours. Removing the skins optional. Blend them in their own soak water until a creamy (thick shake) consistency is achieved. Select a thin skinned, unwaxed green cucumber and slice it in half lengthwise. A quality cucumber is required since it is the primary ingredient in this dish. Pour the cream directly onto the center of the sliced cucumber and sprinkle the dulse flakes on top. Add the alfalfa and garlic sprouts. Put both halves together and voilà—*La Cucumber sandwich.*

Spicy Cucumber Sandwich

Ingredients

Pinch	Cayenne pepper
Spread of	Almond yoghurt

For a spicier version, sprinkle a pinch of cayenne pepper onto the cream prior to adding the dulse and sprouts. Instead of almond cream, use almond cream yoghurt. Almond cream yoghurt is cultured almond cream with a tart taste. *(see p.102.)*

NUT & SEED CHEESE

Basic Seed Cheese

Ingredients

1 cup	Sunflower Seeds
1 cup	Pure Water

Optional Ingredients: Herbs
Cayenne, Garlic, Onion,
Oregano, Savory, Thyme, Basil

Cheeses are related to yoghurts in preparation. Making yoghurt is the first step in making cheese. Make your nut yoghurt according to the basic yoghurt instructions. *(See p. 102.)* Taste test the yoghurt to make sure it is has that tart, lemon–like flavor. Pour out the excess water (whey), if present. Now, you arc ready to make soft cheese simply by aging the yoghurt. Two recipes follow. *Sunflower Farmer Cheese* recipe is akin to high moisture dairy cheeses such as cottage, farmer and ricotta. While dry and hard cheeses like *parmesan,* can be substituted with *Sunflower Parmesan, see p. 162 and Sun–Cheese p. 160.*

Sunflower Farmer Cheese

Ingredients

1 cup	Sunflower Seeds
1 cup	Pure Water

Sunflower Farmer Cheese can be made simply by first preparing seed yoghurt *(see p. 102)*, then pouring it into a sprout bag or cheese cloth and hanging it up to age and dry. You are simply hanging your yoghurt up to dry! A sprout bag is the best choice for this. The "cheese" drains, dries and ages all at the same time. It will be ready in approximately 8–12 hours or overnight at room temperature of 70°–75°F. It should have a denser consistency than regular farmer cheese and a tart, sour taste. Cottage cheese can be made in the same way but starts with a coarser blend of the seeds.

Cashew Cottage Cheese

Ingredients

1 cup	Cashews
1 cup	Pure Water

Yield: 1 pint of soft cheese

Grind the cashews and water together in your blender with the dial set to "chop." The result should be a partially blended, lumpy batch. Proceed to age it as you would regular yoghurt. Let sit in an uncovered jar for approximately 20 hours at room temperature or about 8 hours at 90 degrees F. As with yoghurt, it is done when large air bubbles appear and it has a tart lemon–like taste. Generally the whey is poured out before serving, but you may mix it in, if desired for texture and taste. Chill and serve.

Seed Cheese Loaf

Ingredients

1 cup	Sesame Seed Cheese
1 cup	Sunflower Seed Cheese
½ cup	Carrots, shredded
½ cup	Celery, diced
1 small	Red Onion, chopped
2	Garlic Cloves, pressed
1 cup	Mustard Sprouts or 1 tsp mustard)
1 tsp	Fennel
1 tsp	Celery Seed
3 Tbsp	Tamari
1	Lemon, juiced

This cheese is similar to our "farmer cheese" but is a mixture of two seeds and is full of your favorite vegetables. First prepare one good batch each of sesame and sunflower yoghurt. Pour off the whey and mix the two together. Now add the vegetables, sprouts, spices and lemon. Mix thoroughly and let sit in a covered bowl for 24 hours. It is like making your own sour dough.

An optional but delicious touch is to age this dish in a food dehydrator. Spread to ½ inch thick and dry it. Serve on a platter with paprika, sprouts and shredded carrot. Experiment with other versions; include different herbs, vegetable broth powders and kelp. This hearty, aged loaf has a strong flavor and a "meaty" taste. It should be eaten as a side dish with vegetables and salads. Store for 1 week in the refrigerator. Do not drive under the influence of seed loaf!

Hard Cheese

Hard cheese is made by drying the yoghurt mixture in a dehydrator or in the sun. Freshly made yoghurt is spread onto one of the dehydrator trays. The result is a delightful semi-moist, or dry and brittle texture. Since hard cheeses are dehydrated, they are fully discussed in the chapter on food dehydration. Here are some of the recipes you will find there: *Sunny Parmesan Cheese, Hot and Spicy cheese, Herb cheese, Cheese and chips and Cashew Yoghurt cheese.*

Rejuvelac!

What Is It?

After all that sprout bread, sunflower parmesan cheese, nut yoghurt and sprout pizza, you can get thirsty! So, how about some sprout lemonade? Rejuvelac is simply lemonade without the lemon. The lemon–like flavor comes from the culturing and fermenting of the sprouted wheat. It was invented by Dr. Ann Wigmore, founder of the Hippocrates Health Institute and the Ann Wigmore Foundations in Boston and Puerto Rico. *(See Appendix, Resources, p. 305.)* She had been experimenting with irradiated foods to see if they were still healthy. Irradiation is the practice of exposing food to streams of ionizing (gamma or electron) radiation from radioactive Cobalt-60 or

Cesium–137. The fruits, vegetables, grains or meats do not become radioactive themselves (the dosage, approximately 100 to 1,000 kilorads, is too small), but some of their cells are altered and micro–organisms are destroyed, which inhibits spoilage. The commercial advantages to irradiation are the decreased use of pesticides and increased shelf life. Dr. Ann was suspicious, and rightly so, of any food that could keep for 2 or 3 months without refrigeration. So, she decided to experiment by eating these foods and monitoring the effects.

> *After a short period, my body became thin and weak and my digestion was destroyed. I felt sickly with hardly enough energy to move about. When I asked the Creator for an answer, the idea of soaking wheat came to me. So I began to soak wheat and to drink quarts of the water in which the wheat had been soaked. My health began to return and I regained weight. It was as a result of this episode that Rejuvelac was created* [15].

Its abundant source of enzymes, healthful micro–organisms and vitamins gave her the missing elements she needed and the idea to call it "rejuvelac" for its rejuvenating properties.

The theory is simple and so is the technique. The wheat sits in the water for several days exuding its enzymes, vitamins and proteins. Friendly living organisms develop during this time that manufacture more vitamins and partially digest the protein. It tastes tart just like yoghurt and similar to lemonade. Imagine enjoying your own lemonade all year round without having to buy lemons! It's more nutritious, too.

PRESERVE HUMAN LIFE

NOT SHELF LIFE

Basic Rejuvelac

Ingredients

½ cup   Soft Wheat Berries
6–7 cups   Pure Water

Yield: Approximately 2 quarts

First, you will need a half gallon jar, ½ cup of soft wheat berries and your trusty sprout bag or jar. Although Rejuvelac can be made with unsprouted grain, sprouted wheat brings to the water an abundance of vitamins, enzymes and protein. It also provides maltose, the grain sugar, as a by–product of germination. Soft wheat is preferred to hard wheat because of its sweeter, and more delicate flavor.

Start by sprouting ½ cup of soft wheat berries for 3 days in a sprout bag. First soak the berries for 10–12 hours, then rinse twice daily. *(See Appendix, Sprouting, p. 287.)* Mix or chop the 3 day-old sprouts in a blender filled about three–fourths of the way with pure water—about 3 cups. The "chop" should break open the sprouts but not blend them to a paste. If you have an old fashioned blender with just one or two speeds, blend for about 10 seconds. This releases their storehouse of vitamins, proteins and enzymes into the water. Next, pour the water and the sprouts into the half gallon jar. Fill the jar to the top with water and let it sit for three days in a shady spot at approximately 65°–75°F. Cover the top with your sprout bag, cheesecloth or a screen. Your Rejuvelac must breathe. A mason jar is very convenient for this since it has a removable inner lid and allows for easy placement of a cheesecloth or screen. Stir the mixture twice daily. This is very important. It mixes up the enzymes and develops live organisms. A chopstick or other long utensil is helpful. Smell your mixture each day so that you can monitor its maturation. Making Rejuvelac is like baby sitting. Although these baby organisms are too small to see, they still need your tender care. Don't walk out on your Rejuvelac or, like a baby, it will develop a smell.

How To Tell When It's Done

Good Rejuvelac, like good yoghurt, tastes sour. It will smell fresh and taste like sparkling lemon water. In some cases, it may remind you of sauerkraut. The differences in taste have to do with variances in the temperature and the frequency of stirring. The cooler temperatures tend to create a lemon taste, the warmer temperatures, sauerkraut. Stirring is crucial to flavor. Stirring distributes and enlivens the friendly bacteria that break down the starch into sweeter sugars. Smell your Rejuvelac before you drink it. Remember, good Rejuvelac will taste like lemon or sauerkraut, and smell fresh. It may take you a couple of trials to establish the right location and technique. Every environment is unique. If your Rejuvelac smells bad or does not have the characteristic taste, then something is wrong. Let your nose and tongue be your guide. Putrefactive bacteria may have developed. To be safe, throw it out and start over again. Good judgment is part of good health.

How To Take Rejuvelac

If your Rejuvelac is ready, stir it one final time and pour off the liquid through a screen or strainer leaving the sprouts behind. This is the Rejuvelac you will drink. Because it is so "alive" with enzymes and active bacteria, start with only one glass, 6–8 ounces per day, in order to allow your body to adjust to the infusion of new intestinal flora. After approximately two weeks, your system should become acclimated to it and you may increase the volume and frequency of your drinks. But don't chug it down. Always treat Rejuvelac with respect. After all, it is not Coca–Cola. It's *the real thing.*

Storage and Endurance

Place the decanted Rejuvelac—the batch you are drinking from—in the refrigerator. Close the jar with a covered lid so that it does not absorb refrigerator odors. Be sure to open it at least once every few days to release the carbon dioxide that builds up. Rejuvelac has the amazing ability to last for weeks. It is good as long as it has its characteristic flavor. The mother jar—the original batch with the pulp—is not ready to quit. Refill it with water and the old sprouts will get stirred up for another round. The second batch matures faster than the first, taking only 2–3 days. You have just shortened the generation gap! This batch has a milder flavor because it is less virile. You can reap more than two generations from the same mother, but it is not recommended because each one is weaker in potency. Give your mother a break! When you are done with the spent wheat, don't throw your mother down the sink. She is highly cultured. When the time comes, we recommend dehydration *(see p.171)*. The dried, powdered sprouts make a kind of "sprout yeast." Life springs eternal.

Rejuvelac Wine

Ingredients

½ cup	Soft Wheat Berries
3/4 cup	Organic Raisins
2–3 Tbsp	Star Anise
Top off	Pure Water

Yield: 2 quarts

Like Rejuvelac? Fine. While you're still standing up, let's make some wine!

This "wine" is a variation of the standard Rejuvelac recipe. Begin the same way by soaking the wheat berries for 8 hours, then sprouting them in a sprout bag for 3 days. Set your blender to chop, then pour the chopped sprouts into a half gallon mason or other jar. This time add the raisins and anise, then fill to the top with pure water. Place your jar in a cool or shady spot. Temperatures of 65°–75°F. are ideal. Cover the top with a sprouting lid, a screen, a sprout bag or other breathable fabric. Let sit for 3–4 days as before, depending on the season and temperature. Stir twice daily.

After 3 days, decant the wine leaving the raisins, anise and sprout pulp behind. Store as usual in the refrigerator, with a covered lid, for up to 2 weeks; meanwhile refill the mother bottle for a second batch. The second generation will take half the time as the first, but is also less potent.

Rejuvelac wine may actually have a tiny alcoholic content developed from the fermentation of the sugars in the raisins. Although, it's not enough to make you tipsy, the flavor can knock you off your seat! If there is any alcohol content, it is checked by the prolific amount of friendly bacteria and enzymes, B–vitamins and B–12. It promotes a healthy intestinal tract and should keep you walking straight.

California Wine

Ingredients

½ cup	Soft Wheat Berries
4	Figs, dried and chopped
3 sticks	Cinnamon

Yield: 2 quarts

Proceed according to the basic recipe for *Rejuvelac wine (p. 116)*, only this time replace the raisins and anise with dried figs and cinnamon sticks. Chop the figs first for best results.

Other wines could include dill seed, fennel, parsley, basil, peppermint, spearmint, cardamon, sassafras, mace and allspice. Have fun and hold on to your hats!

New York Wine

½ cup	Soft Wheat Berries
3/4 cup	Organic Raisins
¼ cup	Sassafras Bark

Proceed according to the basic recipe for *Rejuvelac wine (p. 116)*. A strong flavored wine made for people who can take it. Uses chopped dates and sassafras bark.

Chablis

½ cup	Soft Wheat Berries
1 cup	Dates, chopped
2 Tbsp	Peppermint Leaves

Proceed according to the basic recipe for *Rejuvelac wine (p. 116)*. A light aperitif made with raisins and 3 Tbsp peppermint leaves for a real surprise. Ooh, la la.

Bordeaux

½ cup	Soft Wheat Berries
3/4 cup	Organic Raisins
2	Licorice Stix

Proceed according to the basic recipe for *Rejuvelac wine, (p. 116)*. This unassuming dinner wine is made with raisins and licorice stix and has an invigorating flavor.

Other Grains

Rejuvelac can be made with any grain. Hard wheat, kamut, rye, barley, oats, millet and rice are all possibilities, but generally do not taste as good. Hard wheat has a stronger flavor than soft wheat. Rye and barley are even more potent. Rice, kamut (Egyptian wheat), oats and millet are the best tasting, but of these, only kamut will sprout. The others will not germinate in the form commonly available to consumers. However, the non-sprouters still make good Rejuvelac. Just follow the recipe eliminating the sprouting step. It will not be as nutritious nor taste as sweet, but it is still Rejuvelac. Of all the alternatives, rice, millet and kamut are my number 2 choices. Though experimenting can be fun, sprouted soft white wheat is still number one.

ICE CREAM

Without Sin

In this modern age of overindulgence, ice cream has become our mascot of gluttony leading us down the path of portliness and sugar–coated transgression. No other food is so burdened by guilt with every bite. Nor is any so tied to reward for its ingestion. One often "sneaks" a taste of ice cream rather than eats it or earns a dish only after some masterly achievement.

The Origin of Ice Cream

Rumor has it that ice cream was first discovered in the late nineteenth century by John Milchedig. John had a reputation as an over-anxious farmer who persisted in milking his cows even in the cold and snow. One day before the onset of a nasty winter storm, he was working feverishly and in his haste accidentally whipped the milk into cream. By the time he got home, the cold had set in and the cream was frozen. Not being the type to let his milk go to waste, he asked his family to help him eat it. No one was very happy having frozen cream with their cereals. But they scraped it and sweetened and, in fact, developed a taste for it. Twenty-four hours and two gallons later, John was back in the cold trying to replicate his frozen cream. He worked for days through some of the winter's iciest weather. So strong was his commitment that his family began to worry. Then, one day, when he did not return for dinner, *Howard, John's son,* went out to fetch him. There in the midst of a bad storm, he found his father fallen at the hoof. "It's done," he gasped, handing Howard the finished product, but he lapsed before he could utter another word. John had finally succeeded and it was delicious. Right then and there, Howard pledged to bring his father's iced cream to restaurants all over the world. The rest is dental history.

Quality vs. Entertainment

Ice cream is a much loved food. The feelings that ice cream supports, celebration, pleasure and reward are laudable. One would not want to besmirch the good name of ice cream or its positive psychological effects. But as with many things, quality makes a difference. Ice cream, as it is commercially available, can contain milk, eggs, artificial flavors, dyes, BHT, BHA, glacial acetic acid, benzyl acetate, propylene glycol or any of one hundred chemical stabilizers, emulsifiers, bactericides and thickeners that are legally permitted. They are *not* required to be stated on the label. Even if it was perfectly pure, it would still be verboten for the strict—vegan—vegetarian. The recipes that follow are dairyless ice creams, made from fruit and/or nuts and natural sweeteners. Now you can enjoy the psychological benefits of ice cream without the disadvantage of unhealthful ingredients.

How To Pick Bananas

A Letter Of Appeal

Bananas have a secret appeal. This soft, sweet, sensuous fruit has served us dutifully through the ages in the form of pies, cakes, cookies, snacks, cereals and fruit salads. Where else can you get a wealth of carbohydrates, vitamins and minerals in a neat, naturally wrapped package! But bananas have never received their deserved respect. Man has mashed it, squeezed it, blended it, composted it and used it as the butt of his jokes. How unfair! This gentle fruit never hurt anyone. Its only fault is its colorful complexion. They come in dark skins or light, with spots or without, firm and strong or soft and sweet. Even the old wrinkled ones are ravishing. They make wonderful snacks as dried banana stix or chips. One of the saddest sights is to see the local grocer throwing out old bananas. It is acknowledged that the truly black bananas are already halfway to heaven, but many of the old softees are still in their prime. If you want to do the humane thing, ask your grocer to let you adopt them at a low price. Give bananas a home and they will give you a treat.

—The Banana Fan Club

PICKING RIPE BANANAS IS THE MOST IMPORTANT PART OF MAKING BANANA ICE CREAM. DON'T SLIP UP. MAKE THE RIPE CHOICE.

Color Me Yellow

Turning disrespect into humiliation, modern day commercial plantation farmers pick bananas green and fumigate all bananas coming into this country from Mexico, the Caribbean, South and Central America. Fumigation is required for bananas, papayas, pineapples and other tropical fruit by the Department of Agriculture in order to prevent the spread of pests, plagues and witch doctors. Health food stores sometimes carry ungassed bananas, so keep looking. But if you really want to do a banana a favor, pick it ripe. It's easy. The first thing to look for is color. No racism here. Bananas are made up of many wonderful shades. A ripe banana is bright golden yellow with brown spots all over. The necks and bottoms should be black, and perhaps shriveled, but not green. Try not to buy bananas housed in plastic. A plastic bag is nothing but cold-blooded murder to a banana as it cuts off its respiration! Avoid green or pale yellow bananas as they are too starchy. Pick them soft with a deep yellow complexion and few, if any, bruises. If your bananas are ripe, sit or hang them in a place where they can get plenty of ventilation. If they are a little green around the edges, so are we all! Simply enclose them in a brown paper bag. This enhances the production of natural ethylene gas that ripens them the way Mother nature intended. If you wish to accelerate the ripening, try singing to them, preferably in Spanish. Above all, if you can't find the banana you love, love the one you find.

How To Find
The Perfect "10" Banana

a. Deep blonde–yellow skin with lots of freckles.

b. No bruises on the body and no green at the neck or feet.

c. Black necks are the most desirable. This is where they are joined with their sisters. A green neck is simply not ready to break away.

d. Soft to the touch, but don't squeeze until he/she is yours.

Ode to a Banana

Good morn, sweet, soft, and gentle fruit.
You who glide to earth from high above in thy armour of gold,
thy suit of yellow.
There is no other fruit before me, so handsomely dressed, so
pleasantly curved.
Let me jump into thy crescent and sleep the night away as if
the very moon were in my lap.
And in the day, I bask in your brightness only to be outshown
by the sun itself.
Lend me your finger sweet arch, that I may savor each
moment before thy fall.

Oh, thou phosphorus-filled friend, feed me your potassium, your
vitamin A, your sweet fruit sugar.
No other fruit could do the same.
Nay, woulds't I even light upon a lime (too green), a lemon (too
sharp), a logenberry (too tart).
An apple has not the pectin for me!
The breadfruit no bread, the date, no date.
I water not for watermelon.
You are my mango, my papaya,
and I your nut.

Dairyless Banana Ice Cream

Ingredients

I bunch   Ripe Bananas

Basic banana ice cream is basically made from bananas. Just peel them, freeze them and homogenize them through an ice cream maker. It's that easy. Start by buying about 4 ripe bananas or as many bananas as you have guests. Remove the peels, wrap them in a plastic bag and freeze. When thoroughly hard, pump one at a time through a Champion juicer set in the homogenizing mode. There are only three elements here: you, the banana and the machine. The last two are most important.

The Ice Cream Machine

The ice cream machine is entrusted with the job of breaking down the ice into tiny pieces and whipping the fruit or other ingredients into a creamy, "custard" consistency. This "homogenizing" action can be achieved with a professional ice cream maker, a food processor or a Champion juicer. A professional ice cream machine is designed to accept ice, cream, milk, fruit, and sugar and mix it all together. If you are just using a frozen banana, you do not need an ice cream maker and will not be using its full capabilities. The other ice cream recipes have more ingredients, but they can easily be mixed in a blender. The ice cream maker would serve only to mix in the ice cubes. Such a minor use for a machine that can only serve one food function may not be the most useful way to spend your kitchen appliance dollars.

Food processors, on the other hand, serve multiple purposes and are in many kitchens already. If you have one, try using it before buying anything else. Cut 2 frozen bananas into one inch pieces and process them with the whipping blade or the stainless steel cutting "S" blade. Whip until smooth. The processor does a good job most of the time but watch out for its two failings. Sometimes large pieces of frozen banana remain unfractionated and detract from the total smooth texture of the ice cream. Also, in your attempt to whip it smooth, you may actually start to defrost the dish. However, if you do not want to purchase any other equipment, this will do.

Ironically, the best machine for making dairyless ice cream is a Champion juicer. This versatile machine makes vegetable and fruit juice, shreds carrots, coconuts, beets and has a "homogenizing" mode that grinds nuts and seeds into butter, sprouts into sprout bread and frozen fruit into ice cream. The result is a velvety textured ice cream that is a lot like the professional swirled type soft ice cream extruders. Do not expect your regular centrifugal vegetable juicer to do the same thing (Save yourself a mess.). Blenders also do not work. If you put a frozen banana in a blender, nothing much happens. Blenders are liquifiers by their nature and require water, which would make your ice cream very watery. The attraction of ice cream is 50% texture and 50% taste.

More Banana Ice Cream

Strawberry Banana

Ingredients

6–8	Ripe Bananas
1 pint	Strawberries

Blueberry Banana

Ingredients

6–8	Ripe bananas
1 pint	Blueberries

Follow the basic banana recipe, but this time add the new ingredients. Always wash your strawberries and blueberries well and buy them organically grown when possible. Remove stems and buds and freeze in a separate plastic bag from the bananas. Once frozen, pump the berries through the Champion juicer by alternating the banana and berries. Try to keep a ratio of 3:1—three parts banana to one part berries. Why, you ask, don't we just use the berries alone? Unfortunately, these berries are too watery and require the thickening and emulsifying properties of banana to resemble ice cream.

Banana–Date Ice Cream

Ingredients

6	Ripe Bananas
12	Dates, pitted

This time, pump those bananas through the Champion while alternating with soaked, chopped dates. Use 2 dates for every banana. Soak the dates first to soften them so as not to overwork your machine. Whatever you do don't forget to pit them, or you'll have a pitiful mess! Serve with chopped filberts or your favorite nut on top.

Sprout Banana Ice Cream

Ingredients

4	Ripe Bananas
1/3 cup	Sunflower Seeds

Here, the prettiest and the strongest foods team up to make a hell (health) of a dish.

Sprout the hulled—steel gray—sunflower seeds in the sprout bag for 2 days. Soak for 10 hours, then drain and rinse twice a day. *(See Appendix, Sprouting, p. 287.)* Freeze in a plastic container. Pump the frozen sprouts through the Champion juicer in alternation with frozen bananas. It's absolutely seedful!

Carob–Banana Ice Cream

Ingredients

2–3	Bananas, ripe
1/3 cup	Carob Powder
¼ cup	Honey
2 Tbsp	Liquid Lecithin
I tsp	Vanilla extract

Yield: Serves 4

Here's a delicious dessert that lets your conscience feel as good as your stomach. First, chop up the bananas and whip them in the food processor along with the carob, lecithin, honey and vanilla. Although food processors are best, you may use a blender. Poke the bananas around with a spatula until they are whipped. When smooth, pour the mixture into an ice cube tray. Cover the tray with wax paper and freeze. When frozen, snap the cubes out of the tray and push them through the Champion juicer one at a time.

An alternative to the ice cube trays is a pint size plastic container—the kind available in deli stores. Freeze your ice cream in it. When ready to serve, loosen by running the container briefly under hot water. Invert onto a cutting board and force out the ice cream. Cut the mold into cubes and pump them one by one into the Champion as in the basic recipe.

SPROUTMAN'S® FAMOUS

Cashew–Vanilla Ice Cream

Ingredients

1 cup	Cashews
1 cup	Pure Water
1	Golden Delicious Apple, cored
1/3 cup	Maple Syrup or ¼ cup Honey
1	Fresh Vanilla Bean or 1 tsp extract
3 Tbsp	Liquid Lecithin

Ain't No Bananas

Bored with bananas? If you're turning yellow and developing freckles, it's time for a change. This is the ice cream of choice for those who have had enough. First blend the cashews and water, then add the apple and lastly the bean and lecithin. Blend until thoroughly smooth, then taste. It has got to taste good now or it will not taste good later. Make any minor adjustments as you desire. It should be the consistency of heavy cream. Pour the liquid into ice cubes or a plastic container as before. When frozen, slice the mold into small parts that will fit down the Champion juicer. Don't forget to take your share before it's too late.

SPROUTMAN'S® FAMOUS
Coffee Ice Cream

Ingredients

1 cup	Cashews
1 cup	Pure Water
1	Golden Delicious Apple, cored
1/3 cup	Maple Syrup or ¼ cup Honey
3 Tbsp	Herbal Grain beverage (Coffee)
1	Fresh Vanilla Bean or
	2 Tbsp vanilla extract
3 Tbsp	Liquid Lecithin

Coffee and ice cream? What kind of health book is this! Don't panic. Keep your Good Humor. This is guaranteed to be the healthiest coffee ice cream in the world.

Follow the same instructions as in the *Cashew–Vanilla* recipe, only this time add your favorite coffee substitute. Some popular brand names are Cafix and Bamboo, but there are others. Blend and freeze in ice cube as before. Run through the Champion for that custard texture.

Mocha Ice Cream

Start with the coffee ice cream recipe. Add 3 tablespoons of raw carob powder to the ingredients. Also add additional water as necessary to compensate for the carob and coffee powders. That's all!

About the Ingredients

Raw carob powder tastes sweeter and lighter than the toasted kind, which is somewhat bitter. Unfortunately, it is harder to find.

Golden delicious apples are recommended because of their neutral color skins and their sweet taste. The apples add lightness, and sweetness and their pectins help hold the mixture together.

Sweeteners. Use good quality maple syrup from organic farmers. Maple syrup adds a lot of flavor. Honey adds smoothness and creaminess.

Cashews are the main ingredient in the non–banana ice creams so find good tasting cashews. As you know, cashews come in different sizes—jumbo, butts, splits and pieces. The jumbos are the best quality and the most expensive. The splits and pieces are just what they sound like and are the most economical. Unfortunately, they expose more surface area to light and air for oxidation. You may notice this in old cashews as a browning around the edges. Pass these by and purchase the cleanest, whitest cashews you can find.

Liquid lecithin is a viscous oil extracted from soybeans. It is an extremely rich source of phosphorus and the B vitamins choline and inositol. It is known for its excellent ability to emulsify oils. Its job in this recipe is to add a thickness and creaminess that is usually provided by an egg. Dry lecithin granules are not as good for this purpose although they are a good supplementary food.

Vanilla. If you choose vanilla extract, try to find one with a low alcohol content, preferably less than 35%. Do not buy "vanillin," which is an artificial flavor. In this recipe, the vanilla bean can be used easily and with great results. Just chop your bean up into pieces and throw it in the blender with the maple syrup. It will blend nicely and you will have lots of brown bean speckles and a few larger pieces that have a pleasant crunchy taste. The long, dark, slender beans are available at natural food stores. Incidentally, you can make your own vanilla without any alcohol. Just blend fresh vanilla beans with water and strain.

For more information on the above ingredients, see Glossary, p. 269.

This ice cream is made of the healthiest ingredients and resembles the texture, color, temperature and flavor of the dairy version. But just like the real thing, it is rich. Overconsumption can be too hard on your system to digest. It's fun food, so eat it, sparingly and for fun.

Sproutman® Meets
THE MARX BROS.
(Even They Like Dairyless Ice Cream!)

N— A Burlesque In One Act —N

Source Unknown

CHICO	Hey, get 'cha tutti-fruitti ice cream...Hey, get 'cha tutti-fruitti ice cream...
GROUCHO	What kind of flavors do you have?
CHICO	I got chocolate, strawberry, and vanilla.
GROUCHO	Okay, I'll take vanilla.
CHICO	Sorry, I don't have any.
GROUCHO	I thought you just said you had vanilla.
CHICO	I do got vanilla. I just ran out of it.
GROUCHO	Okay, I'll take strawberry.
CHICO	Sorry, I don't got no strawberry...Hey, get'cha tutti–fruitti ice cream...
GROUCHO	I suppose you don't have chocolate either?
CHICO	No.

GROUCHO	No what?
CHICO	No, I do have it.
GROUCHO	Oh, well in that case....
CHICO	I just ran out of it that's all.
GROUCHO	I see...I suppose you don't have any tutti-fruitti either.
CHICO	I don't sell the tutti-fruitti.
GROUCHO	You don't sell tutti fruitti,...Why not?
CHICO	It's no good for you, that's why.
GROUCHO	It's no good for me, eh?
CHICO	Yeah, it's got sugar in it.
GROUCHO	It's got sugar in it. Oh, I see...sugar. I should have known...that'll make it taste good.
CHICO	Yeah, but it's a no good for the blood sugar.
GROUCHO	Well, I don't want any blood sugar, I want plain sugar.
CHICO	I don't sell plain sugar.
GROUCHO	Okay, then I'll buy some blood sugar.
CHICO	You can't buy blood sugar, you gotta make it.
GROUCHO	I gotta make it myself, eh?
CHICO	Yeah, you make it in the pancreas.
GROUCHO	All right, I'll buy one.
CHICO	I don't sell any.
GROUCHO	I suppose you ran out of them.
CHICO	Eh, you a nice guy, I'll tell you what I'm gonna do. I'm gonna give you some ice cream that's real good for you.
GROUCHO	You're gonna give me some ice cream? Well, now that's the best news I've heard all day. What flavor?
CHICO	Sprout.
GROUCHO	Would you mind spitting that again?
CHICO	I said sprout. Sprout ice cream.
GROUCHO	That's what I thought you said. I think I'm getting a little indigestion, so long.
CHICO	Just a minute, don't you want any ice cream?
GROUCHO	I'm not sure.
CHICO	This is healthy for you. It's got no sugar, no eggs, no milk.
GROUCHO	What's it made of...air? Ha!
CHICO	It's just made out of fresh fruit...
GROUCHO	What did you call me?
CHICO	. . . And sprouts.

GROUCHO	Look, do you think you could spray somewhere else?
CHICO	Here, try some.
GROUCHO	Uhh . . . You know what it looks like, don't you. Hmmm . . . but not too bad. All right, how much does it cost?
CHICO	Nothing today.
GROUCHO	Nothing? Don't tell me...you don't sell any.
CHICO	I do sell it. I just ran out of it. That's all.
GROUCHO	Now you've got me hooked. Where can I get some of this sprout ice-cream?
CHICO	From the Sproutman.
GROUCHO	The Sproutman...eh? What does this guy do...fly?
CHICO	He doesn't fly, he sprouts.
GROUCHO	I see...well, okay, how do I find him?
CHICO	You don't find him, he finds you.
GROUCHO	Well, what do I do, stand on Main Street and wave a pancreas?
CHICO	Well, if you wave your pancreas, he will come.
GROUCHO	I'll bet he won't be the only one. Well, thanks for the information.
CHICO	Hey...where you going?
GROUCHO	I'm going to look for my pancreas.

☆ *FIN* ☆

REVIEW

Making Non-Dairy Yoghurt And Cheese

Step 1 Collect 1 cup of your favorite seed. Cashew, sunflower, sesame and pumpkin are most popular and the easiest to prepare.

Step 2 Blend with 1 to 1½ cups of pure water until smooth. The consistency should be that of heavy cream or a "thick shake." Add or reduce water accordingly. If you use hard seeds such as almonds, then soak them first for 6 hours.

Step 3 Pour into an uncovered jar or one covered with a sprout bag, screen or cheese cloth. Place in a warm environment: a) Over the pilot light on top of the stove; b) Inside an always warm oven; c) In a yoghurt maker or food dehydrator; d) At room temperature.

Step 4 Let sit for approximately 6 hours if the temperature is 90°–100°F. and a starter is used, or 8 hours if a starter is not used. Lower temperatures take longer. At room temperature, the yoghurt should sit for 20–24 hours or one day.

Step 5 The yoghurt is done when a) Lots of air bubbles become visible indicating the presence of carbon dioxide producing bacteria and yeasts; b) The taste is tart and sour; c) Whey, a white liquid, is visible at the bottom of the jar.

Making Non—Dairy Cheeses

Step 6 To make cheese, follow steps 1–5 and first make yoghurt. Pour off as much of the whey as possible. For best results, pour into a sprout bag and let drain. For soft cheeses like ricotta and farmer cheese, let sit for 12 hours to drain and cool. For cottage cheese, process the cashews only to a chop, allowing some large pieces in the final product. Eat the "cheese" right after draining off the whey or let sit for additional time depending on desired flavor.

Step 7 For hard cheese, pour or drain off the whey and spread the curds out on a non-stick dehydrator sheet 1/8 to ¼ inch thick. Dry for approximately 12 hours at 125°F. Make it perfectly dry and brittle or slightly moist depending on the variety. Length of drying period will vary. Higher temperatures mean shorter drying times. Thicker spreads mean longer drying times.

Step 8 Store yoghurts and "soft" cheeses in the refrigerator for up to a week. Store perfectly dry hard cheeses in a closed jar or plastic bag/container in your cupboard. If they are slightly moist, store in a refrigerator. Most hard cheeses store for months.

Review — Making Rejuvelac

Step 1 Soak ½ cup of soft white wheat berries for 12 hours.

Step 2 Sprout in a sprout bag for 3 days or until the "shoots" are longer than the berry. *(See Appendix, Sprouting, p. 287.)*

Step 3 Pour all sprouts into a blender and mix or chop with 3 cups of pure water for approximately 10 seconds. The sprouts should be macerated but not blended.

Step 4 Pour the entire contents into a 2 quart jar. Top off with more water. Cover the jar with a sprout bag, cheese cloth or screen.

Step 5 Let age for 3–4 days, stirring twice each day. Sit it in a warm place between 68° and 77°F.

Step 6 Taste each day. It is ready when a distinct lemonade or sauerkraut flavor is achieved. Stir, then strain out the liquid and refrigerate in a covered jar. Stores perfectly for up to 2 weeks.

Step 7 If you wish to make a second jar from the same batch, refill the mother jar with water and proceed as in step 5. This time it takes 2–3 days to mature. Potency reduces with each generation. Discard the berries or dehydrate them to make "matzoh."

Questions & Answers
with Sproutman®
(What Could Possibly Go Wrong?)

DEAR SPROUTMAN: I have been sitting with my nut yoghurt now for 8 hours and still I'm not seeing bubbles. Am I blind?
—*Deflated*

DEAR DEFLATED: Don't be depressed. Pump yourself up with some Rejuvelac wine, then go back and blend those nuts. Your temperature is undoubtedly too low...for the nuts. Below 68°F., bacteria won't thrive as vigorously. Once you warm them, you'll see that they will be bubbling with joy—and so will you.

DEAR SPROUTMAN: I've made seed yoghurt now several times and still there's no whey. Why?
—*Dehydrated*

DEAR DEHYDRATED: Water is the most important ingredient in life. Use it. Your yoghurts are suffering from a condition known as lowfluiditis. When blending, add between 1 and 2 cups of water to the 1 cup of nuts or seeds. Remember that some seeds require more water than others. So give it to them, and they will show you the whey.

DEAR SPROUTMAN: You told me to let my Rejuvelac sit one week in the sun, now my whole kitchen smells like a garbage can. Who's going to clean this mess up? —*Stinker*

DEAR STINKER: I'm afraid you've spilled your Rejuvelac over your wheatgrass instructions. Though wheatgrass and Rejuvelac come from the same seed, they are two entirely different processes. Yes, wheatgrass should sit in the sun for one week, but Rejuvelac should not. The heat created by the sun raises the temperature of the Rejuvelac above the maximum 77°F. This is especially true in warm weather. The high temperature cultivates putrefactive bacteria instead of the friendly kind. Throw out the bad batch and start anew keeping your Rejuvelac in a shady spot. Open the windows and air yourself out.

DEAR SPROUTMAN: I never liked the scum that forms on top of cooked beans, so I stopped eating them. The same thing happens when heating milk. I gave that up, too. Now my Rejuvelac has developed scum on top. I hate this! —*Foaming*

DEAR FOAMING: Don't froth, help is on the way. Shakespeare wrote, "...This scum is but a stirless molt." And so it is with Rejuvelac. If you don't stir twice a day, scum will form on the surface of the water. Don't get stirred up, just stir.

Words Of Wisdom from the Food Guru

❀ SWAMI ❀
SPROUTANANDA

We eat for many reasons. Food does much more than feed the physical body. Nutrition is not the only thing we get from food. Food can make us happy or sad; it can stimulate or it can calm. Have you ever eaten a food and then felt unhappy afterwards? Even if it has vitamins, you can still feel unhappy. But if the vibrations of the food are right for you, you will feel good with or without the vitamins.

Food feeds us on many levels. It feeds the energy body and it feeds the mind or mental body. In my country, we drink milk to make us calm. It nourishes our "energy body," our soul. In America, when you eat ice cream, it feeds your mind more than your body. But if the mind is at peace, then the body is at peace too, yes? Who knows, maybe ice cream will bring you nirvana.

Recipes From The

FOOD DEHYDRATOR

Dry It. You'll Like It.

Conservation and preservation are concepts we all need to incorporate in our lives. To that end, a food dehydrator becomes a necessity. It enables us to store the bountiful harvest from our summer garden in the cupboard and enjoy it all year long. The flavors are supremely concentrated and the process is a lot less of a chore than canning. Indeed, dehydrated dishes are a whole cuisine unto themselves and a delightful addition to the family menu.

What is Food Dehydration?

Food dehydration is the process of removing moisture from food via evaporation. This gentle, non-destructive process uses warm air and controlled ventilation. The result—grapes become raisins, plums become prunes and a pear–shaped fruit called syconium turns into a fig. Fruits have always been the most commonly dried foods. Pineapple yokes, papaya spears, dates, apples, pears, apricots and bananas are the most popular and widely available. Although they are nutritious and delicious snacks, they represent only part of the colorful world of dehydrated foods. In this chapter, we explore the rest of the world.

Vegetables, herbs, nuts and seeds, dairy foods and last night's leftovers are some of the foods you can dehydrate. Wait till you taste the sensations that lie ahead. Dry this—zucchini chips, sweet potato and beet chips, tomato leather, sunflower seed yoghurt and cheese, and cashew cottage cheese. Dry up Mom's lasagna and take it on your hiking trip. Dry your summer garden's crop of dill, parsley and basil and make it last throughout the Winter.

Nutrition, Storage, Taste and Quality

Even if you were not interested in its food value or delicious flavor, you would have to appreciate the practical merits of dehydration as a means of food preservation. If you have ever stored food using canning or freezing, you will appreciate the simplicity of dehydration. Canning takes hours to prepare and requires several steps. One of the steps, boiling, changes the food entirely. It kills nutrition and eliminates all hope of preserving fresh original flavor. Both canning and freezing take up space—lots of it. The former quickly fills up cabinets; the latter eats up precious freezer space. Dehydration, on the other hand, shrinks food down to a fraction of its original size and weight. For example, you can dry 25 pounds of tomatoes down to 1–2 pounds and fit them all in a 1 quart jar!

If you find that impressive, wait till you taste them. It is remarkable how rich and vibrant the flavors are. Why? It's simple. Once the water has been removed, all flavors become concentrated. That is why raisins have a more intense flavor than grapes. What's more, foods dried with your home dehydrator taste better than those that are commercially prepared. Commercial drying machines operate at high temperatures to speed the drying process in order to achieve the volumes they must produce. Since you are in control when doing your own drying, you can take your time and allow your favorite foods to dry at gentle temperatures that contribute to better flavor, aroma, color and texture. And there is another advantage to home drying—you control the quality and variety of the food. Good tasting fresh food becomes great tasting dried food. Commercial preparers cannot select premium fruits. They may even use ends or cosmetically undesirable fruit since their cost is lower and such defects will not be noticed. However, you can pick choice produce and create varieties that are never commercially available.

Nutrition and Economics

Your home dehydrator will add sound nutrition to your diet. No other method of food processing—neither baking, frying, boiling, canning or freezing—maintains the nutritional integrity of the food as well as dehydration. It leaves vitamins, minerals, proteins and enzymes virtually intact.

Hopefully, you will want to start drying foods as a way of introducing new flavors and ideas into your diet. But if you are the practical type, you will start dehydrating foods just to save money. If you have ever walked the Appalachian Trail or sailed the high seas, you have experienced those store-bought foil packages of dried foods. Many hikers are critical of their palatability and limited selection. All agree it is a very expensive way to eat. Whether designed to be eaten on the trail or at home, store bought dried foods are expensive. A recent check at the local natural foods store revealed a single one ounce (1 oz.) package of shitake mushrooms selling for $2.95 and a pound of dried tomatoes at $12.00/lb. A tiny jar of dried dill flakes cost $1.95. You can save lots of money by drying these foods yourself.

How To Buy A Food Dehydrator

Since dehydrators are still an uncommon appliance for most of us, the first step is to purchase one. You will find this similar to the chore of selecting a blender, food processor or water filter with one exception—they are not usually stocked in the corner houseware store. In some cases, they have never even heard of them. This somewhat eccentric item is most often sold by specialty stores and mail order catalogues. In fact, there are fewer than ten dehydrator manufacturers in the whole United States.

A smart purchase is one based on price, size, capacity, versatility, energy efficiency and design. These machines range in price from $40 to $600. Obviously, one of your first criteria is to find a comfortable price range. Next, you have to consider the amount of space available in your kitchen or pantry room. While some machines are fairly compact, other are quite large. One of your most important decisions, however, is capacity. How much drying space do you need? First, some other questions must be asked in order to answer this. Do you have your own garden that produces copious amounts of produce? Do you like to store small amounts of foods or do you prefer to stockup in bulk? Would you mind running 3 six hour batches of bananas, for example, as opposed to doing the whole lot in one cycle? These are the questions you need to answer regarding capacity.

CRITERIA FOR SELECTING A DEHYDRATOR	
Size	Does it fit in your kitchen?
Price	Does it fit in your budget?
Capacity	Size and number of trays
Versatility	Accessories for liquids, leathers, etc.
Energy Efficiency	Watts usage, thermostat.
Design	Efficient ventilation. Round or square
Expandability	Can you add more trays later?

To enable you to prepare a variety of recipes, your dehydrator should have the versatility to make yoghurt and jerky as well as leathers, semi-liquid and loose dry foods. Energy efficiency refers to the amount of electricity a machine uses per hour. They can consume 300 to 900 watts of power. Probably the most important feature of a dehydrator is its design. How does it circulate the air? Is it re-circulating the same air or taking in fresh air? Does it dry the edges at the same rate as it dries the center? Is your machine round or square. How many trays does it have? Is it expandable? These are the kinds of questions you need to explore when purchasing a dehydrator.

Not An Oven

A dehydrator is not an oven. Ovens do not dry food, they cook it. Sure, foods will dry out in an oven if left there long enough. They will also become overcooked, brittle and/or charred. Cooking changes food on the molecular level. That means it alters the cell structure, nutrition and taste. A dehydrator, on the other hand, removes moisture by gently evaporating it through warm air exchange. The nutritional integrity of the food remains largely intact.

What If You Do Not Have A Dehydrator?

If you do not have a dehydrator and do not wish to purchase one at this time, you have three choices:

Choice 1. Low Oven. You can use your oven at the lowest possible temperature. Crack open the oven door to create air circulation and to moderate the temperature. This method has the effect of partially cooking the food as well as drying it. It will have mixed results depending on the food being dried and the nature of your oven. A convection oven, if you have one, works best. But in general, temperature control in an oven is difficult and loss of nutrients is far greater than in a dehydrator.

Choice 2. Modified Oven. This method involves your oven and a little handiwork. Install a 150 watt light bulb inside your oven. If you need to, use a worker's lamp (a bulb cage at the end of a long cord). In this approach, the oven stays off and the heat of the bulb does the drying. Improve your results by adding a small fan to circulate the warm air. Leave the door ajar to create circulation. If possible, lay your food on a non-aluminum screen. This affords better air circulation and simulates the mesh screens used in professional dehydrators. Nylon or plastic screening is available from camping, outdoor supply and houseware stores. If screening is unobtainable, use parchment paper.

If your oven has a pilot light that is on constantly, it can substitute the need for a bulb. Raise or lower the temperature by changing the pilot adjusting screw. If you have no pilot light, set your oven to the lowest temperature possible and leave the door open. Electric ovens work better because temperatures can be set very low.

Choice 3. Sun drying. This is how the art was invented in the first place. It requires a hot, sunny, dry climate. Unfortunately, that leaves many of us out. But if the weather is ideal, it can be a fine way to dry food. Hang onions, garlic and leafy herbs on strings, place fruits and vegetables in nets, or lay them out on screens. Rain, cold, clouds, insects, animals, air pollution, acid rain, northern climates and high humidity often make this ancient approach impractical. But, if you are in the right place at the right time, it is the most natural way to dehydrate. Make sure you drink plenty of water.

Practically speaking, your best choice is still to purchase a dedicated dehydrator. These machines usually work faster, use less energy, handle greater volume and provide fool-proof results. For the health-minded consumer, a food dehydrator is just as useful an appliance as the venerable kitchen blender.

About Temperature

Most dehydrators let you adjust the temperature from 85°F. to 145°F. With the exception of yoghurt which only succeeds at temperatures under 100°F., your vegetables and fruits give you complete freedom to select the preferred temperature range. In other words, any food can be dried at any temperature. A zucchini doesn't care if it is 90°F. or 140°F., honest. However, two factors need to be considered in your selection of the proper temperature.

    a.   Higher temperatures mean faster drying.
    b.   Lower temperatures maximize the preservation of enzymes.

Temperature can make a major difference in time. Tomatoes can take 24 hours at 90°F. and 14 hours at 145°F. If a food remains fairly wet after 24 hours, the chances for mold development increases. This is equivalent to leaving food out on the counter on a hot day. It turns bad!

On the other hand, there is no such thing as an over dried tomato. Once a food is dry there is no harm in leaving it in the dehydrator longer. Unlike an oven that continues to bake and burn, a dehydrator can do no harm. So if your zucchini is supposed to be ready in 6 hours and you arrive home after 10 hours, you can still enjoy perfectly delicious zucchini chips.

THE THICKNESS OR THINNESS OF YOUR SLICES AFFECTS THE LENGTH OF TIME IT TAKES TO DRY A FOOD

Laurel & Hardy

The famous comedy duo was identified by their girth. One was fat, the other skinny. Similarly, the thickness or thinness of your slices also affects the length of time it takes to dry a food. The rule of thumb is: thin slices dry quickly; thick slices take longer. A 1/8 inch thin slice of tomato will dry in 8 hours at 90°F., but half a tomato takes 24 hours-plus at the same temperature. Of course, there are other considerations. Thin slices tend to be brittle while the thicker ones are leathery. Slice according to your preferred texture.

Mesh Sheets or Solid Trays

All good dehydrators come with a choice of mesh sheets and solid trays. The mesh sheets are flexible non-stick plastic sheets that allow you to pop food off the sheet easily and with very little cleaning. If you were not to use these sheets, your food would lay on the rack itself. Removal and cleaning would be more difficult.

Solid trays are plastic non-stick sheets designed for wet and dripping foods. They hold liquids and prevent them from leaking down to the other racks. Fruit leathers, yoghurts and all liquid and semi-liquid dishes, require non-stick solid tray inserts. Since these sheets prevent some air circulation, the food takes a little longer to dry. If you are making your own dehydrator, try using butcher's wrap as an alternative non-stick sheet. Avoid using wax paper or freezer wrap. They are ineffectual and result in the loss of your food.

Storage

All dried foods store best in sealed moisture–proof jars or zip-lock bags. If 99%+ of the moisture is removed, many foods will last for years. When a food is brittle, it is an indication that it is perfectly

dry. If the food is still soft and pliable, it probably retains some moisture. These foods last for several weeks but should be refrigerated
for multi-month storage. Refrigeration is not necessary for thoroughly dried foods. Sometimes the addition of silica, a drying agent
often found in vitamin supplements, helps maintain dryness and
thus extends shelf life. Cotton balls also absorb moisture. While
glass jars can be ideal for storage, they have two weaknesses. Light
entering the jar can darken tomatoes and discolor other dried foods.
Colored jars would be ideal. Lids must contain rubber gaskets to
make them moisture proof.

Rehydration

While many dehydrated foods are consumed in the dry state, others may be restored by adding water and rehydrating them. Place 6
dehydrated tomato slices in a pint jar and add water. Let them soak
overnight and voilà—rehydrated tomatoes. Rehydrated foods never
quite taste like the fresh originals. Soaked raisins, for example, are
not equivalent to grapes. They do not turn green, swell up to their
original size or have the same texture. Instead, rehydrated foods
form a new category different in taste and texture from either the
original or the dried version. You may even extend the new flavors
further by soaking in liquids other than water. Soak the tomatoes in
a sauce, in lemon juice or even miso soup. You may soak raisins in
apple juice. The medium has the dramatic effect of opening up
many new taste sensations.

Sproutman's Chart for
F O O D   D R Y I N G

F O O D	Slicing	Temp °F	Hours	Tray	Texture
Apples	¼ inch	115–35	6–12	tray	leather
Apricots	halves	115–45	9–16	mesh	leather
Asparagus	1 inch	115–25	5–10	mesh	dry
Banana Stix	quarters	125–45	12–18	mesh	dry
Banana Leather	blend up	125–45	10–15	sheet	leather
Banana Chips	¼ inch	125–45	7–14	mesh	brittle
Blueberries	whole	115–35	7–14	mesh	dry
Beets	¼ inch	120–30	5–12	mesh	brittle
Carrots	¼ inch	115–25	5–12	mesh	dry
Celery	¼ inch	115–25	5–12	mesh	brittle
Cherries	halves	115–35	8–18	mesh	leather
Corn	husk	120–30	5–15	mesh	brittle
Cucumber	¼ inch	110–20	5–15	mesh	brittle
Eggplant	¼ inch	115–25	5–15	mesh	leather
Grapes	whole	135–45	12–20	tray	leather
Grapes	halves	135–45	12–18	mesh	leather
Green Peppers	quarters	115–30	5–15	tray	brittle
Mushrooms	whole	135–45	5–10	mesh	brittle
Onions	¼ inch	120–35	5–10	mesh	brittle
Oranges	¼ inch	115–25	6–12	sheet	brittle
Parsley/Dill	whole	105–20	3–10	tray	brittle
Peaches	halves	125–45	12–20	tray	leather
Pears	halves	125–45	12–20	tray	leather

Pineapple	3/8 inch	115–25	12–20	sheet	dry
Plum/Prune	halves	125–45	15–24	mesh	leather
Potato chips	¼ inch	115–25	5–12	mesh	brittle
Strawberries	whole	115–35	14–24	mesh	brittle
Squashes	¼ inch	115–35	5–15	mesh	dry
Seed Yoghurt	blend up	90–100	8–12	sheet	soft
Sun–Cheese	blend up	115–130	10–15	sheet	dry
Tomatoes	halves	125–45	15–20	mesh	dry
Tomatoes	¼ inch	115–25	5–12	mesh	brittle
Tomato Leather	blend up	125–35	6–10	sheet	leather
Zucchini	¼ inch	115–25	5–10	mesh	brittle
Yoghurt	¼ inch	90–100	8	sheet	liquid

About The Food Drying Chart

Slicing describes how the food should be cut. *Temperature* is in degrees Farenheit and gives a variable range of drying temperatures. You can always lower the temperature or raise it. It increases or decreases drying time respectively. *Tray* suggests drying the food directly on the dehydrator grill. *Mesh* recommends using a mesh sheet to help easily remove food and simplify cleaning. *Sheet* implies a solid sheet for liquids or semi-liquid preparations such as purées. They are leak-proof. *Texture* refers to how the food will feel when it is ready to eat.

Food is not uniform merchandise. Tomatoes, for example, can be big or small and different varieties such as beefsteak will have more moisture than a plum tomato. Because of the inherent differences in fruit and vegetables, the amount of time it takes to dry a food may vary. Your dehydrator may also yield different results than other machines using the same temperature. This is the "art" of dehydrating. Predicting the finish times can be an elusive game. Nevertheless, you cannot make a mistake. It will taste good no matter what you do. It only gets better.

Zucchini Chips!

Ingredients

4–5   Zucchini's, medium size

Drying Time: 5–10 hours. Temperature 115°–125°F.

Tired of parties that serve potato chips and pretzels? Frustrated and fatigued with frivolous fried foods filled with fat? Feel like feeding your friends a fantastic fiber–filled fun food? Not frivolous, not fatuous, not flawed or fried, each forkful is fine, functional fuel for fundamental nutrition and fabulous flavor....Zucchini chips!

Slice up your fresh, clean zucchinis into circular slivers 1/8 inch thick. Place them on a dehydrator tray and dry at 125°F. The slivers will dry into chips in as little as 5 hours. You'll find they are crisp and delicious. So forget your former folly, finally feel free for the future from foul, fatty foods.

Hotcha Zucchini

Ingredients

4–5   Zucchini's, medium size
3 Tbsp   Tamari sauce
½ Tbsp   Dehydrated Garlic granules
2 Tbsp   Dehydrated Onion powder
1 pinch   Cayenne Pepper

Drying Time: 5–10 hours. Temperature 115°–125°F.

It's easy. Prepare your zucchini as in the recipe for zucchini chips. Marinate your zucchini slices in a sauce prepared from the tamari, garlic, onion. Make sure the zucchini is fully covered by the sauce. Let soak for up to 45 minutes for best results or just 5 minutes if in a rush. Now dehydrate as in the basic zucchini chip recipe. Wow!

Dried Whole Tomatoes

Ingredients

Just tomatoes...that's all.

Drying Time: 15–24 hours. Temperature 125°–145°F.

This is the tomato's response to the potato chip.

Select the juiciest, rosiest, most delicious tomatoes you can find. Good tasting, fresh fruit makes good tasting dried fruit. Shop for tomatoes when they are in season locally for the best buys and best quality. Buy a box full and dry enough for the Winter.

How to Slice

You have a choice. Drying the whole tomato can be done, but it takes a long time to dry. Instead, cut your tomatoes in half or quarters and dry the pieces for more efficient results. Dry at 125°–145°F.

Slice your tomatoes into 1/8 or ¼ inch cuts. The thicker the slice, the longer it takes to dry. As with zucchini, the thicker slices can be more leathery while the thinner ones are more brittle. Both are good; the texture is purely a matter of personal preference.

Lay the tomatoes out slice by slice on the dehydrator mesh sheet. Or if they are especially juicy, use a solid sheet. The thin slices should dry at lower temperatures, 115°–125°F. and take less time, 5–12 hours.

How To Select Tomatoes

The most important ingredient in these recipes is, of course, tomatoes. But getting good tomatoes is sometimes difficult. At a certain time of year, corrugated cardboard can be tastier than a trans-continentally transported tomato. The best time to make dried tomatoes is when tomatoes are in season. That is when you get the ripest, richest tasting tomatoes at the best price. Then dry a box full of them and enjoy them all year long.

Ripe tomatoes are rich in color, soft to the touch, plump, and yes, they even smell like tomatoes! Often farmers are forced to dump ripe tomatoes because consumers refuse to buy them when they get too soft. If you plan it right, you can buy them at half price and get perfectly ripe tomatoes plus a few squashed ones that will be just right for tomato leather. *(See also recipe for Tomato Sun Cheese, p. 166.)*

Ode to a Tomato

Plump, soft and mellow, the Queen of Red.
Castle? Nay, just a vine divine.
A scrumptious wonder whose bounty is every
              connoisseur's dream.
Covet her gently, but do not squeeze.
Feel her tenderness, but carefully caress.
Gaze at her design, perfection of shape sublime.
Armour of red crowned by leaves of green.
Stem of stature standing straight and strong.
All in perfect contrast to a richness of red resulting
              from a daily diet of nourishing light.
Hot is the colour, but not the taste.
Ripeness is a term this Queen defined.
Uh Oh . . . careful not to tear, for therefrom gushes a
              river of juice uncompared. Be prepared.
Like a weakness breached. A birth bursting of flavour and fluid.
Napkins are but a feeble barricade against its eminent stream.
There is no similitude, no peer, no plump contender nor one more
              slender.
God gave roses aroma, but this red's the best
Just plant the seed, she'll do the rest
In tastebud heaven we are ever blessed
Long live the Q u e e n.

Tomato Leather

Ingredients

4 Rosy Ripe Tomatoes

Drying Time: 6–10 hours. Temperature 125°–135°F.

Here's a snack that's chewy, tasty and fun to eat for children and adults.

Quarter your tomatoes and blend them one at a time or whip them in a food processor until smooth. Pour onto a non-stick dehydrator sheet. Spread evenly with a spatula approximately ¼ inch thick. The thick spread is deliciously chewy. A thinner spread is crisp and flaky. Dry at 135°F. for 6–10 hours or until evenly dry.

Hotcha Tomato Leather

Ingredients

4	Tomatoes, ripe
1 tsp	Garlic Granules
2 Tbsp	Onion Powder
3 Tbsp	Miso Paste
pinch	Cayenne Pepper

Drying Time: 6–10 hours. Temperature 125°–135°F.

Puree your tomatoes in a blender or food processor with the herbs and spices. Spread the semi-liquid mix on a solid non-stick dehydrator tray and dry at 135°F. until evenly dry. Approximately 6–10 hours. Dat's a spicy tomato!

Herby Tomato

Ingredients

4	Tomatoes, ripe
1	Lemon, juiced
1 tsp	Garlic granules
1 tsp	Oregano
1 tsp	Thyme
1 tsp	Basil

Drying Time: 7–12 hours. Temperature 120°–135°F.

Again, select the best tomatoes you can find. Slice them into ¼ inch pieces. Soak the tomatoes in the herbal mixture and let sit for at least 10 minutes, longer if possible. After soaking, lay the slices onto a dehydrator mesh sheet.

Beet Treats

Ingredients

3   Beets (bulbs only)

Drying Time: 6–10 hours. Temp. 120°–130°F.

This snack will turn your tongue red with excitement.

Clean your beets, removing the tops. Slice approximately 1/8 inch thick by hand or with a food processor. Lay slices out on a dehydrator mesh screen. Dry at 125°F. for about 6–10 hours or until perfectly dry and brittle. Store in a sealed jar or plastic bag. Serve with zucchini chips and a tofu dip at parties or for hors d'oeuvres.

Dried Onion Rings

Ingredients

2   Onions, large

Drying Time: 6–10 hours. Temperature 120°–135°F.

This snack is so special it will make you cry!

Clean, peel and slice the onions either by hand or with a food processor. Onions can be sliced thicker than beets or zucchini and still be efficiently dried. Lay them out evenly on the dehydrator screen and dry at 120°–135°F. for approximately 6–10 hours or until dry. Should be brittle when done.

To reduce your onion tears, rinse the slices and the knife frequently to keep down the pernicious onion vapors. When slicing, cut the top of the onion first and the root last.

Banana Chips

Ingredients

4–5   Ripe Bananas

Drying Time: 7–14 hours. Temperature 125°–140°F.

Here's a snack that is a naturally sweet and fun to eat for all ages.

Select the ripest bananas you can find. Look for the ones that have a rich yellow color and brown freckles. *(See How to Pick Bananas and Banana Ice Cream p. 121.)* Cut your bananas into 1/8 inch slices by hand. Lay them out on a non-stick mesh sheet. The slices may touch one another but should not overlap. Dehydrate at 125°–140°F. for 7–14 hours or until dry.

Banana Stix

Ingredients

4–5   Sweet, Ripe peeled Bananas

Drying Time: 12–18 hours. Temperature 125°–145°F.

A stick is a block off the old chip. . . a banana chip, that is. Proceed the same way as in the chip recipe above except this time slice the banana lengthwise into four long sections. Place them on a mesh sheet and dry at 145°F. It takes 12–18 hours. A luscious snack. Great for teething babies, too. Provides gum exercise and nourishment at the same time.

Banana Leather

Ingredients

4–5   Sweet, Ripe peeled Bananas

Drying Time: 10–15 hours. Temperature 125°–145°F.

Yet another magical incarnation of the banana! This time instead of slicing the bananas one way or the other, simply purée them in a food processor. Pour the purée onto a non-stick solid dehydrator tray. If you do not have these trays, use parchment paper. Do not use wax or freezer paper because they are impossible to separate from the banana. Spread with a spatula until approximately 1/8–¼ inch thick. Leather takes longer to dry than chips—approximately 10–15 hours at 125°–145°F. Note: Bananas are best puréed in a food processor. Blenders will not work without the addition of water. If all you have is a blender, add apple juice or amazake since these liquids will enhance the taste.

Banana chips, sticks and banana leather are wonderful sweet treats. Chill in the refrigerator if you like them brittle, or slice them thicker if you like them chewy. Store in a jar or zip–lock bag for many months of happy snacking.

MAKING SUN-CHEESE

Here is the first of many performances by the talented and versatile sunflower seed. You will be amazed at how cheesy these little seeds taste when prepared in this special way.

Step 1. Make Yoghurt

The first step is to make sunflower yoghurt. Begin by blending the seeds. Add water slowly until you achieve a smooth puree. It should have the consistency of a thick shake. Pour into an uncovered jar or cover with a cloth or hand towel. Let the mixture sit in a warm spot until air bubbles become visible through the side of the jar. This can take up to 20 hours at room temperature or as little as 8 hours in a warm spot (90°–100°F.). A good spot is the pilot light on the stove. Test the yoghurt by tasting it. It should taste sour with a tart, lemon-like flavor. *(See p. 102, Basic Nut & Seed Yoghurt.)*

Finished yoghurt can be identified by three criteria:

a.   Air bubbles
b.   Sour or tart taste
c.   Curds separate from whey.

The dairy terms "curds and whey" are used loosely here since this is not a dairy product. The water portion, which we call "whey" settles to the bottom. The "curds," or solid portion, float above it. Carefully pour out the excess water (whey) using a knife or chopstick to create a small path for the water to sneak out past the curds. The amount of whey present is determined by the amount of water used during the blending process. If you use less water to begin with, you will have less whey to scoop out later. Whey, by the "way", is considered healthful, rich in B-vitamins and enzymes. Feel free to save it and drink it separately, if you like the taste.

Basic Sunflower Sun Cheese

Ingredients

Home made Sunflower Yoghurt

Drying Time: 12–15 hours. Temperature 125°–145°F.

Spread freshly made yoghurt onto a non-stick dehydrator sheet. If unavailable, use butcher's wrap. Wax paper does not work *(see p. 147.)* The thinner you spread it, the faster it dries. If your yoghurt is fluid enough, you can easily spread it over the sheet by tilting the tray at different angles until the mixture is spread. If it is not fluid enough, put back a little of the whey you poured out. A thick spread–¼ inch–is delightfully chewy and takes about 12–15 hours to dry at a temperature of 135°F. A thin–as–possible spread (about 1/8 inch) takes approximately 6 hours at the same temperature. The cheese is done when thoroughly dry and brittle.

GOOD TASTING YOGHURT MAKES GOOD TASTING CHEESE. CHECK YOUR YOGHURT AND MAKE SURE IT IS JUST RIGHT BEFORE DRYING.

Alternative Method

The culturing of the sunflower/water puree into a "yoghurt" can also be done directly on the solid dehydrator sheets, thus eliminating the jar method described above. Just pour the seed purée directly onto the solid sheets and set your dehydrator temperature to 90°–100°F. Taste test your yoghurt periodically for tartness. There are no air bubbles in this approach to provide clues as to its readiness. It may take as long as 20 hours to achieve the proper sour taste. Continue dehydrating until thoroughly dry. If you are in a hurry, you may raise the temperature to 125°F. to speed the drying but only after the desired flavor is achieved.

Sunny Parmesan Cheese

Ingredients

Sunflower Sun-Cheese, Already prepared

Sunny Parmesan Cheese is made by crushing the brittle sun-flower sun-cheese made in your dehydrator—that's all! Once crushed, sprinkle it on you favorite foods. Store it in a closed spice bottle and place it in the cupboard. It need not be refrigerated. Make sure, however, that it is completely dry before storing and that no moisture leaks into the bottle. It will last months if thoroughly dry. Mama mia—Dat's a sharp cheese!

Hot Cheese

Ingredients

1 cup	Sunflower Seeds
1¼ cup	Pure Water
1 tsp	Garlic, granules
1 tsp	Onion, powder
pinch	Cayenne Pepper

Drying Time: 12–15 hours. Temp 125°–135°F.

How does garlic, onion and cayenne pepper sound? Add a pinch or more of these herbs in their powdered or granulated form and mix into the yoghurt after draining the whey. Spread the new mix-ture on the solid dehydrator sheet and dry as in the basic sun-cheese recipe *(see p. 160).*

Herbal Sun–Cheese

Ingredients

1 cup	Sunflower Seeds
1¼ cup	Pure Water
2 Tbsp	Miso, blonde
1 tsp	Thyme
1 tsp	Basil or oregano
1 tsp	Savory or sweet marjoram

Drying Time: 12–15 hours. Temperature 125°–135°F.

It's hot. It's spicy! Just add your favorite herbs to your basic sun-flower yoghurt. Some suggested herbs are garlic, onion and cayenne, oregano, thyme, basil, sweet marjoram and savory. Spread the new mixture on the solid dehydrator sheet and dry as in the basic sun-cheese recipe *(p. 160)*. For more fun and flavor, add the garlic and onion as in the *Hot Cheese* recipe.

Cashew Yoghurt Sun–Cheese

Ingredients

1 cup	Cashews
1 cup	Pure Water

Drying Time: 10–15 hours. Temperature 115°–130°F.

So far we have been making our cheese and variations from sun-flower seeds. Now it is cashew's turn to cheese it up.

First, prepare the yoghurt by blending 1 cup of cashews with approximately 1 cup of water. Proceed to age it following the instructions for making cashew yoghurt *(see p.102)*. Let sit in an uncovered jar for approximately 20 hours at room temperature or about 7–8 hours at 90°–100°F. Pour off the whey, if any, and spread the yoghurt onto the non-stick dehydrator sheet. The yoghurt can be paper thin or as thick as ¼ inch. Some settling and evening out will occur as it dries. It can take 10–15 hours in the dehydrator at 125°F. before it is done. It should be dry and brittle and have a sweet, cheesy taste. Use it as fun food instead of straight cashews, cheese doodles, cheese chips, bread sticks, potato chips or other crunchy, cheesy snacks.

CHEESE N' CHIPS

Zucchini Chips *plus* Sunflower Sun–Cheese

Ingredients

4–5	Zucchinis, mid-size
1 cup	Sunflower Seeds
1¼ cup	Pure Water

Drying Time: 12–15 hours. Temperature 130°–145°F.

This recipe combines two other recipes and sandwiches them together into a fabulous snack. Zucchini Chips *(p. 151)* and Sunflower Sun–Cheese *(p. 160)*.

First make zucchini chips. Slice up a handsome zucchini in 1/8–¼ inch slices and place it on a solid dehydrator sheet one layer thick. Next, take a jar of pre-made sunflower yoghurt and spoon it on top of each zucchini slice. Dry at 130°–145°F. for approximately 12–15 hours or until crispy. Well worth the wait.

Hotcha Zucchini Cheese Chips

Same recipe as above only this time, garnish the chips with a sprinkling of radish or garlic sprouts—your choice. In addition, add two pinches of cayenne pepper to the sunflower yoghurt and mix in before spooning it on top of the chips.

If you do not have sunflower yoghurt made in advance, you can save a step by curing the blended seeds while they dry on top of the chips. Cure at 100°F. for 20 hours. *(See Sun–Cheese p. 160)*

Tomato n' Sun–Cheese

Ingredients

4	Rosy Ripe Tomatoes
1 cup	Sunflower Seeds
1¼ cup	Pure Water
2	Red Onions, sliced
1 tsp	Garlic Granules
3 Tbsp	Miso Paste
pinch	Cayenne Pepper
1 tsp ea	Favorite Herbs (optional)

Drying Time: 16–18 hours. Temperature 130°–145°F.

Prepare sunflower yoghurt by blending the sunflower seeds with water and aging *(see p. 160)*. Pour off any excess whey (water). Mix the garlic, miso and cayenne together with the yoghurt in a bowl.

Next, prepare the tomatoes by slicing them approximately ¼ inch thick and do the same with the red onions. Set the tomatoes out on a solid dehydrator sheet and top them with 1–2 rings of red onion. Spoon the yoghurt–spice mixture generously on top of each tomato and dry at 130°–145°F. in the dehydrator. It dries in approximately 16–18 hours. Don't be in a rush, it is worth the wait. If you have extra yoghurt sauce, dry that too, as a spicy cheese.

Herby Sun Tomato

As an alternative, you may create an herbal version of this dish by adding one teaspoon each of your favorite herbs. Some recommended herbs are oregano, basil, savory, thyme and sweet marjoram. *(See recipe for Herbal Sun–Cheese.)*

Dr. Ann Wigmore's
Energy Biscuits

Ingredients

1	Apple, large, cored & skinned
1 cup	Sunflower sprouts
1 cup	Buckwheat sprouts
¼ cup	Dulse
½ cup	Pure Water or as necessary

Drying Time: 10–15 hours at 100°–110°F.

This is the famous wheatgrass healer's favorite snack. While snacks in America are typically sugar based and ultimately enervating, this treat is completely nourishing and energizing. It is sweet, but only from the concentrated natural sugars in the apple. Pick a good tasting apple, since it is the pivotal ingredient in this dish.

Gather your sunflower and buckwheat greens. Sunflowers can be purchased in many natural food stores, however, buckwheat sprouts are not commercially available. Both can be grown in 1½ inches of soil or in a hydroponic sprouter *(See Appendix: Sprouting p. 287)*. For information on dulse see *p.206*. Slice the large apple in 8 parts and remove the skin (optional).

First soak the dulse in the water. Next, pour the water into the blender restraining the dulse. Add the buckwheat and sunflower slowly. Make sure the blender continues to churn. If there is no whirlpool motion in the blender, add more water. Do not create a tornado in your blender. A simple churning motion will do. Next add the dulse and the pieces of apple, one at a time. Again, add water only as necessary to maintain a grinding motion in the blender. The end result should have the consistency of a thick shake.

Pour the contents onto a solid dehydrator sheet. Tilt the tray to create an even spread ¼ inch thick. Dry at 100°–110°F. for 10–15 hours. Break apart and enjoy as energy wafers.

Sprout Nuggets

Ingredients

1	Apple, large, cored & skinned
1 cup	Sunflower Sprouts
6–12	Grapes, green pitted
1 cup	Sunflower seeds
1–1½ cups	Pure Water or as necessary

Drying Time: 10–15 hours at 100°–110°F.

Start by blending the fruit first, then the greens and finally the seeds. Choose a delicious tasting apple—variety of your choice. Slice it into eight pieces and remove the seeds and core. It is preferable to peel off the skin. Add the pieces of apple and the washed grapes to the blender one piece at a time. Add a small amount of water only as necessary to maintain blender motion. Next, slowly add the sunflower sprouts. This ingredient provides the green energy quotient to this recipe. If you do not have home grown sunflower sprouts on hand or cannot purchase them, you may substitute with a green food powder. Many such powders are available. They may contain spirulina, chlorella or blue–green algae, or wheatgrass and alfalfa or a mixture of them all. Two tablespoons should be sufficient. Make sure the entire mixture is churning with sufficient blender action. Now you are ready to add the sunflower seeds.

Be careful to select seeds that are good tasting, have a pure steel gray color and are free of rancid odors. *(See Glossary, p. 269.)* Add the sunflowers and water to the blender in stages. Make sure the churning motion of the blender continues at all times. Too many seeds at once and too little water will stall the blender action. The end result should have the consistency of a semi–liquid paste.

Spoon the contents onto a solid non–stick dehydrator sheet in dollops approximately the size of macaroons. Dry at 115°–135°F. for 10–15 hours. The finished nuggets can be semi–moist on the inside but should be dry on the outside. Enjoy like green cookies.

Sprout Herbs n' Spice
Grow Your Own Condiments

Ingredients

Any of the following sprouts

3 Tbsp	Garlic Sprouts, dry
3 Tbsp	Radish Sprouts, dry
3 Tbsp	Cabbage Sprouts, dry
3 Tbsp	Onion Sprouts, dry
3 Tbsp	Mustard Sprouts, dry
5 Tbsp	Alfalfa Sprouts, dry

Drying Time: 2–3 hours at 100°–115°F.

> *Give me your tired, your poor, your leftovers*
> *yearning to serve thee.*

Excess food that remains uneaten for too long gets thrown out. It is a waste of good food. One of the advantages of having a food dehydrator is the opportunity to preserve food for enjoyment at a later date. This is especially useful if you are gardener. Nature is bountiful and gardeners tend to have more food than they can consume. This includes indoor gardeners, too. If you have more sprouts than you can handle, consider dehydrating them. *(Some varieties may also be juiced. See Raw Juice, p. 208.)*

It's easy. Let's use radish sprouts as our example. Take your excess radish sprouts and wash them. Clear them of as many hulls and bad seeds as possible. Then spread them directly onto the dehydrator tray. Drying time is a fast 2 or 3 hours. Once dry, place the dehydrated sprouts into a food processor and chop into a powder. A blender will also perform this function. Manual method: place the dried sprouts in a plastic zip lock food bag. Seal the end pushing out all the air. Crush the sprouts by pressing and rolling the bag. Place the powdered sprouts into a condiment jar (save your old jars). Your sprouts have now incarnated as condiments to serve you yet again. Too spicy? Mix with alfalfa to make more mild.

Marinated Dried Tomatoes

Ingredients

1 oz.	Dried Tomatoes
1	Lemon, juiced
4–6 Tbsp	Olive Oil
1 finger	Garlic, fresh squeezed
2–3 Tbsp	Tamari
¼ cup	Water, pure

We have done many things with dried foods, but one thing we have not done is reconstitute them. Dehydrated food goes through a type of reincarnation. First the food has one life as fresh, then another as dehydrated and still another as reconstituted. Each has a different taste and texture despite the fact they are all the very same food. Tomatoes provide a wonderful example of this transformation.

Take your pieces of dried tomato whether they are quartered or sliced and place them in a glass container with high walls. A cylindrical container, like a drinking glass, is ideal because it keeps the tomatoes submerged in the "sauce." If possible, cut or break the tomatoes into smaller pieces. If you end up using a drinking glass, as opposed to a bowl, make sure the top is covered by a lid or a wrap to keep the moisture inside.

Add the water, lemon juice, tamari, fresh garlic and olive oil. Stir and let sit at room temperature for at least 24 hours. Stir periodically if possible. This dish makes a wonderful side salad or adjunct to any primary salad.

Rejuvelac Sprout Bread

Ingredients

Spent wheat left over from making Rejuvelac drink

This recipe is the ultimate example of recycling and it is a great story of how one food can keep providing nourishment over and over again. Like a cat, this wheat has many lives. First it was sprouted and eaten as a party snack (see p. 67), then the leftovers were blended with water to make rejuvelac. The first batch matured in a few days and was consumed. The same batch of sprouted wheat had more water added to it creating another cultured (rejuvelac) drink. This drink was also consumed and the process repeated once again. After this third batch of rejuvelac, should this wheat be discarded? No!

The rejuvelac wheat, although spent in the process of making 3 batches of rejuvelac (see p. 113), still contains a reservoir of yeasts, enzymes and vitamins. It is very low in starch because of all the enzymatic activity and is easily digestible even though it never heated.

Grind the wheat in a blender with a minimum amount of left over rejuvelac. Just add enough to churn the wheat and create a smooth paste. A food processor or Champion juicer will also perform this function without requiring any liquid. Spoon out the wheat paste onto a solid dehydrator sheet at minimal thickness, approximately 1/8 inch. Dry at 110°–125°F. for approximately 6 hours. It is done when completely dry. Break off pieces and enjoy as wafers of wheat. Unlike regular wheat, this bread may be consumed by most wheat sensitive persons because the common allergenic protein, gluten, is gone. It is one of the few opportunities for eating raw grain, without any kind of cooking or baking.

Sprouted Wheat Malt

Ingredients

1 cup   Soft white wheat, dry grain

Drying Time: 10 hours at 125°F.

This simple recipe involves the sprouting of soft wheat. Soft wheat is the low gluten brother of hard wheat. Malt is the short name for the sugar naturally found in grains. This sugar called maltose is commonly derived from barley (barley malt) as a by–product of the brewing industry. Barley malt is boiled until it achieves a dark viscous state similar to that of a dark honey. Although similar in consistency to honey, grain malt is darker in color and stronger in flavor.

Sprout malt, however, made from soft white sprouted wheat, is blonde in color and fairly delicate in flavor. Grow the sprouts for 5 days. Their shoots should be approximately ½ inch long or about 1–2 times the length of the berry. Wash the sprouts well and place them directly on the dehydrator grill. Dry at 125°F. for approximately 10 hours or until dry.

Blend the sprouts into a powder in a blender or a food processor (using the "S" blade). Add the powder to cereals like a wheat germ. Even use it in recipes that call for malt. Although it is by no means as sweet as sugar, it has enough natural sweetness and goodness to satisfy anyone.

Dried Lentils

The Lentil's Answer to the Potato Chip

Ingredients

1 quart	Lentil Sprouts, fresh
2 Tbsp	Dehydrated Onion Powder
1 tsp	Garlic Powder
3 Tbsp	Tamari

Drying Time: 6–8 hours at 145°F.

First, grow your lentil sprouts according to the basic sprouting instructions. (See *Appendix, Sprouting, p. 287.*) Lentils are simple to sprout and are ready in 5 days. Wash the finished sprouts thoroughly and mix in the garlic, onion and tamari. Mix well until the sprouts are coated with this sauce. Ideally, the sprouts should remain refrigerated for 24 hours while they marinate. However, the use of powdered or granular garlic and onion creates an almost instant marination. Spread the sprouts out loosely onto a solid dehydrator sheet and dry at 125°F. for approximately 6–8 hours.

Should you desire to use fresh herbs instead of dried ones, simply dice and blend 1–2 garlic cloves and ½ an onion in the blender with the tamari. Add a few tablespoons of water to help churn the herbs. Pour the sauce into a bowl and mix the lentils in thoroughly. Marinate for 24 hours outside the refrigerator or 48 hours inside the refrigerator before dehydrating. The dried sprouts have a crunchy texture but if they are too hard, germinate and marinate them longer. Once perfectly dry, store them in a sealed jar or ziplock plastic bag to maintain their crispness. They last for months with no refrigeration, if kept perfectly dry. Take them on a hike, put them in the lunchbox or serve them as snacks at parties. See also *Party Sprouts, p. 225.*

Sunflower & Garlic

Mature baby sunflower greens (left, 8 days old) and garlic chives
(right, 12 days old) growing in bamboo without soil or other additives.

SALADS &
SALAD DRESSINGS

The Average American Salad

If you ask an average American to describe a salad, he or she will probably paint a sorrowful picture of white iceberg lettuce and a hardened tomato. More optimistic versions might include a leaf of red cabbage and some grated carrot. For such reasons, salad has scored low on the list of "most desired" foods. It is not a very exciting dish. We quickly learned to shun the salad for beans, burgers, cheese, chips, etc.—for almost anything else tasted better.

With this as our benchmark, it will take a giant leap to arrive at a multi—sprout, vegetarian, gourmet super-salad. Even the "vegetarian" part is a step forward because many restaurant salads include ingredients like ham and bacon bits. However, in the pages that follow, we will take that leap and you will find it is well worth the jump.

Vegetarian Super-Salad

To start with, salads are usually the central food of a vegetarian's diet. As such they are obliged to provide more nutrition than a head of iceberg lettuce can supply. Iceberg is actually an accurate name because it has about as much nutrition as an ice cube. A Super-Salad, on the other hand, is a work of art constructed from a world of nutritious foods. Like an artist drawing from his palate of colors, a super-salad may be created from a palate of ingredients.

Palate of Salad Ingredients

a. Green leafy sprouts—alfalfa, red clover, fenugreek, buckwheat lettuce, baby sunflower greens, garlic chives, red pea lettuce—and hearty lettuce greens like romaine, spinach, Boston, bibb, chicory and endive.

b. Juicy vegetables such as tomatoes, red and green peppers, cucumbers, pickles. Artichokes.

c. Fatty acid rich vegetables such as olives and avocado.

d. Sea vegetables such as hijiki, nori, kelp, arame and raw dulse.

e. Spicy herbs such as chopped onion, shallots, chives, scallions, garlic, dill, parsley, leeks, celery, savory, thyme, oregano.

f. Root vegetables such as shredded carrots, beets, Jerusalem artichokes, turnips, parsnips. Baked or steamed potatoes cut in chunks and mixed in. Raw shredded squash such as summer squash and acorn.

g. Raw bean sprouts such as lentil, mung, adzuki, red pea and smaller amounts of either raw or lightly steamed chick pea, green pea and peanut sprouts.

h. Sunflower, almonds or pumpkin seeds sprinkled on top.

i. Cooked grains such as rice, millet, quinoa and buckwheat, served hot or cold and mixed with the salad.

j. Spicy sprouts: radish, garlic chives, onion, cabbage, mustard.

k. Specialty foods and condiments such as mustard, lemon, tamari, natto (and other) misos, dark sesame oil, tofu, apple cider vinegar, ginger, cayenne pepper, nutritional yeast, gomazio (sesame seeds & sea salt), spirulina.

l. Dressings made from tofu, tahini, sunflower seeds, cashews, almonds, tomatoes and other vegetables, olive oil, tamari, ginger, basil, lemon, vinegar, garlic.

The Super-Salad presents a new concept in eating salads. Here the salad can function as a whole meal and plays a central role in the nutrition of a vegetarian regime. In a sense, it is similar to soup in that it can include a wide variety of vegetables and grains making it a "meal in itself." If you are in a rush, a salad can be a modest collaboration of sprouts, greens and dressing. Or it can become an elaborate affair that, with the addition of grains, beans and seeds, can be hearty and filling. And although salads are known for low calories, they can be very rich and filling with the addition of avocados, olives, artichokes, yeast, blue-green algae, natto miso and potato.

Meatatarians often ask: "what do vegetarians eat?" Iceberg lettuce and a cardboard tomato, after all, make a pretty grim menu. But with our super-salad, there are hundreds of combinations, shapes, sizes, colors and tastes, that can be created. The simple variance of salad dressings can make a whole new salad out of the very same ingredients. Dressings, as you will witness in this chapter, can also be elaborate (or simple). Save your appetite, skip lunch, do a short fast and prepare to feast from the following salads sensationale.

SUPER SALADS

Quinoa Salad

Ingredients

1 cup	Alfalfa sprouts
1 cup	Buckwheat lettuce
¼ cup	Cabbage sprouts
½ cup	Fenugreek sprouts
1 cup	Quinoa, pre-cooked
generous	Tofu-Tahini dressing

Serves 2

Serve the quinoa hot or cold. Mix all ingredients. Alfalfa and buckwheat are mild and can be substituted with other mild tasting sprouts or greens.

Potato Salad

Ingredients

1 cup	Red Pea lettuce sprouts
1 cup	Alfalfa sprouts
¼ cup	Cabbage sprouts
¼ cup	Fenugreek sprouts
2 cups	Potatoes, pre-cooked
to taste	Cucumber dressing

Serves 2

Serve the potatoes cold. Cut into quarters. Mix all.

Root Salad

Ingredients

1 cup	Sunflower sprouts
1 cup	Alfalfa sprouts
1 cup	Cabbage sprouts
1 cup	Carrots, shredded
¼ cup	Beets, shredded
generous	Sun-Power dressing

Yield: Serves 2

Middle Eastern

Ingredients

1 cup	Sunflower sprouts
1 cup	Red Clover sprouts
½ cup	Fenugreek sprouts
½ cup	Olives
1 cup	Jerusalem artichokes, shredded
½	Avocado, chopped
to taste	Garlic Olive dressing

Yield: Serves 2

Millet Salad

Ingredients

1 cup	Buckwheat lettuce
1 cup	Clover sprouts
1 cup	Alfalfa sprouts
¼ cup	Radish sprouts
½ cup	Hijiki, steamed
¼ cup	Garlic chives, sprouts
1 ½ cups	Millet, pre-cooked
generous	Basil-Tahini dressing

Yield: Serves 2

Toss sprouts. Mix in the millet, hot or cold. Cover with dressing.

Tofu Salad

Ingredients

1 cup	Clover sprouts
1 cup	Sunflower sprouts
1 cup	Alfalfa sprouts
¼ cup	Radish sprouts
½ pound	Tofu, soft or firm, cubed
generous	Tahini-Ginger dressing

Yield: Serves 2

Mix all together.

Chick-Pea Salad

Ingredients

1 cup	Alfalfa sprouts
1 cup	Sunflower sprouts
1 cup	Fenugreek sprouts
½ cup	Cabbage sprouts
2 cups	Chick Pea sprouts, pre-cooked
1 cup	Tofu-Tahini dressing

Yield: Serves 2

Marinated Beansprout Salad

Ingredients

2 cups	Sprouted Lentils
1 cup	Sprouted Mung Beans
¼ cup	Sprouted Adzuki (optional)
2 Tbsp	Dehydrated Onion Powder
1 tsp	Garlic Powder
3 Tbsp	Tamari
1 pinch	Cayenne Powder

Yield: Serves 4–6

Sprout the lentils, mung and adzuki (or red pea) for 5 days, rinsing twice daily. *(See Appendix, Sprouting, p. 287.)*

Mix the spices and tamari together in a large serving bowl. Toss the sprouts into the seasoning and mix until coated evenly. This "marinade" can be ready instantly, but is fully marinated by the next day. Keep refrigerated

Garlic Sprout & Avocado Salad

Ingredients

1 cup	Garlic sprouts
1	Tomato, ripe
1	Avocado, ripe
1	Pepper (sweet)
1 Tbsp	Mustard
3 Tbsp	Tamari
2 Tbsp	Olive oil

Your Italian neighbors from all corners will start "dropping in" once word about this salad gets out. And why not? They know good food. They've been eating it for centuries! Their secret...and yours now...is simple: "good tasting ingredients make good tasting meals."

Selecting vegetables is something you should be fussy about. Start with the tomato. A ripe tomato is more than a fruit, it is an example of fine art designed by nature. Pick them soft and ripe and rich in color. Buy only when in season. Tomatoes can vary from the tasteless and out-of-season to the superbly flavorful and vine ripe. *(For more on tomatoes, see p.154 and Glossary. p. 269.)* Avocados also require sensitive selection. They must be firm but ripe. Too hard and they are immature. Too soft and they are beyond repair. The best approach is to buy them firm and select them as they ripen in your home. Pepper is an easier pick. Choose red, yellow or the common green. Sweet peppers are never hot. Garlic sprouts are ripe when 3 inches tall—about 12 days growth—and look like miniature chives.

Chop the sprouts, tomato, avocado and pepper into ½ inch pieces. Pour the mustard, tamari and olive oil on top. Take time to repeatedly turn the salad and mix the latter into the fruits. Crushing the tomato and avocado in the process only improves your success as their juices and oils are the essence of this simple dish. Why add multiple spices and complicate your dishes with different herbs? Ripe fruits and vegetables, organically grown and rich in natural flavor are all you ever need.

SALAD

DRESSINGS

Dressing
Room

Welcome

Olive Oil Dressing

Ingredients

5 Tbsp	Olive Oil
2 Tbsp	Tamari

In terms of the refinement of taste, dressings are among the most challenging dishes to create. In a salad dressing, even subtle changes in ingredients can affect flavor dramatically. So, the most important first step in making a good tasting dressing is to start with good-tasting ingredients.

Olive oil and tamari themselves require discerning taste buds. Good olive oil can be hard to find. The key to good olive oil lies in its color and aroma. Look for a deep green color and a distinct olive aroma. Reading labels is absolutely necessary. Some of the key words are "extra virgin"—the first pressing using the choicest olives is the most expensive. "Virgin" —a first pressing using lower quality olives. "Pure olive oil" may be a combination of refined olive oils made from later pressings. Unfortunately, the word "imported" on the bottle does not guarantee quality. In fact, many are discouragingly tasteless. Some excellent American brands are available from natural food stores. Let your nose do the walking. *(For more on olive oil, see Glossary, p. 269.)*

Tamari is the excess liquid resulting from making miso—a fermented soybean paste. Good tamari should have no preservatives, and ideally, no wheat. It should be low in salt, dark in color and rich in flavor and aroma. Try different brands until, like a fine wine, you find the one you like the best.

Shake the two ingredients together in a jar and toss with your favorite salad. This dressing is simple but sublime and never misses. It is the healthful alternative to the conventional oil and vinegar dressing. Once you've become an expert, try the following variations.

Garlic Olive Oil Dressing

Ingredients

5 Tbsp	Olive Oil
2 Tbsp	Tamari
1–2 cloves	Garlic, pressed

Just shake in a jar or toss in your salad. Press the garlic well.

Lemon Olive Oil Dressing

Ingredients

5 Tbsp	Olive Oil
2 Tbsp	Tamari
1–2 cloves	Garlic, pressed
2 Tbsp	Lemon, juiced

Macrobiotic Olive Dressing

Ingredients

5 Tbsp	Olive Oil
2 Tbsp	Tamari
1–2 cloves	Garlic, pressed
2 Tbsp	Lemon, juiced
1–2 Tbsp	Dark Sesame Oil
2 Tbsp	Natto Miso

Just shake all ingredients together in a jar, then mix well into the salad. Dark sesame oil is the oil pressed from toasted sesame seeds. It has a very rich flavor. Natto miso is a variety of soybean paste made with ginger, barley, seaweed and barley malt. It is exquisite and a wonderful addition to many recipes. Both these ingredients are available in oriental and natural food stores.

Tofu-Tahini-Ginger

Ingredients

1 cup	Pure Water
1+ inch	Ginger Root, diced
1 small	Onion, peeled and quartered
½ cup	Lemon Juice (fresh)
2–3 Tbsp	Tamari
½ cup	Tahini (prefer raw)
8 oz	Firm Tofu, sliced (organic)
pinch	Cayenne pepper, (optional)
1 clove	Garlic pressed, (optional)

Yield: 3 cups

Combine the first five ingredients in a blender until the ginger is thoroughly blended. Peel and remove the ends of a very small (or ½) onion and cut in small enough parts to be easily consumed by your blender. Slowly add the tahini while the blender is running. When thoroughly mixed, add the sliced cakes of tofu one piece at a time. You now have a creamy, white, high protein dressing with plenty of ginger snap. Protein from soy (tofu) and sesame (tahini) make a superbly balanced amino acid combination. Add more ginger or the optional garlic and cayenne pepper if you want it snappier.

Use raw tahini found in better natural food stores. It is thicker and has a true sesame flavor. Regular tahini made from toasted sesame seeds, is darker and has a roasted flavor. If you like that flavor, you can get it by adding a teaspoon of toasted sesame oil to the raw tahini. This way you are not eating roasted seeds. Heated oils, whether from fried foods like tempura, natural potato chips or roasted nuts, should be avoided. Tamari is the liquid that results from making miso. Miso is aged soybean paste. That is why tamari is known generically as "soy sauce." Good tasting tamari makes a difference. An alternative to tamari would be the popular *"Dr. Bronner's Soya Bouillon."* This dark, salty liquid has no added salt, but is made with salty ingredients like sea vegetables.

Tahini-Ginger Dressing

Ingredients

1 ½ cups	Pure Water
1 ½ inch	Ginger, diced
1 cup	Tahini, raw
1 Tbsp	Tamari
1	Lemon, juiced

Yields: 2 cups

Here is a simplified version of the previous recipe sans tofu. It makes the dressing slightly easier to digest and instead of having your tofu as part of your dressing, you can place it directly in the salad.

Always blend the diced ginger first, since it is the main flavor ingredient and needs an unencumbered blender environment in order to succeed. Slowly add the tahini while blending. As the tahini slows down the whirlpool effect in the blender, add the tamari and lemon juice to quicken it. Or, if you prefer, add a small amount of additional water.

Basil-Tahini Dressing

Ingredients

1 ½ cups	Water
½ bunch	Basil, fresh
1 cup	Tahini
1–2 Tbsp	Tamari
1	Lemon, juiced

Yield: 2 cups

This is simply delicious. Fresh garden basil and good tasting raw tahini are a marriage made in tastebud heaven. Add the lemon and you have reached the stars! Fresh basil is only available certain times of year, so grab the opportunity and grab some basil.

Blend your basil using the leaves only. Peel the leaves from 2–4 average size stalks. Stalks are usually about 8 inches long. Although the stalk is usable, it has much fiber and less flavor. If you use the stalk, chop it well. Pulse your blender until all the basil is puréed. You cannot overdose on basil. Next, add the tahini. If the mixture becomes too thick to turn in the blender, add the tamari and lemon juice. If still too thick, add small amounts of water. It makes your salad come alive! Warning: some basil—tahini fans have been known to consume the dressing prior to its reaching the salad!

Tomato-Basil-Tahini Dressing

Ingredients

1	Tomato, rosy ripe medium
1 ½ cups	Water
½ bunch	Basil, fresh
1 cup	Tahini
1—2 Tbsp	Tamari
1	Lemon, juiced

Yield: 2 cups

Move over basil. A fresh ripe garden tomato is about to mix it up with you. Start making the previous *Basil Tahini Dressing* by blending the water and basil first, then add the tomato. Slowly pour in the tahini while the blender is working. If the whirlpool in the blender stops, "pulse" the blender (short off and on periods), then, add the tamari and lemon. Add more water if necessary.

Oregano—Tomato

Ever see fresh oregano? If you do, substitute fresh oregano for fresh basil in this recipe for a truly "Italiano" dressing that will make mama mia sing Polyeucte. Bellaisimo!

Sun-Power Dressing

Ingredients

1 ½ cup	Pure Water
I cup	Sunflower Seeds
3 Tbsp	Tamari
½ cup	Fresh Lemon Juice
I	Onion, quartered (medium)
I clove	Garlic, pressed
¼ cup	Olive Oil
½ cup	Grapefruit Juice, fresh
2 Tbsp	Kelp flakes
Pinch	Cayenne Pepper

Yield: 4 cups

Combine the water, seeds, tamari and lemon juice in a blender and blend until creamy. Slowly add the remaining ingredients until all is blended.

This is a creamy, refreshing dressing that really perks up a salad and adds lots of nutrition. Sunflower seeds are a rich source of protein, essential fatty acids and minerals such as potassium, phosphorus and zinc as well as vitamin B–1.

Buy kelp flakes or granules or, better yet, make your own. Buy whole kelp and dry it to the brittle stage in your dehydrator or other warm spot. Then crush the brittle kelp into flakes.

The olive oil and fresh grapefruit juice can be considered optional. Olive oil adds a smoothness and creaminess to the recipe. The grapefruit sweetens the dressing without the use of honey and it combines perfectly with lemon. More or less lemon may be used according to taste. A very healthful and versatile dressing. Enjoy.

Sprouty Gazpacho Dressing

Ingredients

2 Rosy	Ripe Tomatoes
2 cups	Sprouted Sunflower Greens
2 cups	Pure Water
¼ cup	Cabbage Sprouts
1–2	Garlic Cloves, chopped
3 Tbsp	Tamari
pinch	Cayenne Pepper (optional)
½ bunch	Fresh Dill
1/3 cup	Fresh Lemon Juice

Yield: 3–4 cups

Quarter your ripe tomatoes and blend them slowly with the water. Add the garlic, tamari and half of the lemon juice. Blend again, then slowly add the dill, cabbage sprouts and sunflower greens. Blend until finely chopped. Substitutes: If no sunflower greens are available, use a medium size avocado instead. Substitute radish sprouts for cabbage sprouts or just use regular cabbage. Add the remaining lemon juice and cayenne, if desired. If you do not have sunflower sprouts, it's time to start growing them. It takes 8–10 days to grow sunflower greens and is worth it. *(See Glossary, p. 269.)*

If your dressing becomes too thick, it may be the result of too much avocado or tomato. Because these fruits are of variable size, you may have to use a little less fruit or a little more water. The texture should be somewhat coarse with vegetable pieces that are large enough to chew.

Stores in the refrigerator for approximately 3 days.

Live Tomato Ketchup

Ingredients

2–3	Tomatoes, medium size
1 Tbsp	Mustard
2 Tbsp	Miso Paste
1 clove	Garlic
2 Tbsp	Olive oil
2 Tbsp	Vinegar

Just blend together. Not quite ketchup, but a "live" homemade version that can be used in similar fashion. First, blend the tomatoes with the mustard, miso paste and garlic. Adding these ingredients early has the benefit of ensuring they get well mixed. In the case of the garlic, it ensures you won't get a surprise chunk that sets off your salivary smoke alarm. The olive oil adds smoothness to this recipe while the vinegar adds the necessary bite.

Tomatoes are everything here and picking good ones can at certain times of the year be a fine art. If you use tomatoes that taste like cardboard, your recipe will not taste much better. Select very ripe, red, soft, plump tomatoes, as these are the richest in flavor. Hard tomatoes are fine for standard ketchup since they are cooked. But in "live" ketchup, what you taste is what you get. *(For more on tomatoes see "Ode to a Tomato," p. 154 and Glossary, p. 269.)*

Mustard and miso can also substantially affect your results. A mild dijon mustard is recommended over the hot Chinese variety. Miso comes in several varieties with great variances in taste. Use a "mellow" light miso for best results. *(See Glossary, p. 269.)*

The selection of quality olive oil is discussed in the *Olive Oil Dressing*. Use the best olive oil available. Vinegar comes in different varieties. Many are steeped in herbs such as tarragon, thyme, basil and others. Or just use a good apple cider vinegar. Natural and specialty food stores have excellent selections.

Radishire Sauce

Ingredients

1 cup	Radish sprouts
2 Tbsp	Cabbage or Mustard sprouts
4 Tbsp	Rice Vinegar
2 Tbsp	Pure Water
2 Tbsp	Tamari
1 tsp	Umeboshi Plum
1 tsp	Dark Sesame oil
2 Tbsp	Ginger, minced
½ tsp	Garlic, minced
2 Tbsp	Honey
1 tsp	Kuzu

Worcestershire never had it so good! This sauce is made from sprouts and other healthful ingredients. Not only will it spice your food, but the natural ingredients in this sauce are known to open and relieve congestion in the respiratory system.

In your food processor, add the liquid ingredients first, then the honey, spices and lastly sprouts. Blend until puréed. Substitutions: You may use 1 Tbsp of yellow mustard instead of mustard sprouts; apple cider vinegar instead of rice vinegar; rice syrup instead of honey. Umeboshi plum, also known as Japanese plum, should be in the form of a liquid concentrate. Dark sesame oil is also known as toasted sesame oil. Most ingredients are readily available in better health food stores. The unique flavors of this sauce will be reminiscent of Chinese Szechuan cooking and all-American shish kabobs. Use in stir fries; add to vegetables and seafood.

Pinacolavo Dressing

Ingredients

1 slice	Pineapple, ½–¾in thick
1 large	Avocado
1 ½ cup	Pure Water
1+ Tbsp	Miso, blonde
1	Lime, juiced
1 pinch	Cayenne Pepper

Yield: 2 cups

Select a medium-ripe avocado and a sweet pineapple and they will reward you with a refreshing summer salad dressing that is scrumptiously special. Because these are the main ingredients, it is critical you pick the best fruits at their peak of flavor.

Haas avocado, the variety with the rough dark green skin, is preferred. Pick avocados firm, but not hard. Picking pineapple is yet another art. Most important is the smell. If you cannot smell the sweet fruit aroma, you will probably not taste it. A ripe pineapple has a rich gold and yellow color and is soft to the touch but not mushy. Use "mellow" light miso paste.

Blend the two fruits with water. Slowly add the miso, lime juice and pinch of cayenne pepper. That's all! No oil, no vinegar, just fresh fruit and vegetables. Breathes life into your salad. Ahh...refreshing.

In a rush? Use 1 cup of natural pineapple-coconut or pina-colada juice instead of pineapple and reduce the water by ½ cup. Makes a slightly sweeter and smoother dressing.

If you are concerned about the effrontery of combining fruits and vegetables, you can relax. Pineapple and lime are highly acidic citrus fruits similar to lemon and mix very well with oil rich foods like avocado. In addition, in a strictly technical sense, avocado is considered a fruit because it contains a pit.

Sunflower Pesto Dressing

Ingredients

1 handful	Basil, fresh
1 ½ cups	Water
1 cup	Sunflower seeds
1	Lemon, juiced
1 Tbsp	Tamari

Yield: 2½ cups

It only pays to make pesto when fresh basil can be obtained. Wash the basil thoroughly and blend all leaves and the leafy portions of the stalks in 1 cup of water. Your handful of basil will consist of approximately 5–7, 6 inch stalks. Your blender will turn dark green. Then add the steel gray shelled sunflower seeds and blend thoroughly, adding more water as necessary to maintain a speedy whirlpool motion. Add the juice of 1 lemon (about ¼ cup of juice) and 1 Tbsp of tamari. Add the rest of the tamari and lemon according to taste. Achieve a consistency similar to milk.

Sunflower Cheeze Pesto

Ingredients

10+	Basil leaves, fresh
1 cup	Sunflower yoghurt "cheeze"
4 Tbsp	Olive oil
1	Lemon, juiced
½ tsp	Umeboshi plum paste
Garnish	Garlic sprouts

Yield: 1½ cups

Good fresh basil in season is necessary to make good pesto. While traditional pesto uses pine nuts, this recipe uses sunflower seeds. The cheesy taste of the cultured sunflower seed "cheeze" lends itself perfectly to the sharp pesto flavor. Make sunflower seed cheeze by blending one cup of sunflower seeds with one cup of water and aging it in a sprout bag or cheese cloth. *(For the complete recipe, see Sunflower Cheese, p. 109.)*

Wash the basil leaves well. Use the leaves only. Do not use the stalks in this recipe. Blend the leaves in the blender with the lemon juice and olive oil. Add a tiny amount of water if necessary and stop occasionally to move the leaves off the sidewall with a spatula. The result is to dice the basil leaves which can, if you prefer, also be done with a knife and cutting board. Mix in the umeboshi paste *(See Glossary, p. 269.)* and all ingredients together. The consistency should be similar to cottage cheese. Add the garlic sprouts as a garnish on top or stir them in. Or, use a small clove of garlic, diced.

Cucumber Cashew Dressing

Ingredients

1 cup	Cucumber, chopped
1 cup	Cashews
1 cup	Pure Water
2 tsp	Miso, blonde mellow
2 Tbsp	Dulse flakes

Yield: 2 cups

This is a non-dairy version of the popular cucumber-yoghurt dressing. It's simple, sweet and delicious.

Blend the cashews and water until smooth. Purchase kirby cucumbers. These are the thin skinned kind that are commonly used for pickling. You may use green cucumbers if you peel off their skins. Chop the cucumbers into 1 inch pieces and add them a few at a time into the cashew milk while the blender is in motion. Add the dulse flakes and then the miso according to your taste. Mellow miso is a light flavor, low in sodium miso available in most natural food stores. *(For more on miso see Glossary, p. 269.)*

Cashew Dream Dressing

Ingredients

1 cup	Water
1 cup	Cashews, whole or pieces
1	Lemon, juiced
1+ Tbsp	Tamari
1 tsp	Kelp flakes
2 Tbsp	Olive oil
½ pinch	Cayenne pepper (optional)

Yield: 12 ounces

It's white, it's creamy, it's sweet, it's a dream come true.

Blend one cup of clean, white whole cashews (cup overflows) or 1 level cup of cashew pieces in 1 cup of water. Juice one lemon, add the kelp flakes and olive oil. Blend all together until smooth.

For the finishing stage we add the remaining ingredients, the tamari, cayenne and water slowly and according to taste. Add all or part of the additional water as necessary in order to achieve a milkshake consistency. Add the cayenne if you like it hot. Your dream has come true.

❀ LIQUIDS ❀

Soup, Juice, Soda Pop, Beverages

Breakfast Drinks

Start Your Day with Pure Water

The real first drink of the day should always be fresh water. Just as you take your ablutions externally, take them internally. Your stomach and intestines need washing before beginning the day's intake. Between each meal, there should be a period of cleansing and rest. If you rode a camel across the treacherous desert, it would behoove you to rest it, bathe it, nourish it and treat it with great care. Your stomach and body carry you across life's long journey. It is an engine that runs all day, every day. Part of its daily maintenance is washing and resting. Ironically, some people take better care of their cars then they do their stomachs. You are not a walking garbage dump. Your stomach is not a blind pit into which you stuff whatever your eyes behold. It is your one and only engine which must last the rest of your life. Water and rest are essential to its endurance. *(For more on water purification, read 'Wetter is Better' also by this author.)*

Lemon Breakfast Drink

Fresh squeezed citrus juice is one of the best early morning cleansers. Grapefruit, lemon and pineapple are the strongest. Squeeze the juice of half a lemon into a glass of water. That's all. Choose hot or cold water depending on personal preference. If you find straight lemon too strong, do not use a sweetener. Cut it with the juice of one grapefruit. The addition of a tablespoon of olive oil turns this cleansing drink into a liver flush. Use good tasting olive oil. *(See Glossary, p. 269.)*   Add garlic and it becomes a blood cleanser. This simple drink, if taken daily, is a powerful tool for health and longevity.

Flax Drink & Cleanser

Ingredients

2 Tbsp	Flax seeds
1 cup	Apple Juice
1	Banana

It's simple. Blend 2 tablespoons of flax seeds until you achieve a semi-smooth flour. Add 1 cup of apple juice and blend. Then add the small banana and blend all until smooth. It should have the consistency of a thick shake. Take on an empty stomach. Drink plenty of fluids afterwards and wait 1 hour before eating solid foods.

Flax has the ability to function as a bulk laxative because of its gelatinous nature. It moves through the intestinal tract like a broom sweeping everything in its path. Follow this drink with plenty of water to keep the mass moving. Chia seed is also gelatinous and has a similar effect. Try this recipe with chia instead of flax or mix both together. The colon is a two-way membrane that absorbs nutrients and oxygen but can also reabsorb poisons. You may have heard the expression: *the source of all disease begins in the colon.* Good colon health is fundamental to good health. *(For more on the health benefits of flax, see Glossary, p. 269.)*

The Coffee Ritual

Americans are famous for their inability to function before imbibing their morning brew. The pick-up power of coffee is clearly not nutritional. Rather, its effect is four-fold:

a) *Ritual.* The routine has a ceremonial sacredness. We covet the cup and worship the power within it. b) *Emotional.* There is an emotional attachment to it and the perceived result. c) *Chemical.* Addiction to caffeine. The test of any chemical addiction is the presence of physical withdrawal symptoms upon quitting. d) *Mental Program.* The effect of these three factors is to create a subconscious mental program necessitating the early morning coffee in order to function. Those who have missed their morning beverage often complain of being out of synch during the day or not having truly awakened. Food addictions are common and coffee is probably not as deleterious as sugar or alcohol. However, it is a cultural habit that can be replaced with more better beverage choices. One such alternative follows.

Sproutman's Morning Beverage

Ingredients

1 cup	Apple Juice
1	Banana (Ripe)
2 Tbsp	Sesame seed meal (hulled)
1 Tbsp	Spirulina, Chlorella or blue-green algae
1 Tbsp	Bee Pollen
1 Tbsp	Lecithin granules
1 Tbsp	Slippery Elm
12–15	Almonds (chopped)
1–2	Dates (pitted)

For those of you who do not like to eat a large breakfast or who do not have time for one, you can launch your day with this superb breakfast drink. After cleansing your intestinal tract with fresh, pure water and following the *Recipe for Entering the 21st Century (see p. 2)*, this healing green breakfast drink will coat the intestinal tract with its purifying, oxygenating chlorophyll and nourish your cells with highly assimilable nutrition. It is your first step to a healthier day.

It is practically a liquid meal. The natural sugars in the banana, date, apple juice and bee pollen provide immediate energy. The protein in the algae, sesame and almonds offer long term stamina. Lecithin insures efficient fat digestion and all provide delicious flavor and texture. This nourishment comes in one concentrated, easy-to-take package. Carry it along to work in a jar or thermos, sip it during the day or have it as a liquitarian lunch. It is satisfying in a way that is only a consequence of true nourishment.

Begin with the apple juice and banana. Blend, then add the sesame meal, algae and bee pollen. These are the core ingredients. If nothing else, these ingredients alone will suffice. Add the remaining ingredients in the order listed. Blend after introducing each one. Add more juice or water if the mixture becomes too thick to maintain blender motion. Aim for a "milk shake" consistency.

To make sesame meal, blend ½ cup of dry, hulled (blond) sesame seed. Stop and stir with a wooden spoon or chopstick until all seed is fractionated. *(See 'Sesame' p. 278.)*

Options. You may use almonds instead of sesame and water instead of juice. The last four ingredients lecithin, almonds, slippery elm and dates, are all optional and may be used according to personal preference.

Manhattan Sprout Chowder

Ingredients

2	Tomatoes
1 cup	Pure Water
1	Garlic Clove
2 Tbsp	Tamari
2 cups	Sunflower Sprout Greens
1/3 cup	Cabbage Sprouts
1 cup	Radish Sprouts
¼ cup	Dulse Sea Lettuce, soaked
1 bunch	Favorite Fresh Herb
1 pinch	Cayenne Pepper

Yield: 2½–3 cups

Here is a "hot" soup that never needs to be cooked!

First, make sure you have plenty of sprouts on hand. This soup is a great idea when you have too many sprouts and don't know what to do with them! Home grown sunflower sprouts or those purchased from a natural food store are at the heart of this recipe. *(See Appendix, Sprouting, p. 287.)* If none are available, substitute with organically grown spinach.

Blend the tomatoes, water and garlic first, then slowly add the rest of the ingredients making sure they are only chopped and not fully blended.

This is the kind of soup to which you can add almost anything. Fresh herbs such as dill, parsley, chives or basil are excellent. Use a different one each time to vary the flavor and delicacy of your soup. Add more or less water depending on the desired thickness. Instead of cabbage sprouts, you may use regular cabbage or kale. Miso paste can be used instead of tamari. Add extra water if needed. Onion sprouts or scallions are always welcome. As long as the soup base is established,—the first five ingredients—your imagination and taste buds are free to roam. One caution: please do not cook. The heat from this raw soup comes only from its spices, sprouts and delicate herbs. Let them perform their nutritional miracle without devitalizing the ingredients by cooking. You'll feel warm inside and healthier for it.

Dulse

Dulse is a red colored sea vegetable that grows off the coast of Maine, Canada, Oregon and Alaska. Japan grows no dulse so this is one seaweed that is strictly North American. Its texture is so soft and chewy that it needs no cooking. Just soak for a few minutes in water or eat it as a snack right from the bag. Dulse is high in iron, protein and vitamins A & B. *(For more on dulse, see Glossary, p. 269.)*

Dr. Ann Wigmore's Energy Soup

Ingredients

1	Apple, peeled
1 handful (2oz)	Buckwheat lettuce
1 handful (2oz)	Baby Sunflowers
1 small	Apple, cored + cut
¼ cup	Dulse, soaked
½	Avocado, ripe

This is the famous wheatgrass doctor's daily health soup. She probably took it everyday for the last 30 years of her life. It is so simple, it is divine. Simply blend up the ingredients in a food processor or blender. If you use a blender, constant assistance with a spatula and the addition of a small amount of water may be necessary to maintain blender motion.

Peel the apple, core it and cut it into eighths. Cut the avocado in half and remove the pit. Using a tablespoon, spoon out the "meat." Process the sunflower, buckwheat and apple first, add the dulse and avocado last. Blend or process into a coarse or lumpy consistency. Good for breakfast, lunch or dinner. This green soup won't stick to your ribs or your colon. It simply converts into raw energy.

Sunflower is available already grown at many natural food stores. Buckwheat must be home-grown. In the Ann Wigmore method, both are grown in 1 inch of soil. However, they may also be grown hydroponically. (See Appendix, Sprouting, p. 287.)

Sproutman's
Sprout Vegetable Soup

Ingredients

3–4 cups	Pure water
½ inch	Ginger root
¼ cup	Radish sprouts
¾ cup	Cabbage sprouts
1	Lemon, juiced
3 Tbsp	Tamari
2 Tbsp	Olive oil
1 ½ cups	Sunflower greens
1 cup	Buckwheat lettuce sprouts
1 bunch	Garlic or Onion sprouts

Here's a soup that's hot without being heated! Just blend the ingredients together, that's all. It's easier than opening a can. Start with half the water. Add the ingredients in sequence, then slowly adding the rest of the water as needed. The last 3 ingredients should not be fully blended, only chopped. This gives your soup a thick, hearty texture. Vary the recipe by adding your own favorite spices. Hot spice enthusiasts may add cayenne pepper. No chives? Substitute with 1 or 2 scallion greens. If you are out of buckwheat sprouts (perish the thought!), substitute with alfalfa. If you are out of sunflower greens, substitute with spinach. (Try not to run out; even Popeye prefers sunflower greens.) These sprouts make a great tasting, nutritious soup. Mmm, mmm good!

RAW FRUIT &

VEGETABLE JUICES

Drink Raw Juice!

When you get an intravenous feeding in the hospital, you are getting 100% of that nourishment sent directly into your bloodstream. You don't have to worry about the ability of your digestive system—stomach, liver, pancreas and intestines—to absorb it. Sadly, the average American is in such poor shape that his/her ability to convert solid food into cellular absorbable nutrients (called assimilation), is only a fraction of what it should be. Just because food goes down and out, does not mean it gets used for cellular nourishment. With age, our production of hydrochloric acid and digestive enzymes is reduced. Unfortunately, the "food" in the intravenous feeding is mostly sugar water. You could make a diet of vitamin pills, but even some of them can be difficult to digest and often require solid food in order to work. But there is a way you can get nearly 100% assimilation of fruits and vegetables–raw fruit and vegetable juice.

Here's The Juice!

Too much alfalfa sprouts? Cabbage and radish sprouts sitting in the refrigerator uneaten? Do your buckwheat or sunflower crops have too many hulls still standing? If you have more sprouts than you can eat, put them through your vegetable juicer and transform them into a rich, nutritive enzyme drink. Juicers separate the fiber from the liquid leaving you pure juice. No sense throwing those sprouts or other excess vegetables into the compost. Juice them before they go bad. All the green leafy sprouts make juice. Avoid the beans such as green pea, mung, lentil and adzuki. They are too starchy, yield very little juice and can upset your stomach. Rinse and examine your sprouts before juicing them. If they have turned sour or smell at all, compost them.

Here are some happy juice combinations.

<u>a</u>	<u>b</u>	<u>c</u>
4 oz Carrot	4 oz Carrot	4 oz Carrot
½ oz Radish	1 oz Alfalfa	2 oz Sunflower
1 oz oz Alfalfa	1 oz Cabbage	

<u>d</u>	<u>e</u>	<u>f</u>
4 oz Carrot	5 oz Carrot	5 oz Carrot
2 oz Buckwheat	1 oz Garlic	1 oz Fenugreek

Why Drink Juice?

Nothing is more nutritious than juice. Imagine eating a meal of spinach, parsley, sprouts, tomatoes, lemon, celery, radishes, green pepper and cucumber. Ordinarily, considering the normal state of our digestive systems, we would only digest half of it. But once we extract the liquid portion of these vital foods, we can assimilate and absorb up to 99 percent of their food value even with weak digestion. In fact, it barely takes any digestive energy at all to assimilate the nutrients extracted from fruit and vegetable juice. The concentration of pounds of valuable foods into a single glass of juice maximizes digestion and is the major benefit of fresh squeezed juice. Carrots are a good example. It takes 10 average size carrots to make a glass of carrot juice. Could you consume that many carrots? Absolutely not! Yet, in the process of extracting the juice from these vegetables, all of the enzymes, water soluble vitamins, minerals and trace elements are both liberated and concentrated in the juice, assuming you are using a quality juicer. If you are trying to heal your body, choose live cellular nutrition. The best source is the fresh squeezed juice of living plants.

What No Fiber?

Many people wonder about the value of drinking juice after all the promotion and praise they have heard about the value of fiber. If the fiber in carrots is so healthy, why eliminate it?

Juice frees the vital nutrients in plants and makes them readily available for digestion. The fiber in carrots does indeed serve an important digestive function. Carrots should also be consumed whole. Raw vegetable juice is not recommended in place of whole food but as a supplement. By all means, eat a diet rich in fresh vegetables and fruits and consider your juices as power drinks of liquid vitamins.

ONE GLASS OF CARROT JUICE CONTAINS	
(8.68 ounces or 246 grams total)	
Water	219 grams
Vitamin A - Carotene	6,318 RE
Vitamin C	21 mg
Calcium	58 mg
Magnesium	34 mg
Phosphorus	1102 mg
Potassium	716 mg
Protein	2.32 grams
Carbohydrate	22.8 grams
Calories	98

Pasteurized Juice vs. Fresh Juice

Don't race to guzzle down bottles of apple, grape, orange and tomato juice unless you plan to make them yourself. Bottled juices must be pasteurized in order to ensure shelf life. Pasteurized juices are boiled to sanitize them against bacteria and disease organisms that occur normally when fresh food ages. Unfortunately, enzymes and many vitamins are destroyed in this process. Though they taste good, there is no live nutrition left in bottled juices—only sugar, flavor and water. Even the taste and color are no match for the fresh-squeezed version. Which do you prefer—fresh squeezed orange juice or the pasteurized container variety? If you answer 'fresh,' then wait till you taste the difference between bottled and fresh squeezed apple juice! Fresh apple juice is white—just like the color of an apple when you bite into it. Bottled apple juice is brown because nutrients have been lost to oxidation upon contact with the air. Just exposing live nutrients to air and light is enough to destroy some of these fragile friends. Live food is perishable and that is the way it is supposed to be. Enabling a container of orange juice to sit on a supermarket shelf for a month is a miracle of distribution but a mockery of nutrition.

Get Color Therapy from Your Food	
Yellow	Glowing, freeing, illuminating, extroverted, relaxing.
Orange	Invigorating, energizing, positive, festive, anti-depressive, joyful.
Red	Energizing, vital, active, expanding, accelerating, attracting, loud.
Purple	Deepening, dampening, relaxing, unsteady, mysterious, hypnotic, mystical, introverted.
Blue	Quiet, sedative, concentrating, spiritual, embracing
Green	Soothing, passive, calming, hoping, protective, regenerating.
Brown	Stabilizing.

Green Juice Cocktail

Ingredients

3 oz	Celery, juiced
3 oz	Spinach, juiced
2 oz	Tomato, juiced
½ oz	Cabbage, juiced
¼ oz	Dill, juiced
1	Lemon, juiced
1 clove	Garlic, juiced
1–2 inch	Ginger root, juiced
1–2 Tbsp	Tamari
pinch	Cayenne

Here's an elixir that is potent enough to fit in as one of the hard drinks at the corner bar. The difference is that the potency of this drink fortifies your body instead of debilitating it. It's the natural V-8.

This recipe, and all juice recipes, are measured in terms of ounces. This is because one cannot measure all vegetables in cups or tablespoons. In this case, 3 ounces of celery juice and 3 ounces of spinach juice combine with 2 ounces of tomato juice all made from fresh vegetables. Using a measuring cup as the collecting container, juice the celery up to the 3 ounce line. Switch to spinach and juice up to the 6 ounce line, then the tomato up to 8 ounces. These three are the core ingredients.

The other ingredients in this recipe are more herbal in nature, providing spice in addition to healing. In this regard, you may exercise personal preference by adding or eliminating them. However, this cocktail is beautifully balanced and will reward you nutritionally for experiencing it in full. Green juices have a strengthening and calming influence. Enjoy them before dinner or in the early evening.

Carotene Energizer

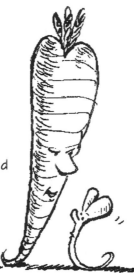

Ingredients

6 oz	Carrot, juiced
1 oz	Beet, juiced
1 oz	Green Pepper, juiced
1 oz	Cucumber, juiced
½ oz	Parsley, juiced

Orange colored juices are rich in carotene which is the plant kingdom's form of vitamin A. With carotene, our bodies are able to manufacture vitamin A. Orange colored juices are generally energizing in nature. In other words, they are pick-me-ups. It is no coincidence that "orange juice" is America's favorite breakfast drink.

Carrot juice, with its abundance of carotene, is as orange as orange juice and not at all acidic. Its sweetness offers quick energy. Mix this juice with beets, a liver stimulant, and you have one of the most healthful elixirs. The addition of cucumber and parsley, while not core ingredients, offsets the sweetness of the carrots. Both are known as cleansers for the kidneys and urinary system. Their chlorophyll–rich healing green color added to the orange makes this a nicely balanced drink. Athletes should use this energizing juice instead of the commercial powdered milk protein formulas.

Juice Suite

Ingredients

6 oz	Carrot, juiced
1 oz	Apple, juiced
1 oz	Alfalfa sprouts, juiced
1 oz	Watermelon rind, juiced
1 inch	Ginger root, juiced

And how sweet it is! A colorful and delicious combination. First of all the sweet combination of carrot and apple is unsurpassed. You will never know the true taste of apple juice until you have had it freshly squeezed. It is the equivalent of eating a liquid apple!

Some people suggest that vegetables and fruits should not be mixed because the stomach requires different enzymes to process them. This is true of solid food. However, digestion of juices does not take place in the stomach. Juice passes through the stomach into the duodenum, the beginning part of the small intestine where pancreatic enzymes are introduced. Juice requires minimal digestive action and therefore is not subject to the more complex digestive criteria of solid food.

Alfalfa sprouts add the color green to the orange of this juice to lend balance. The watermelon rind, also partly green, adds sweetness and a wealth of minerals. Watermelon rind is known for its effectiveness as a kidney cleansing agent. The hot flavor of ginger root balances the sweetness of the carrot and apple and is an excellent conditioner for the stomach and lungs. These added ingredients create a more balanced drink, nutritionally and energetically, than drinking carrot alone.

The Venerable Smoothie

The smoothie is a wonderful, nutritionally rich, non-dairy beverage. The combination of blended fruits, with banana as the top banana, is guaranteed to hit a home run. First start with a ripe banana. *(For selecting bananas, see p. 121.)* Slice and blend it with some apple juice and fruits like strawberry or blueberry. Then blend in the additional ingredients in the recipes below. They make a non-dairy malted or thick shake that's great for getting you going in the morning or anytime you want a sweet and nourishing treat.

Soothie

1	Banana
1+ cups	Apple Juice
1 Tbsp	Lecithin granules
¼ cup	Sunflower seeds
1	Date, chopped
1 Tbsp	Spirulina

Bluthie

1	Banana, ripe
½	Apple, cored
1+ cups	Apple Juice
1 Tbsp	Bee Pollen
½ cup	Blueberries or
6	Strawberries

Doosie

1	Banana
½	Apple, cored
1+ cups	Apple Juice
¼ cup	Raw Carob Powder
¼ cup	Cashews
1 Tbsp	Nutritional Yeast
1	Vanilla Bean, chopped

Cantaloupsie

1	Cantaloupe, ripe

Chop into chunks and blend.

HOMEMADE

NATURAL SODAS

Soda is arguably America's most popular drink. It is considered the "thirst that quenches." It is also one of the most unhealthful liquids America consumes. Coke drinkers, who in the original drink got high from the real cocaine in it, are now getting their high from the caffeine and "non-prescription drugs" included in the form of artificial flavors, colored dyes and preservatives. If that doesn't make you spriteful enough, the many forms of sugar—dextrose, sucrose and corn sweeteners—should. Of course, if you would rather switch than fight, there are always the diet sodas with artificial sugars—cyclamates, saccharines and nutrasweets. Big advertising campaigns have successfully sold young America on the idea that drinking soda pop is fashionable. The "Pepsi Generation" is losing its teeth and risking its health for the sake of being "cool." All is not lost, however. Soda can be a refreshing and satisfying drink, if made simply and wholesomely.....*Sproutman* to the rescue!

Vanilla Soda

Ingredients

1 quart	Sparkling Mineral Water
1	Vanilla Bean

The best kind of soda is made by Nature herself. Naturally sparkling mineral water springs forth from the belly of the earth in Arkansas, France, Switzerland and other pristine places around the world. Your natural foods store has a wide selection. The number 1 seller, Perrier, is a mere baby in the marketplace compared to Coke, yet a giant in its own field.

Now for the recipe. Slice a whole vanilla bean right down the middle, lengthwise, and set the two long halves inside your favorite bottle of sparkling water. Store your bottle in or out of the refrigerator according to your usual procedure. Let it sit there until you have imbibed the last drop. The longer it sits, the more natural vanilla you will taste. Voilà! It's that simple, quick and delicious.

Proceed from this basic recipe to create the following fountain delights.

OTHER FOUNTAIN DELIGHTS

Homemade Maple-Vanilla Soda

1 quart	Sparkling Mineral Water
2 Tbsp	Maple Syrup
1	Vanilla Bean

Honey-Vanilla Soda

1 quart	Sparkling Mineral Water
2 Tbsp	Honey
1	Vanilla Bean

Honey-Cinnamon Soda

1 quart	Sparkling Mineral Water
2 Tbsp	Maple Syrup
2	Cinnamon sticks

Homemade Root Beer

1 quart	Sparkling Mineral Water
2 Tbsp	Maple Syrup
¼ cup	Sassafras bark

Root Beer Float

1 quart	Sparkling Mineral Water
2 Tbsp	Maple Syrup
¼ cup	Sassafras bark
1 scoop	Vanilla ice scream (p.129 top)

Vanilla Ice Cream Soda

1 quart	Sparkling Mineral Water
2 Tbsp	Maple syrup
1	Vanilla Bean
1 scoop	Vanilla ice scream (p.129 top)

NATURAL FRUIT SODAS

Grape Soda

2 cups	Sparkling Mineral Water
½ cup	Grape juice

Orange Soda

2 cups	Sparkling Mineral Water
½ cup	Orange juice, fresh squeezed

Lemon-Up

2 cups	Sparkling Mineral Water
1 twist	Lemon
1 twist	Lime

Pineapple Soda

2 cups	Sparkling Mineral Water
½ cup	Pineapple juice

With these homemade sodas, you and your family will never be thirsty...or bored. Kids, too! Now you can enjoy variety and flavor without compromising health. L'Chaim!

Radish Sprouts
Six day old radish sprouts grown hydroponically in bamboo.

Natural Sesame Halvah

Ingredients

```
1 cup        Sesame Seeds, hulled
1–2 Tbsp     Honey, raw organic
```

Yields: 5–10 sesame balls

Finally, this fabulous snack is restored to its original pristine nature. Those of you who have learned to love this dish know that it is commercially prepared with glucose, hydrogenated vegetable oil, cottonseed oil, dried egg albumin, artificial color and artificial flavor. For this reason you may have eliminated it from your list of healthy snacks. Sacrifice no more! Natural halvah is back. It's nutritious, delicious and easy to make.

A Sticky Job, but Someone's Got to Do It

First step in making halvah is to grind your hulled sesame seeds into sesame meal. A food processor, blender, nut-seed or coffee grinder will all work for this purpose. When using a blender, a spatula or chopstick is recommended to dislodge seeds on the blender walls and nurse them back into the blades.

Find a wide bowl with tall sides or use a cooking pot. Put the seed meal in first, then add the honey. Mix thoroughly with a strong rubber spatula or wooden spoon. Do not be discouraged if it does not combine well at first. It needs lots of kneading. This dish gives plenty of exercise in addition to plenty of nutrition. Warming the honey in the pot makes it more fluid and easier to mix. Now wet your hands and get ready for a ball.

Round or Flat

Pull out a quarter size lump of the mixture and roll it into a tight ball. Wet your hands regularly to simplify working with the sticky seeds. If you want flat halvah instead, simply flatten the balls and cut out your favorite shapes using a cookie cutter. If you do not like to get your hands sticky, roll the balls on a cutting board sprinkled with coconut meal. Place in a storage bowl with a lid and store in the refrigerator. C'est toute. Make a million of them, they have excellent shelf life, unless someone finds out where they are!

About Sesame

Some controversy exists regarding whether to consume hulled or unhulled sesame seed. The hull is the branish jacket that encloses the seed. It contains relatively high amounts of oxalic acid—an acid which among other things, binds calcium. We use the hulled variety to make halvah. The hulled seed eliminates concern about oxalic acid. *(For more on sesame seeds, see Glossary, p. 269.)*

Carob Halvah

Ingredients

1 cup	Sesame Seeds, hulled
1–2 Tbsp	Honey, raw organic
2 tsp	Carob powder, raw untoasted

Follow the basic recipe, only this time mix carob powder into the honey, then work it into the sesame meal. Warming the honey first makes it easier to mix.

Coconut Halvah

Ingredients

1 cup	Sesame Seeds, hulled
1–2 Tbsp	Honey, raw organic
¼ cup	Coconut, shredded

Just mix the ground sesame seeds in with the honey as in the basic halvah recipe. Place your coconut shreds in a dish or on the cutting board and roll the balls into it until completely coated.

Raisin Halvah

Ingredients

1 cup	Sesame Seeds, hulled
1–2 Tbsp	Honey, raw organic
¼ cup	Raisins

Same recipe. Mix the honey in first and then the raisins.

Deluxe Halvah

Ingredients

1 cup	Sesame Seeds, hulled
1 Tbsp	Maple Syrup
¼ Tbsp	Vanilla Extract
2 Tbsp	Raw Honey
½ cup	Oatmeal, flour

Same basic recipe but this time with maple syrup and vanilla. It may be looser because of the extra fluids, so add some oatmeal flour as needed to firm things up. Oatmeal also adds flavor and nutrition. Mix it in as the last ingredient. If you cannot find oatmeal flour, powder regular oatmeal flakes in your blender.

Super-Green Halvah

A Super Charged Snack

Ingredients

2 cups	Sesame meal
¼ cup	Honey, raw
1 tsp	Vanilla extract
2 Tbsp	Bee pollen
2 Tbsp	Spirulina, chlorella, or blue-green algae

Grind raw, hulled sesame seeds into sesame meal using a food processor or blender as described in the basic *Natural Halvah* recipe. The entire procedure can be accomplished in a food processor. However, if you only have a blender, grind the seeds there and do all the mixing by hand. The manual method works just fine and has the added advantage of contributing to your daily upper arm exercises!

Combine the raw, unpasteurized honey with vanilla extract, then work into the sesame meal. Once the mixture begins to stiffen, sprinkle on the bee pollen and algae and mix well. Remove the "dough" and form into 1 inch balls, wetting your hands regularly to prevent sticking. Refrigerate for extra firmness and storage.

About the Ingredients

Use raw, unpasteurized buckwheat or clover honey. Try to find a vanilla that is alcohol-free. One variety is made from Madagascar bourbon vanilla beans with a glycerin base. Bee pollen should be refrigerated for maximum potency. *(For information on green algae foods, vanilla and bee pollen, see Glossary, p. 269.)*

Party Sprouts

Ingredients

2 cups	Lentil Sprouts
2 Tbsp	Onion Powder
1 tsp	Garlic Powder
3 Tbsp	Tamari Sauce
pinch	Cayenne Pepper (optional)

There's going to be a party. Throw out the commercial pretzels and potato chips and start up the sprout bags!

Soak ½ cup of lentils for 8–10 hours and sprout for 5 days rinsing twice each day. *(See Appendix, Sprouting, p. 287.)* Place the matured sprouts in a bowl and garnish with the onion, garlic powder and tamari. Mix the spices in thoroughly. If necessary, make a separate batch with cayenne pepper for those who like it hot. Spread on a cookie sheet and bake at 250°F. until brittle and crispy. It takes approximately one hour depending on your oven. For a similar dehydrated version of this recipe, see *Dried Lentils p. 173,* in the dehydrator chapter. The looser you pack them, the faster they will finish.

Once perfectly dry, store them in a storage bowl with a lid or a ziplock plastic bag to maintain their crispness and prevent moisture from infiltrating. Do not refrigerate. They last for months if kept perfectly dry. Take them on a hike, put them in the lunchbox or serve them at the party. They are crispy, crunchy and spicy. Imagine, all this without salt, deep fried fats, flour, sugar, artificial flavor, BHT or BHA, cottonseed and palm oils, hydrogenated fat or red dye #2. Let the party begin!

Dry Roasted
Sprout Peanuts

Ingredients

1–2 cups	Raw Shelled Peanuts
1/3 cup	Tamari Sauce
2 tsp	Garlic Granules
3 Tbsp	Onion Powder

Are you nuts about peanuts, but can't digest them? Peanut sprouts to the rescue—one of the most delicious treats in our sprout repertoire.

Peanuts are generally misunderstood. Partly a bean and partly a nut, they are known to be very difficult to digest. Their digestion is complicated by the availability of shelled nuts that enable us to over consume them. Sprouted peanuts go a long way toward simplifying the digestion problem. As the peanut germinates, it begins to resolve its identity problem and becomes a pea. It tastes and looks like a fresh pea and can be cooked and served like one. In fact, it makes a great cooked vegetable side dish. But the true talent of the peanut unfolds in the roasting process. The sprouted, dry-roasted peanut is truly rewarding and simple to prepare.

Selecting & Sprouting

The most important ingredient is the nut itself. Peanuts are frequently difficult to sprout and unless you get the right variety, success will evade you. Organically raised, raw, red skin Valencia is the best variety. Sprout 1 cup of nuts in a sprout bag rinsing 3 times per day. *(See Appendix, Sprouting, p. 287.)* The soaking period is a long 12 hours. They take 7–8 days to reach maturity. Do not sprout peanuts in a jar. Limited ventilation and drainage reduce germination dramatically. Big peas and beans—a peanut is a pea—can have germination rates as low as 50%–75%. If you get a batch that does better, stock up. Peanuts like to be rinsed 3 times per day. The more you rinse, the more success you will have. Rinsing washes away mold and fungus created by non-germinating seed and debris. Cloudy rinse water is common for peanuts but is indicative that better rinsing is required. Before roasting, remove any discolored or damaged seed.

Baking

The mature sprout should develop shoots that are 1–2 times the length of the nut. Mix them in a bowl with the tamari and garlic. Dried garlic granules are preferable because of their ability to spread evenly over the beans. Lay them one layer deep on a cookie sheet with approximately one inch sides. Please avoid using aluminum trays. No oil is needed. Dry roasted means they are roasted in their own oil. Turn them over with a metal spatula about half-way through. Bake in the oven for approximately 2½ hours at 250°F.

If the peanut sprouts are still soft and moist at the end of the cooking period, let them harden in the oven with the heat turned off. If they are fairly hard already, remove them from the oven and let them cool. Do not let them get overly hard in the oven. They dry as they cool. Their texture should be firm and mildly crunchy. If they are soft, they need more cooking. Soft, semi-moist peanuts are not bad, just less crunchy. They require refrigeration since they are more perishable. Completely dry peanuts may be stored in a jar in the cupboard for months. The long sprout tails on these peas remind you that germination has converted the proteins into more digestible amino acids, the fats into more soluble fatty acids and simplified many starches. Not only that, but they're delicious, too. Enjoy.

A sprouting tray and greenhouse designed by Sproutman
The versatile dividers allow for one, two or four varieties to be grown
simultaneously. The tallest sprout shown is red pea lettuce.

ALTERNATIVES TO SALT

Throughout history, salt has held a position of unique importance. Wars have been fought over it and civilizations have been built up around it. Even the Bible refers to salt as a measurement of value: "Ye are the salt of the earth." The Greeks used it as a medium of exchange from which comes the expression "worth his weight in salt" and salt is the root of the word "salary."

While salt has many applications, we are concerned with its use as a condiment or flavor enhancer. Excess salt consumption has been one of America's biggest dietary problems, leading to high blood pressure and hypertension. In 1981, for the first time, food manufacturers were required to list the salt content of their foods on the label. Then Secretary of Health and Human Services, Richard S. Schweiker commented: "Sixty million Americans suffer from hypertension, which can lead to strokes and heart attacks."

Salt Alternatives

The potential dangers of excess salt consumption can be controlled through prudent diet. Upon withdrawing from a high daily salt intake, one discovers that natural flavors become brighter. A strict no salt diet is probably not possible because sodium chloride is a natural ingredient in many man-made foods as well as vegetables. On the other hand, commercial table salt is not pure salt, but rather a combination of salt, iodine, non-caking agents, dehydrants and even sugar (in the form of dextrose). Natural salt is a one-ingredient food whose source is either the ocean or rock. Many supplemental foods are "salty" making them good substitutes for the pure thing.

Foods That Can Substitute for Salt		
Miso paste	Kelp granules	Scallions
Tamari or soy sauce	Dulse flakes	Radish sprouts, dried
Cayenne pepper	Seaweeds	Mustard
Yeast	Soy Bullion	Oregano
Herbs (various)	Garlic granules	Basil
Umeboshi Plum	Onion powder	Thyme

Natural and specialty food stores carry herbal salts that are a combination of dried, powdered vegetables and herbs mixed with sea or earth salt. Some may also include yeast and isolated soy protein. Sample a few from your natural foods store until you find one you like best. Cut down on the use of salt by including it as one of a group of flavor enhancers. The following recipes are home–made salt alternatives that use herbs, seeds and mixes with reduced sea salt and still provide plenty of flavor and spice.

(See Glossary, p. 269, for more information on Kelp, Dulse and other seaweeds.)

Sprout Salt

Ingredients

5 tsp	Alfalfa sprouts, powdered
1 tsp	Natural Sea Salt
1 tsp	Radish sprouts, powdered
1 tsp	Cabbage sprouts, powdered
1 tsp	Garlic sprouts, powdered
1 tsp	Dulse, dried flakes

A wonderfully healthy condiment using dehydrated sprouts. Simply dehydrate your excess sprouts, then store them in a zip sealed plastic bag. Once you have collected the different varieties, grind them in a blender and sift together according to this recipe. *(For more on dehydrated sprouts, refer to Sprouts n' Spice, p. 169.)*

Sesame Salt

Ingredients

1 cup	Sesame seeds, hulled + ground
1–2 Tbsp	Sea Salt
1+ tsp	Garlic granules
2 tsp	Onion powder

Sesame is one of our miracle foods. It is the highest source of calcium of any land or sea plant (1160 mg per 100 grams). It is also a superb source of essential fatty acids and amino acids. For many years, the Japanese have used a sesame salt preparation known as gomazio. In the Japanese recipe, the whole seed, including the brown seed jacket, is used. In this recipe, the blonde hulled seed is purchased, toasted and ground into a meal. To toast hulled sesame seeds, spread the seeds one layer thick on a cookie sheet and place in an oven of 300°F. Or, you may use a broiler or toaster oven. Let the seeds brown but be watchful. Sections of the tray may toast faster than others. They are done when the majority are golden brown. *(For more about sesame seed, see Glossary, p. 269.)*

Grind the seeds into a meal using a blender, nut/seed grinder or food processor. *(See making Natural Halvah, p. 222.)* Add the sea salt, garlic and onion powder, and shake well. Keep refrigerated in a sealed jar. Use generously on grain dishes, bean sprout dishes, even salads. Very versatile, very delicious, very healthy.

Salt N' Spice

Ingredients

¼–½ cup	Sea Salt
1 tsp	Kelp, granules
½ tsp	Paprika
½ tsp	Garlic powder
1 tsp	Oregano
1 tsp	Basil
1 tsp	Thyme

A true herbal salt using some of nature's most flavorful herbs and a rainbow of colors. Use freshly dried herbs for maximum flavor and nutrition. Blend all herbs together in a blender or nut/seed mill. The finer the powder, the smoother the mixture. Add in the sea salt last and mix thoroughly. Although this mixture is primarily salt, you cut down the salt ratio by simply using less of it.

Rice Salt

Ingredients

1 cup	Rice powder
2+ tsp	Sea Salt
2 tsp	Garlic granules

As a grain, rice is a natural combination with salt. Rice powder becomes the primary ingredient of this condiment as is sesame in sesame salt. The result is a less salty, flavorful grain condiment.

Rice powder can be made by dehydrating rice cereal made from blended cooked rice. But the fastest and easiest way to obtain rice powder for this recipe is to grind up some store purchased rice cakes. Use unsalted, plain organic rice cakes and blend into a powder in your blender. It takes approximately 3 rice crackers to make about 1 cup of rice powder. Mix in the sea salt and garlic and store in the cupboard in a moisture proof container.

Green Salt

Ingredients

1 tsp	Chlorella
1 cup	Rice powder
2+ tsp	Sea Salt
2 tsp	Garlic powder

Prepare as in recipe for *Rice Salt*, only here the salt is green.

Red Salt

Ingredients

2 tsp	Dried Tomatoes, powdered
1 cup	Rice powder
2 tsp	Sea Salt
2 tsp	Dulse flakes
1 tsp	Paprika

More rice powder, but this time with dried tomatoes and paprika. Dried tomatoes and dulse must be brittle and not pliable. Warm them in a low oven or dehydrator to make them brittle dry. Then blend them into flakes using a blender or nut/seed mill. Prepare as in recipe fore *rice salt,* then mix together and store in a jar with a sealed lid.

Blue Green Salt

Ingredients

¼ cup	Sea Salt
1 tsp	Blue Green Algae

Prepare as in recipe for *rice salt.*

LIGHT COOKING

Low Temperature + Long-Time = Maximum Nutrition

This chapter represents a minor departure from the other recipes in this book in two ways. First, low–temperature cooking is used. Secondly, this section is not 100% vegan because an animal by-product (butter) is used in two of the recipes. (Veganism is a form of vegetarianism that excludes dairy and egg products.) While this cookbook does not aim to be 100% raw foods, it is 100% vegetarian.

Sprouts–To Cook or Not to Cook

Sprouts and raw foods are sometimes considered synonymous. One would never consider cooking a salad, for example. But sprout seeds extend beyond the salad domain.

The choice of seeds is distinguished by those varieties that develop a green leaf and those that do not. The green, chlorophyll developing seeds are for salads and should be grown vertically, like lettuce in your garden. Radish, cabbage, clover, buckwheat, sunflower and alfalfa, to name a few, are such seeds. Beans, on the other hand, are not chlorophyll developing, do not need light nor vertical development, and are commonly grown in a jar or, even better, a sprout bag. *(See Appendix, Sprouting, p. 287.)* Some popular varieties are mung, lentil, chick pea (garbanzo), green pea, soy, adzuki and red pea. They are usually sprouted for 3 to 5 days and look very much like beans with a tail. There is no metamorphosis of these big beans as with alfalfa, which transforms itself from a legume into a completely different entity—a green plant. Although the sprouted beans are truly easier to digest, higher in protein, lower in starch and require less time to cook, they are still mostly raw and one does not consume raw beans.

This certainly holds true for the bigger beans like soy and garbanzo. They should be cooked until soft all the way through. Cooking time for the sprouted bean is usually half that of the regular bean. A good policy is to use low heat, long term cooking.

Low Heat, Long Term

This technique is good for both sprouted and un-sprouted beans, grains and even vegetables. It's simple. Turn the flame on low, put on the lid and simmer until done. Near the end of the cooking process, the lid should be left slightly ajar to relieve escaping gasses. Stir periodically and never let all the water cook out.

More of the smaller size beans—mung, lentil, adzuki or red pea—can be eaten raw but still should be cooked when any sizable portion is consumed to get optimum digestibility. Cooking time is even quicker for these beans. Another approach is to heat the beans to a boil, then shut the heat off, cover and let steep.

Grains such as hard wheat, rye, spelt, kamut and soft wheat are also sprouted in a bag or jar like the beans. Technically, grains are chlorophyll developing plants because they are grasses. Grasses are, of course, green, but they are not salad foods, at least by human standards. Cows and horses consider them haute cuisine! Grains are usually sprouted for 2 to 5 days and yield a seedling that is 1 to 2 times the size of the berry. The grain sprouts can be ground into sprout dough for making sprouted breads, crackers and cookies, dried and pulverized into flour, or toasted for snacks. They can also be eaten raw as snacks or mixed with dried fruit in small quantities. As with raw beans, raw grains are not normally consumed and sprouted raw grains are still not fully digestible. They need judicious cooking to become completely digestible. Baking sprouted grain as in sprout bread, however, can be accomplished at temperatures much lower than standard bread baking. *(See chapter on making sprout bread.)* Sprout bread usually bakes at 250°F. (normal bread is baked at 450°F.). Because these temperatures are so low, sprout bread can take as long as 3+ hours to bake. The bread is dried as much as it is baked. In summary, grains or big beans, should be cooked when consumed in quantity for maximum digestibility.

Green Pea Melt

Ingredients

2 cups	Green pea sprouts
2 Tbsp	Butter, raw
¼ tsp	Salt, herbal
3–4 ounces	Tofu mozzarella "cheese"

Yield: Serves 3

The proud pea deserves better than to be merely thought of as thick soup. Here's a creative pea dish that's different and delicious.

First sprout a cup of whole green peas for 4–5 days. *(See Appendix, Sprouting, p. 287.)* This should yield approximately 2 cups of fresh green pea sprouts. Cook the pea sprouts in water for approximately 30–45 minutes on a low flame. They are ready when soft. Pour off the water and sauté for 3–5 minutes in a skillet with butter and salt. Add the tofu mozzarella "cheese" in thin slices on top and allow to melt.

About the Ingredients

Whole sproutable green peas, preferably organically grown, are, of course, the essential ingredient. For butter, we use Alta-Dena brand butter made from raw milk. The mozzarella is a non-dairy cheese fashioned from tofu. Several brands are available at natural food stores. Pick one that you like and read the package to make sure it melts.

Green Pea Mash

Ingredients

2 cups	Green pea sprouts
2 Tbsp	Butter, raw
¼ tsp	Salt, herbal
1/3 cup	Soy milk *(or substitute)*

Yield: Serves 3

Sprout 1 cup of whole green peas which will grow to approximately 2 cups of green pea sprouts. Cook the pea sprouts just as in the *Green Pea Melt*. Place the drained peas in your food processor and add the butter, salt and soy milk. Puree and serve. That's all.

This dish also makes for a great baby food. Just use the peas and soy milk and eliminate the salt and butter.

As a substitute for soy milk, use almond milk, or rice milk. The recipe for almond milk is in the dairy section of this book. Rice milk and almond milk are both available in natural food stores.

Braised Tofu

Ingredients

8 oz. cake	Tofu
2 stalks	Scallions
2 Tbsp	Olive oil
1 tsp	Dark sesame oil
1–2 cloves	Garlic
2–3 stalks	Celery, chopped
½ inch	Ginger root, diced
1 Tbsp	Mustard, dijon
1–2 Tbsp	Natto Miso

Yield: Serves 2

No household should be devoid of meal ideas as long as there is tofu on hand. As you stare into the refrigerator searching desperately for the fettucine, the nut-burger, the quiche, the guacamole, the parmesan and the pot pie, staring back at you is the bland and unglamorous tofu. But don't let this jello-like fellow fool you. Despite his white pallor and vacuous demeanor, he can whip up quite a colorful meal.

A true culinary chameleon, the tofu can play as many parts as Lawrence Olivier without ever disappointing the audience. In one role he's a meat substitute, in another a salad mainstay, or he can dress like a dressing, simulate a soup, cheat as a cheese and double as a dessert. Today, this brazen fellow plays a small fry who gives a stirring performance.

Oil your skillet with quality olive oil. Olive oil is one of the best oils to cook with because it has a high smoking temperature. Cut your cake of tofu into small half-inch cubes, then add it to the skillet after the oil is hot. Stir the tofu and, after it gets hot, add the scallions and garlic. If the skillet becomes dry, add the sesame oil. If still too dry, add more olive oil. When the tofu begins to brown, add the celery, the ginger, the miso and mustard. Stir well and serve.

Ingredients

The final ingredients do not have to be cooked. They only need to be heated so their flavors blend into the mix. The celery should be chopped into small ½ inch sections. Any variety of dark miso can be used. However, natto miso is made with barley, ginger, seaweed and malt and is particularly flavorful. Ginger root can be scraped with a mincer for best results. Onion or onion sprouts can be substituted if you are out of scallions.

This is an amazingly simple dish that is quick to prepare, full of flavor, has a variety of textures and is rich in nutrition.

Braised Tofu & Rice

Ingredients

1 cup	Rice, cooked
1 cake, 8oz.	Tofu
3 stalks	Scallions, chopped
2 Tbsp	Olive oil
1 tsp	Dark sesame oil
1–2 cloves	Garlic
3 stalks	Celery, chopped
½-1 inch	Ginger root, diced
1 Tbsp	Mustard, dijon
2 Tbsp	Natto Miso

Yield: Serves 2

This is another quick dinner that is thoroughly satisfying and nutritious. Once you have become an expert at making braised tofu, add 1 cup of cooked rice to the mixture and stir it in.

Cook the rice first in a separate pot. Organically grown short grain rice is preferred. Normally, ½ cup of dry grain will yield 1+ cups of cooked grain. Make sure the rice is thoroughly cooked and softened. Since it is cooked separately, add it when the tofu is nearly done. It simply needs to be mixed in. Notice some of the ingredient amounts are increased from the tofu version in order to balance the addition of the rice.

Hearty appetite.

Hijiki Sea Salad

Ingredients

1 cup	Hijiki, pre-cooked
2 tsp	Tamari
1–2 Tbsp	Olive oil
1	Lemon, juiced
1 tsp	Umeboshi plum paste
1 heaping Tbsp	Garlic sprouts (or 1 clove)
1 Tbsp	Yellow mustard (optional)
Yield:	Serves 2

Hijiki is a black seaweed made up of hundreds of rich black curls or fronds several inches long. It has a strong sea flavor and firm texture and will expand 4 times its volume when cooked. Hijiki is too tough to eat in the raw state, but softens when simmered in water for 10 minutes. The Japanese, who cultivate more Hijiki than anyone, use it as a side vegetable dish or appetizer and often eat it with rice. In a typical dish, the cooked Hijiki might be sautéed with onions, carrots, peas, tamari and sesame oil. Or it can easily be added to soups, stews, casseroles or served cold with salads.

Nutrition

Hijiki is a great treat for vegetarians. It is a magnificent source of minerals and although strictly a vegetable, it has the smell and flavor of seafood. The tiny branches float 3–6 feet below the ocean surface soaking up valuable nutrients. Hijiki has more potassium than rice, bananas, or wheat bran; more sodium than olives, spinach, swiss chard, celery or beets; more magnesium than almonds, cashews, or peanuts; more iron than rice or wheat germ; more calcium than kale, collard greens, spinach, or parsley. Such an impressive food deserves to be enjoyed more in this country.

Cover approximately 1 cup of Hijiki in a pot of water and simmer for 15 minutes or until soft. Hijiki can swell 5–6 times its size. Drain off most, but not all, of the water and add 2 Tbsp of good quality olive oil, 2 tsp of tamari and the juice of 1 lemon. Stir in 1 tsp of umeboshi paste and a heaping tablespoon of garlic sprouts. Squeeze in the juice of a small garlic clove if you have no sprouts. Serve hot as a side dish or cold as a seaweed salad.

Optional ingredients: Use Dr. Bronner's bullion instead of tamari. Miso paste is another wonderful addition. You can also embellish your dish by adding ½ cup of either garlic chives, french onion sprouts or chopped scallions. Grated ginger is another favorite. This is one dish that is delightfully different from typical American cuisine and rich in flavor and nutrition. So, go to your natural health or oriental food store and ask for Hijiki. Enjoy.

Spinach Marinade

Ingredients

½ lb	Spinach
1 clove	Garlic, pressed
2 Tbsp	Olive oil
1 Tbsp	Tamari

This is the original *Popeye* recipe.

First, clean the spinach well removing all grit and sand. Steam the greens lightly in a steamer or place the freshly washed leaves in a pot, cover and simmer. The water remaining on the leaves from the rinsing is usually enough for steaming. Simply throw the wet spinach in a skillet, cover it and use a very low flame. Monitor closely and remove once the leaves have softened. Remove from heat immediately as these leaves are delicate, add the olive oil, tamari and garlic. Stir well and serve.

A superb summer dish or whenever spinach is in season. Use local organic spinach whenever possible. Popeye got his "muskels" this way.

Oil & Fat
America'S #1 Dietary Enemy

The average American consumes 42% of his/her calories from fat–over 50 pounds per year. It could be in the form of french fries, steaks, burgers, ice cream, butter, milk, eggs or processed foods made from these ingredients. All these foods contain saturated, high cholesterol fat, which has been linked to the nation's top killers: cardiovascular disease and cancer. Even when Americans dine on the leaner Chinese and Indian cuisines, as typically prepared in this country, they are eating excessively oily food. Even sautéed/fried "health foods" such as tempura tofu, potato chips, home fries, tempeh burgers and natural cheeses are full of fat. The *Standard American Diet (S.A.D.)* is in a sad state of affairs.

A F.U.N. diet *(Fruit & vegetables for Ultimate Nutrition),* on the other hand, consists of 90% fruits and vegetables and complex carbohydrates like grains and beans. The SAD diet contains excessive amounts of refined sugars that are linked to hypoglycemia and diabetes, the number 3 killer in the USA. Only 10% of the FUN diet is fat and that is from natural oil rich foods such as avocados, olives, nuts and grains. Protein is in the form of non-toxic plant protein. The SAD diet is 2.5 times higher in protein. Excessive protein produces uric acid by-products, a known contributor to heart disease.

AT YOUR NEXT MEAL, CONSIDER FEEDING YOUR CELLS IN ADDITION TO YOURSELVES.

The SAD diet also includes 15 pounds of table salt per year. Salt (sodium chloride) retains fluids, including many poisons. The engine that drives our bodies is the human cell. It absorbs nutrients and excretes waste. When you prevent it from excreting its waste, you create a fundamental breakdown in the cycle of growth and repair. So, not only must we nourish our cells, we must also keep them clean.

Americans routinely use food as entertainment and therapy. We please our palate first and our cells last. Our palates have the wonderful ability to express themselves immediately through the taste buds. Cells, on the other hand, do not let us know how they are doing until years later with either normal or abnormal growth. Normal growth is good health. Abnormal growth is a tumor, cancer or cardiovascular disease. At your next meal, consider feeding your cells in addition to yourselves.

Oils & Chinese Food

Chinese food has a reputation for being healthy cuisine. True...if you eat it in China. In a major survey of 6,500 Chinese conducted by Cornell University's T. Colin Campbell, only 4 Chinese men per 100,000 were found to die of heart disease compared to 67 Americans. For every Chinese woman who dies of breast cancer, 5 more American women die and eight times as many American women die of cervical cancer. Although the Chinese eat more calories and carbohydrates than Americans, they weigh less and have less body fat. The Chinese are also far less likely to develop colon cancer or diabetes and it is apparently their diet that does it. Rice and noodles are their basic food and vegetables and meat just complement the rice. A mere 7% of their diet is meat, poultry and fish, while Americans get 70% of their protein from animal products.

The Real Chinese Food

Unfortunately, American Chinese cuisine has developed into something much closer to a hamburger stand than to a meal in China. "Crispy" usually means deep-fried. "Sweet and sour" means deep-fried and stir-fried, then soaked in a sauce of fat, sugar and cornstarch. Stir fried is supposed to be a quick, light frying technique that minimizes cooking and maximizes flavor. But in practice, you can squeeze puddles of oil out of a typical stir-fried dish. Worse yet, the economy-family restaurants invariably use the least expensive oil—cottonseed. Cottonseed contains 27% saturated fat—the most saturated of all the vegetable oils. The cotton plant is also one of the most pesticide treated crops primarily because it is not controlled by the regulations governing consumable vegetables. Pesticides are fat soluble so guess where they end up? In the fatty parts of the plant.

Our Relationship with Oil

Oil is one of the hardest of all foods to digest. It is not a natural food, but an extraction from grains, seeds and, in a few cases, vegetables like olives and avocados. If you want oil, the best quality comes from oil rich foods. If you extract oil from foods, there is a risk of it becoming adulterated. Commercial extraction processes use chemicals and high heat. High quality mechanical extraction is good as long as the oils are fresh and properly stored. Exposure to light, air and heat destroy them. Rancid oils form aldehydes that are toxic and allegedly carcinogenic. Oils heated to the smoking point or reused, as is often done in commercial food preparation, become harmful, unmetabolized solids that impair the production of prostaglandins. Just because cooking with oil is common, does not mean it is healthy. Please do not give up on Chinese cuisine. The healthiest Chinese food between here and China is the dish you prepare at home.

No Fat Chow Sprout
(Translation: Chinese Food Without Oil)

Ingredients

5	Celery stalks, chopped
10	Water Chestnuts
1 small	Onion, cut in rings
8 oz	Cellophane Noodles
1 cup	Silken Tofu, puréed
2+ Tbsp	Peanut Butter
3 Tbsp	Tamari
2 Tbsp	Lecithin
½ cup	Water
1 cup	Adzuki sprouts
1 cup	Mung sprouts
garnish	Radish sprouts
garnish	Garlic sprouts

Yield: Serves 3–4

Steam the water chestnuts, celery, and onion rings in a steamer or a covered saucepan with ¼ inch of water for approximately 10 minutes. While steaming, prepare the peanut sauce by blending the silken tofu, peanut butter, tamari, lecithin and water. A food processor is best for this. Blenders are difficult to use. If you must use a blender, pulsing the motor and poking the food with a spatula will help. It should have a creamy, pudding-like consistency.

When the vegetables are ready, pour off the excess water and save it. Add the tofu-peanut butter sauce to the veggies along with the cellophane noodles. Add back some of the excess vegetable water as necessary to cook the dry noodles and keep the dish fluid. Once the noodles are soft and moist, simply garnish the dish with the mung, adzuki, radish and garlic sprouts. Turn the flame off, put the cover back on and serve.

Unlike American noodles, Chinese cellophane noodles have no wheat content. They are made entirely of potato starch. This dish has lots of familiar Chinese vegetables and flavors making it very Chinese without the added oils. Commercial Asian cooking as it is practiced in the USA, uses oils excessively and of questionable quality. Here we use peanut butter instead of peanut oil which delivers the flavor without the grease. It is filling, delicious, and good for you.

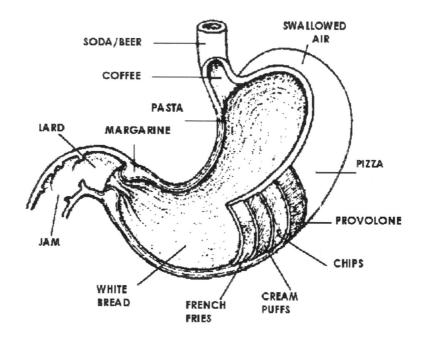

Oil-Free Refried Beans

Ingredients

5 cups	Pinto beans
3–4 Tbsp	Green and red salsa
2 Tbsp	Onion powder
1 tsp	Garlic powder
1 Tbsp	Sea Salt

Yield: 2½ quarts of refried beans

Here's a healthy salsa bean dip that is oil-free and still perfectly Latin.

Soak the pinto beans for 12 hours, then sprout them in a sprout bag *(See Appendix, Sprouting, p. 287.)* for 2 days maximum. Cook the beans on a low flame, approximately 40–60 minutes or until soft. Scoop off any foam that builds up during cooking. When soft, pour off half to 2/3 of the cooking water.

Mash up the softened beans with a mashing tool or a food processor. Add the salsa sauce and spices.

Traditionally, bean dips are used with corn chips, tostadas and burritos. As an alternative, serve this dip on the side with cooked quinoa (a grain) and salad.

Creamed Potato Mash

Ingredients

3	Potatoes, medium size
½ cup	Soy milk
¼ cup	Water from potatoes
½ tsp	Salt, herbal
2 Tbsp	Butter, raw

Yield: Serves 2

Mash is a smash . . . according to children and adults.

First, clean the potatoes well, carving away any potato eyes (potato sprouts should not be eaten) or bad spots. Use brown (nongreen) organic potatoes. Boil in water for 35–45 minutes on a low flame or until soft. Test by puncturing the potato with a fork. It should travel through the potato easily. Remove the soft potatoes, quarter them and place in food processor with a partial amount of the cooking water and soy milk. Process until chopped. Add the butter and herbal salt. Add more water and soy milk if the potatoes are still too dry and thick. It has a tendency to thicken after it sits and cools.

For children, use less butter and herbal salt as per taste. Pick a delicious soy milk, one that you find enjoyable as a drink, but is plain and not flavored. Potatoes are one of the staple foods of the world and this is a very nourishing and satisfying meal for the whole family.

Cream of Rice Cereal

Ingredients

3 Tbsp	Rice flour
1 cup	Pure water
1 Tbsp	Butter, raw
¼ tsp	Salt, herbal

Yield: 1 cup hot rice cereal

A hearty cereal for kids and adults and so very easy to prepare.

First make rice flour by blending short grain organic rice in a nut/seed mill or use your grain mill if you have one. Oster blender owners can use their blender with the 4 ounce blend 'n store cup. Or use with a 4–8 ounce mason jar. Invert the mason jar and screw it onto the blade. Only a few ounces of rice flour needs to be made at any one time. Blend until a flour consistency is achieved. (Makes a loud noise when first blending.)

Add the rice flour slowly to boiling water, stirring continuously to avoid lumping. Continue stirring on a low flame until it thickens. Use of a manual rotary blender or egg beater is essential. Add more water if too thick. Add herbal salt and raw butter to taste.

This hot cereal, made from freshly milled rice, is very nourishing. Builds strength for the whole day.

Wheat-Free Sprout Tabouli

Ingredients

1 cup	Lentil sprouts
1 small bunch	Kale
2–3	Tomatoes, ripe
4 stalks	Basil, fresh
1 inch	Garlic Sprouts (or 1 clove crushed)
1 Tbsp	Miso paste, mellow light
1–2 Tbsp	Olive oil

Yield: Serves 2

Tabouli is a popular, traditional middle eastern dish that is considered very healthy. Unfortunately, tabouli is made with cracked wheat and is thus another wheat product in our already overly wheat–centric diet. In addition, the wheat is often uncooked which is contrary to our philosophy against the consumption of raw grain.

First, sprout 1 cup of lentils for 5 days or until the shoot is approximately 1 inch long. *(See Appendix, Sprouting, p. 287.)* When mature, steam the sprouts to partially soften them. Do not overcook. They should remain crispy but not crunchy.

The sprouts and kale can be steamed simultaneously, if you have a large enough skillet. First, thoroughly wash the kale and chop into 1–2 inch pieces. Kale is tough raw. Steam it on a low flame until it begins to soften—about 10 minutes. The lentils take twice as long to steam as the kale, so start the lentils first, then add the kale.

This dish is best prepared whenever good ripe tomatoes and fresh basil are available. Dice your tomatoes or chop each into 16 pieces. Dice the basil, too. Mix the tomato and basil into the kale and lentil sprouts. Mix the crushed garlic (if using clove), olive oil and miso paste in a bowl, then pour the contents onto the tabouli and mix thoroughly. Last but not least, mix in the garlic sprouts. This dish needs to be mixed well. Tastes better the longer it sits.

LET'S GO SHOPPING

A Comparison Of Common Foods With "Live" & Whole Food Alternatives

The following list includes a variety of popular foods available in groceries and supermarkets and eaten as part of a typical American breakfast, lunch, dinner or snack. Each food is followed by a commentary and a suggested alternative. The alternatives exemplify our philosophy to choose whole foods, unadulterated and unprocessed, and containing "live" nutrition.

Ingredient listings for the following foods were taken directly from their product labels. The products were purchased at a famous name national supermarket chain. Food manufacturers may have changed their product ingredients or packaging since this study was written.

The author and publisher make no claims as to the fitness or unfitness of the brand name foods listed here. The philosophical differences indicated in the suggestions for alternative foods should not be construed as an attempt to slander the good name of the many manufacturers listed. In general, these companies are providing the best products they know. They have all been approved for consumption by the United States Food and Drug Administration and/or the U.S. Department of Agriculture. The author welcomes the efforts by many national brands to achieve more natural standards.

CONVENTIONAL: 100% Pure Florida Orange Juice from Concentrate

INGREDIENTS: All natural, no sugar or preservatives added.

ALTERNATIVE: Fresh Squeezed Juice

This orange juice was squeezed, boiled, concentrated, frozen and then reconstituted. It is four steps removed from the original fruit. B-vitamins, vitamin C and enzymes cannot survive this much processing. This product may have excellent shelf life and taste, but it has lost the gift that oranges are meant to give us. Drink fresh squeezed orange juice. Prolong human life, not shelf life.

CONVENTIONAL: Minute Maid 100% Pure Lemon Juice

From Concentrate. No additives or preservatives.
INGREDIENTS: Water, concentrated lemon juice. Frozen.

ALTERNATIVE: Fresh Squeezed Lemon

Lemon is a wonderful and powerful cleansing fruit especially for the liver. But not after it has been boiled and frozen. *See Orange Juice above.*

CONVENTIONAL: Musselman's Natural Apple Sauce

Sodium Free, No sugar added. *INGREDIENTS:* Apples and water.

ALTERNATIVE: Blended Apples

Commercial apple sauce is made from boiled apples. It cannot be bottled any other way. Since they are going to be made into sauce, apple quality is usually very low. But you can easily make your own "live" apple sauce. Just quarter your apples, remove the seeds and blend in your food processor. You control the quality of the apples. It takes seconds to blend a few apples, which is faster than it takes to locate them on the supermarket shelves.

CONVENTIONAL: Breakstone's Grade A Sour Cream

A cultured product made from pasteurized dairy ingredients.
INGREDIENTS: Cultured milk, cream, skim milk, enzyme.

ALTERNATIVE: Non-Dairy Yoghurt

Commercial sour cream is frequently cultured with rennet, an animal enzyme taken from the lining of a cow's stomach. The souring is done with pasteurized (boiled) milk. Sour cream is attractive because of its smooth, creamy texture and delightful sour flavor. But these same qualities can be achieved with unpasteurized, dairy and animal-free cashew yoghurt. *(See p. 102.)*

CONVENTIONAL: Kretchmer's Wheat Germ

INGREDIENTS: 100% toasted wheat germ.

ALTERNATIVE: Soft Sprouted Wheat

Kretchmer makes a delicious tasting vacuum–packed product and is to be commended for promoting the virtues of wheat germ.

Unfortunately, wheat germ is highly perishable and can spoil within hours after milling. There is even potential for spoilage prior to packaging. The best way to take advantage of this super-nutritious, highly perishable product, is to sprout the grain yourself and eat the sprouts. Three day old sprouted wheat increases B-vitamin content 400%–1200%. Germinate to increase the value of your germ.

CONVENTIONAL: **Sunsweet Prunes**

INGREDIENTS: Plums Pre-Cooked in water. Vacuum sealed.

ALTERNATIVE: **Soaked Prunes**

Prune juice is a misnomer. It is not juiced fruit, but "flavored water" accomplished thanks to the process of osmosis from soaking prunes. For your personal use, you do not have to boil the fruit as the commercial companies must. Since fruit can be digested raw, why cook and kill the delicate nutrition. Simply soak prunes in enough water to cover them and let sit at room temperature for 24 hours. Drink the "juice" then enjoy the reconstituted plums. Or, pit the plums and blend them with the juice water to thicken the juice. Refrigerate.

CONVENTIONAL: **Polanar All Fruit Apricot Spreadable Fruit**

INGREDIENTS: Grape juice concentrate, apricots, pear juice concentrate, citrus pectin, natural flavor.

ALTERNATIVE: **Blended Fruit Jam**

Choose your favorite jelly fruit like strawberry, blueberry or apricot. Why cook fruit? Just blend your favorite fruit in the food processor. Remove all pits and leaves. Add honey for added sweetness (optional). Use Agar–agar, a natural gelling agent if you prefer "jelly" rather than "preserves."

CONVENTIONAL: **Regular Milk, Grade A**

Homogenized, pasteurized Vitamin A and D Lowfat Milk. (2% Milkfat).
INGREDIENTS: Lowfat milk, Vitamin A Palmitate, Vitamin D3 added.

ALTERNATIVE: **Raw Cow or Goat Milk**

If you drink milk, try to obtain it from a raw dairy. Two raw milk brands found in natural foods stores are Steuve's and Alta Dena. If you were to 1) boil milk (pasteurization), 2) disperse its fat content with a centrifuge (homogenization) and 3) add synthetic vitamins (palmitate and D3) or hormones, a young calf would probably refuse to drink it. So why should you? Synthetic vitamins are not necessary if you take milk in its original state. Obtain raw milk whenever possible. As long as you are wanting to drink non-human milk, try goat milk. The mammary glands of a goat produce a milk whose fat and protein content more closely resemble human milk.

CONVENTIONAL: **Second Nature No Cholesterol Egg Product**

INGREDIENTS: A Pasteurized blend containing egg whites, water, nonfat dry milk, modified food starch (corn), corn oil, sodium stearoyl lactylate, cellulose gum, magnesium chloride, beta carotene, ferric orthophosphate, zinc sulfate, vitamin E acetate, Calcium pantothenate, TBHQ (to maintain freshness), vitamins: cholecalciferol (D3), Riboflavin (B2), pyridoxine hydrochloride (B6), thiamine (B1), cyanocobalamin (B12), folic acid.

ALTERNATIVE: : **Real Eggs**

Let's face it. An egg is the end product of a female chicken's ovulation cycle. If this is what you choose to eat, then why not have the real thing? The cholesterol scare has created many substitute products. Unfortunately, most of them are filled with artificial ingredients whose effects could be worse than the original product. The dietary intake of cholesterol from food does not dramatically affect serum cholesterol–the kind we manufacture in our blood. Our self-made cholesterol is distorted more by our intake of excess sugar than cholesterol–rich foods. An egg, by the way, despite what it is, is a wonderfully nutritious food. Eat it or leave it alone.

CONVENTIONAL: Chocolate Flavored Balanced Dietary Food Supplement

INGREDIENTS: Calcium caseinate, fructose, cocoa, corn syrup solids, partially hydrogenated coconut oil, salt, microcrystalline cellulose, dipotassium phosphate, natural and artificial flavors, magnesium oxide, aspartame, ascorbic acid, Vitamin E, Vitamin A palmitate, niacinamide, zinc oxide, electrolytic iron, copper gluconate, D calcium pantothenate, Vitamin D2, pyridoxine hydrochloride, riboflavin thiamine mononitrate, Vitamin B12, folic acid, biotin, potassium iodide.

ALTERNATIVE:
Sproutman's Morning Beverage

This is one of many powdered diet "smoothie" drinks that fill you up and satisfy your hunger without adding many calories. Basically, these drinks are milk and sugar with added synthetic vitamins. Who can be hungry after drinking milk and sugar?

Instead, try *Sproutman's Morning Beverage* recipe for a real pick me up and hunger satisfier. *(See p. 202.)*

CONVENTIONAL: Frito Lay Santitas Tortilla Chips

INGREDIENTS: Corn, vegetable oil (one or more of the following: corn oil, sunflower oil, cottonseed oil, peanut oil, partially hydrogenated soybean oil, or partially hydrogenated sunflower oil) and salt.

ALTERNATIVE:
Baked Crackers Or Chips

Corn is one of the most abundant grains on the planet and very nourishing. It is also one of the few grains that can be digested without cooking. If you haven't eaten a fresh picked, raw corn on the cob, please do. Like wheat, this grain is very versatile. But frying it in oil, or several oils, as in this product, is verboten. Baked chips and baked crackers made of corn, rice or wheat are better alternatives. *(See oily foods, p. 246.)*

CONVENTIONAL: **Chachies Fresh Mild Salsa**

INGREDIENTS: Fresh tomatoes, onions, peppers,
cilantro, water, salt, garlic, spices, natural flavor, citric acid,
sodium bisulfite added to protect flavor.

ALTERNATIVE: **Raw Tomato Sauce**

Spicy tomato sauce is fine, but why cook this raw fruit to death and then add preservatives. Simply blend your ripe tomatoes in the food processor with your spices. *(See Raw Tomato Sauce, p. 45.)*

CONVENTIONAL: **Heinz Tomato Ketchup (Est'd 1869)**

INGREDIENTS: Tomato paste made from red ripe tomatoes, distilled vinegar, corn syrup, salt, onion powder, spice, natural flavoring.

ALTERNATIVE: **Raw Ketchup**

What is the difference between tomato sauce and ketchup? Both consist of blended tomatoes but the flavor and texture is different. Ketchup is smoother and has a sweet (sugar or, in the above case, corn syrup) and sour (vinegar) flavor. As with the tomato sauce and salsa above, no need to cook the tomatoes.

CONVENTIONAL: Wish Bone Lite Classic Dijon Vinaigrette Dressing

INGREDIENTS: Water, vinegar, soybean oil, dijon mustard, lemon juice, sugar, salt, onion, spices, garlic, natural flavors, red bell pepper, potassium sorbate and calcium disodium EDTA to preserve freshness, xanthan gum for consistency, artificial flavor, annato for color.

ALTERNATIVE: Olive Oil Dressing

Too many unnecessary ingredients make up this spicy dressing. The first five ingredients would have been enough. But even there, the use of lemon juice and vinegar are redundant. Needless to say, we're opposed to preservatives and artificial flavor. With powerful spices such as onion, garlic and mustard, why is artificial flavor needed? If quality ingredients are used, natural flavors should be enough. *(See p. 184.)*

CONVENTIONAL: Chinese Fortune Cookie

INGREDIENTS: Enriched wheat flour (niacin, reduced iron, thiamine mononitrate, riboflavin), malted barley flour, potassium bromate, sugar, eggs, vegetable shortening (soybean, cottonseed and or canola oils), salt, artificial flavor (vanillin), lecithin, baking soda.

— or —

CONVENTIONAL: Pepperidge Farm Chocolate Chunk Cookies

INGREDIENTS: Unbleached wheat flour, sweet chocolate (with lecithin added) sugar, partially hydrogenated vegetable shortening (soybean, cottonseed and/or canola oils) butter, whole eggs, brown sugar, leavening (baking soda, ammonium bicarbonate, cream of tartar), vanilla extract, salt and caramel color.

ALTERNATIVE: Natural Cookie

Since a cookie is simply a delicate, sweetened flour product, why not keep it simple with whole grain and naturally sweet dried fruits? The two commercial cookie products above complicate a simple idea with eggs and oils (shortening). As a society, we concentrate too much on getting the food in–the sensations of taste and texture. We totally ignore getting it out–digestibility. *(See p. 47.)*

CONVENTIONAL: **Red Oval Farms Stoned Wheat Thins**

INGREDIENTS: Enriched wheat flour (containing niacin, reduced iron, thiamine mononitrate, riboflavin), cracked wheat, hydrogenated vegetable oil, shortening (containing one or more of the following: soybean oil, canola oil, cottonseed oil), salt, sodium bicarbonate, whey powder, malt flour, yeast.

— or —

CONVENTIONAL: **Nabisco Original Wheat Thins**

INGREDIENTS: Whole wheat flour, enriched wheat flour {contains reduced iron, thiamine mononitrate (B1) riboflavin (B2)}, vegetable shortening (partially hydrogenated soybean oil), sugar, salt, high fructose corn syrup, malted barley flour, vegetable colors (annatto extract, turmeric and paprika oleoresins).

ALTERNATIVE: **Sprout Cracker**

Enriched wheat flour is simply flour with the synthetic vitamins listed in parenthesis added back in. Both of these products contain sugar although the Canadian brand disguises their sweetener with the words "malt flour." Nabisco adds three sugars including corn syrup and malted barley flour. To its credit, Nabisco uses whole wheat and natural vegetable colors.

Our Sprout Cracker uses one ingredient: sprouted wheat. The sweetness is natural to the sprouts–so are the vitamins.

CONVENTIONAL: Cadbury's Fruit & Nut Bar

INGREDIENTS: Milk Chocolate, raisins and almonds. {Milk chocolate contains sugar, milk, cocoa butter, chocolate, lecithin, artificial and natural flavorings.}

CONVENTIONAL: Belgian Chocolate

INGREDIENTS: Sugar, cocoa butter, powdered milk, lecithin E322, vanillin (artificial vanilla flavor), cocoa solids.

ALTERNATIVE: Natural Snacks

Basic chocolate bars are surprisingly one of the simplest packaged foods you will find. The six ingredients in the Belgian chocolate are very standard. Read labels carefully. The fruit and nut bar contains milk chocolate–a complex ingredient itself within a list of ingredients. Chocolate and milk are both highly allergic foods for allergy sensitive persons. Cocoa is a strong stimulant. *(See p. 221.)*

CONVENTIONAL: Morton Lite Salt

INGREDIENTS: Salt, potassium chloride, sodium silicoaluminate, magnesium carbonate, dextrose, potassium iodide. Each ½ teaspoon contains 550 mg sodium and 733 mg potassium. "Lite Salt" is a trademark of Morton Thiokol, Inc. (The aerospace company)

CONVENTIONAL: Iodized Salt

INGREDIENTS: Salt, sodium silico aluminate, .01% poassium iodide stabilized with sodium thiosulfate.

ALTERNATIVE: Dulse, Natural Salt

One of the most fundamental mineral foods, salt, has been commercialized into a complex formula of artificial chemical ingredients. Why must a simple food be so adulterated? Is not the taste of salt enough in itself? In these two salt products, much has been added in an attempt to make a generic product unique. Stabilizers, synthetic vitamins, fillers to reduce the sodium, and even sugar (dextrose) are added to salt. This is a preposterous act of culinary perversion! Salt and sugar represent basic, distinct and opposing flavors. Would you put salt on your dessert?

Some of the more natural alternatives to commercial salt would be earth salt, rock salt, sea salt, sea vegetables like kelp and dulse, nutritional yeast, tamari, miso paste and gomazio (sesame salt). *(For more on these these foods, see Glossary, p. 269, and salt, p. 229.)* Powdered kelp and dulse mixed with sea salt and herbs is a healthy condiment that reduces the percentage of direct salt. One popular salt substitute is Dr. Bronner's Balanced Mineral Bouillon, which is made from mineral salts, soy, lemon and sea dulse.

$$\backsim$$

CONVENTIONAL: **Big Wheat Enriched Bread**

INGREDIENTS: Made with unbleached wheat flour (enriched with: niacin, iron, thiamine mononitrate and riboflavin), water, wheat bran, cracked wheat, corn syrup, modified wheat gluten, yeast, soybean oil, salt, honey, non-fat dry milk solids, sweet dairy whey, monoglycerides, sodium stearoyl lactylate, caramel color, calcium propionate (to retard spoilage), monocalcium phosphate, calcium sulfate, wheat starch, ammonium chloride, potassium bromate and calcium iodate.

ALTERNATIVE: **Sprouted Wheat Bread**

The above bread, baked by a major bakery and packaged under the private labels of major supermarket chains contains 26 separate ingredients. Sprouted wheat bread contains 1 (one) ingredient: sprouted wheat. "Unbleached wheat flour" is a euphemism for white flour without the bleach. It is also lacking the germ and the bran and all of the flavor and nutrition that comes with it. That is why this recipe includes synthetic vitamins. They are necessary to re-place the natural ones that were removed during milling. Sweeten-ers and salt are necessary to bring back some of the lost flavor.

This comparison is symbolic of much that has gone wrong with mass food production and the reason for the return to "natural" foods. Only a couple of generations ago, bread was made by grinding whole grains in the kitchen. Manufacturers of modern breads are busy trying to replicate old fashioned bread while maintaining shelf life. Sprout bread improves upon old fashioned bread because it does not require a grain mill and the sprouts have increased the vitamin levels as well as the bran.

Prolong human life, not shelf life.

CONVENTIONAL: Green Giant Baked Beans

INGREDIENTS: Soaked navy pea beans in a sauce containing water, brown sugar, sugar, bacon (cured with water, salt, sugar, dextrose, sodium erythorbate, sodium nitrite, may also contain sodium phosphate, dextrose, spice and coloring, artificial flavor), salt, tomato paste, modified corn-starch, dextrose, artificial color, sodium phosphate, natural flavor.

ALTERNATIVE: Navy Pea Beans

It is symbolic that the last ingredient in this long list is natural flavor. It represents the lowest level of importance for before it comes 4 sugars, 2 salts and artificial flavor. Yet, the first two ingredients give away the secret of this dish, beans and water. A natural version of this dish could be prepared by cooking the navy beans in water until soft. Then, pour off water and mix in a casserole baking dish with blended fresh tomatoes, tamari and a minimal amount of molasses. Bake until semi-dry.

CONVENTIONAL: **Kingston Corn Flakes**

INGREDIENTS: Milled yellow corn, sugar, salt, partially hydrated vegetable oil (contains one or more of the following: canola, soybean), malt syrup, corn syrup, BHT (a preservative). Enriched with vitamin C sodium ascorbate, vitamin B3 niacinamide, reduced iron, vitamin B6 pyridoxine hydrochloride, vitamin A palmitate, vitamin B2 riboflavin, vitamin B1 thiamine mononitrate, folic acid and vitamin D.

ALTERNATIVE: **Nature's Path Corn Flakes**

INGREDIENTS: Organic flaked yellow corn, clover honey, corn bran, trace of sea salt.

It doesn't take much to make simple corn flakes. The natural brand simply uses organic corn and honey. The commercial brand uses milled corn in which the bran and the germ are separated and then removed. Hydrogenated oils and three kinds of sugar are then added. A preservative is now necessary because this processed food unstable in this unnatural state and therefore perishable. Synthetic vitamins are added to "enrich" this denatured corn product. The natural product left all the nutrients in as nature designed it.

A sprouting bag designed by Sproutman
Sprout bags breathe and drain on all sides unlike a jar which is
limited to one outlet for both. This bag is made of flax, a raw linen
fabric that is resistant to mold and mildew and durable enough in
water to last for years. Green pea is growing out the top surrounded
left to right by lentil, red pea and mung bean.

GLOSSARY
OF FOODS

More Information About Some Of The Special Foods Used In This Book

— A —

Avocado

Avocados require sensitive selection. They must be firm but ripe. Too hard and they are immature. Too soft and they are beyond repair. The best approach is to buy them firm and select them as they ripen in your home. Haas avocado, the variety with the rough dark green skin, is the most popular.

— B —

Bee Pollen

Another wonder food created for us by the bee. Rich in vitamins and minerals and slightly sweet, pollen is an excellent way to add super-nutrition to smoothies, cereals and snacks like halvah. Bee pollen is perishable and should be refrigerated for maximum potency.

— C —

Carob Powder, Raw

Raw carob powder tastes sweeter and lighter than the toasted variety. The latter is somewhat bitter. Unfortunately, the raw powder is harder to find.

Cashews

Cashews are the main ingredient in the non-banana ice creams so find good tasting cashews. As you know, cashews come in different sizes—jumbo, butts, splits and pieces. The jumbos are the best quality and the most expensive. The splits and pieces are just what they sound like and are the most economical. Unfortunately, they expose more surface area to light and air for oxidation. You may notice this in old cashews as a browning around the edges. Pass these by and purchase the cleanest, whitest cashews you can find.

Coconut, shredded

Coconut is actually a dried fruit. It is, however, vastly different from a raisin. Size is not the primary difference. The most important distinction is that coconut is the only dried fruit with a high fat content. Even more unusual for a fruit, coconut is a saturated fat. Nevertheless, shredded coconut is used in many of the same kinds of recipes as raisins.

Traditionally, coconut is made by shredding the fresh coconut and dehydrating it to remove its water content. Making your own coconut is easy. Simply chop up a fresh coconut and shred it in food processor or juicer/grinder. Keep it refrigerated. It is perishable; that is why it is dehydrated when commercially made. For longer storage, freeze chunks of coconut and shred when ready to use.

— D —

Dulse

Dulse is a red-colored sea vegetable that grows off the coast of Maine, Canada, Oregon and Alaska. Japan grows no dulse so this is one seaweed that is strictly North American. Its texture is so soft and chewy that it needs no cooking. Just soak for a few minutes in water or eat it as a snack right from the bag. Dulse is high in iron, protein, vitamins A & B. *(Recipe on p.204 & 206.)*

NUTRITION IN DULSE			
The following is provided from 1 oz of dulse (28grams)			
Protein	6 grams	Manganese	0.3 mg
Fat	0.5 grams	Copper	0.11 mg
Carbohydrates	13 grams	Chromium	0.04 mg
Calories	75 calories	Fluoride	1.5 mg
Total Fiber	9 grams	Zinc	0.81 mg
Soluble Fiber	4.5 grams	Vitamin A	188 I.U.
Sodium	493 mg	Vitamin B1	0.02 mg
Potassium	2217 mg	Vitamin B2	0.54 mg
Calcium	60 mg	Vitamin B3	0.53 mg
Magnesium	77 mg	Vitamin B6	2.55 mg
Phosphorus	116 mg	Vitamin B12	1.9 mcg
Iron	9 mg	Vitamin C	1.8 mg
Iodine	1.5 mg	Vitamin E	0.5 mg

— F —

Flax Oil, Health Benefits Of

Flax or linseed oil, is our best source of vitamin F and has been an important health product for a long time. But now, it is becoming the latest rage. Dr. Max Gerson first recommended it for his cancer patients. Research in Germany, Austria and India confirms that linseed oil stimulates the immune system, inhibits the growth of cancer cells, and controls cholesterol and hypertension. Edible linseed oil is cold pressed from the flax seed. This wonderful plant not only gives us this special oil, but also linen, the raw material used to manufacture the *Flax Sprout Bag* (hence its name). The seed is also very healthful, providing a mucilage which, like psyllium, helps cleanse the intestinal tract. *(See recipe p. 200.)*

You can enjoy the benefits of this wonderful seed simply by blending 1/3 cup of flaxseed to a meal in a dry blender. Then add 1 cup of apple juice and 1 banana. Drink the mixture before it thickens. Follow it with more water or juice.

— G —

Green Algae Foods

This group includes such super-foods as spirulina, chlorella and blue green algae. These microscopic water-borne plants are among the richest sources of protein, vitamin B–12, minerals and trace minerals on the planet. Per tablespoon (60 grams), chlorella contains 33,300 IU of vitamin A, 881 mg of chlorophyll and 75 mcg of vitamin B-12. It is 55%–65% protein. 71% of spirulina is protein. Used in the form of dried powder, these foods lend themselves perfectly to smoothies and other health drinks.

Ginger Root

Ginger root belongs alongside garlic as one of the most important plant products that grow under the soil. It is common in Asian cuisine and is known in herbal medicine as a tool for "heating" the body. We use it mostly for dressings and dips.

— *H* —

Herbs

Allspice. Not a man-made compendium of herbs as some think. Comes from the berry of Pimenta diocia whose taste relates to cinnamon, nutmeg and cloves.

Basil. Common basil is loved worldwide and can be found extensively in the cooking of the Greeks, Italians and French. The Hindus consider it sacred and place some near temples and outside nearly every house. Egyptians scatter it over the dead. An excellent companion to tomatoes and potatoes. Medicinally it has been used for stomach troubles, vomiting and constipation. Excellent for all soups, sauces, dressings and salads.

Cayenne. Very, very hot in taste. Use sparingly. Cayenne is a member of the capsicum family. Unlike black pepper, it is non-irritating to the mucous membrane. It is actually very soothing and healing and is a natural body purifier and disinfectant. Like garlic, it has many medicinal applications.

Oregano. Popular Italian cooking herb.

Paprika. A capsicum herb but with a mild and sweet flavor. It has the color of red pepper but only a subtle peppery taste.

Savory. A member of the mint family with a peppery flavor somewhere in-between parsley and thyme. Perfect for vegetables, beans and grain dishes. Medicinally used for indigestion.

Slippery Elm. Pleasant tasting with a nut-like flavor. Excellent old-fashioned remedy for sore throats.

Sweet Marjoram. A sweet tasting herb. Flavor is destroyed by cooking so add at the very end. Very popular in Italian food. Excellent in salads and soups. Medicinally, marjoram oil has been used for indigestion, insomnia, toothache and headache.

Tarragon. Has a tangy-sweet flavor and an aroma reminiscent of anise. Great for all vegetable dishes.

Thyme. An aromatic herb, part of the mint family, that was used as an incense to drive away insects. Bees and butterflies, however, love it. Medicinally, it is used to relieve cramps from menstruation and rubbed on the chest and throat for coughs. Oil of "thymol" is used as an antiseptic in mouthwashes and toothpastes and externally as a liniment for rheumatisim.

Hijiki

Hijiki is a black seaweed that is made up of hundreds of rich black curls or fronds several inches long. It has a strong flavor and firm texture and expands 4 times its volume when cooked. Hijiki is tough in the raw state, but softens when boiled or simmered for 15 minutes. The Japanese, who cultivate more Hijiki than anyone, use it as a side vegetable dish or appetizer and often eat it with rice or other grain. In a typical dish, the cooked Hijiki might be sautéed with onions, carrots, peas, tamari and sesame oil. It can easily be added to soups, stews, casseroles or served cold with salads.

Hijiki is a great treat for vegetarians. It is a magnificent source of minerals and, although a vegetable, it has the smell and flavor of seafood. The tiny branches float 3–6 feet below the ocean surface soaking up valuable nutrients. Hijiki has more potassium than either rice, bananas or wheat bran, more sodium than olives, spinach, swiss chard, celery or carrots, more magnesium than almonds, cashews or peanuts, more iron than rice or wheat germ, more calcium than kale, collard greens, spinach, or parsley. Such an impressive food deserves to be enjoyed more in this country. *(Recipe on p. 243.)*

Honey, Raw

Use raw, unpasteurized buckwheat or clover honey. Heating honey alters its crystalline structure. Honey does not need to be heated or pasteurized for the purpose of extending shelf life. Raw, unfiltered honey is naturally resistant to souring and molding and, in fact, extends the shelf life of foods to which it is added.

— K —

Kelp

Kelp flakes are prepared from fresh whole kelp that is dried in a dehydrator or a low temperature oven until brittle. Crumble it in your hands or powder it in a blender. This is much more flavorful than the commercially made kelp powder. Kelp is an excellent substitute for salt because of its natural salt content. As a sea vegetable, it is one of the richest sources of calcium, iron, potassium, magnesium, iodine, manganese, copper, zinc and chromium. Kelp also contains glutamic acid. This acts as a natural tenderizer when cooking beans.

— L —

Lecithin

Liquid lecithin is a viscous oil extracted from soybeans. It is an extremely rich source of phosphorus and the B vitamins choline and inositol. It is known for its excellent ability to emulsify oils. Its job in these recipes is to add a thickness and creaminess that is usually provided by an egg. Dry lecithin granules are not as good for this purpose although they are a good supplementary food.

— M —

Malt

Malt is the short name for the sugar found in grains. This sugar, maltose, is commonly derived from barley (barley malt) as a by-product of the brewing industry. Barley malt is boiled until it achieves a dark viscous state similar to that of a dark honey. Although similar in consistency to honey, grain malt is darker in color and stronger in flavor. *(See recipe for Sprout Malt, p.172.)*

Miso Paste

Miso is a fermented soybean paste that has been used for centuries in oriental cuisine. The mashed soybeans are aged and cured much like cheese. It is used primarily as a seasoning and in the preparation of sauces. If it is not pasteurized, it contains live "friendly" bacteria cultures. Miso comes in a variety of flavors and colors, much like cheese. Hatcho miso is the strongest and darkest. Blonde miso is light in color, mellow in flavor and low in salt. Natto miso is made with ginger, barley, seaweed and barley malt. It is exquisite and a wonderful addition to many recipes.

— N —

Nori

Nori is an edible sea plant like kelp and dulse. Due to the popularity of Japanese sushi, nori is typically recognized as a thin pressed purplish-black sheet with a gleaming luster. Rice and vegetables are rolled into it. This Japanese plant also grows wild off the northern Maine and California coasts and contains up to 25% protein by weight. It also is high in B vitamins including B–12, C and E.

— O —

Olive Oil

Good olive oil can be hard to find. The key to good olive oil lies in its color and aroma. Look for a deep green color and a distinct olive aroma. Reading labels is absolutely necessary. Some of the key words are: "Extra Virgin"—the first pressing using the choicest and most expensive olives. "Virgin"—a first pressing using lower quality olives. "Pure olive oil" is a combination of refined oils made from later pressings. Unfortunately, the word "imported" on the bottle does not guarantee quality. In fact, many are discouragingly tasteless. Some excellent American brands available from natural food stores are Haines, Carothers and Walnut Acre's brands. Let your nose do the walking.

In a study reported in the *Journal of American Medical Association*, olive oil consumption among 4,903 Italians, of mixed age and gender, reduced total cholesterol levels by 9.5% as well as blood pressure and blood glucose. Conversely, butter and margarine consumption raised all three levels. Olive oil contains about 77% monounsaturated fat. Of that, 75% is oleic, 13% palmitic, 9% linoleic, 2% stearic and 1% palmitoleic. 125 calories are contained in a tablespoon of olive oil.[18]. *(See olive oil dressing p. 184.)*

— S —

Sesame

In the Arabian Nights *Open Sesame* was a magical password. This ancient seed was often thought to have mystical powers. No wonder. With 1160 mg per 100 grams, it is the number one dietary source of calcium—more than such nutritional marvels as kelp, dulse, collard greens, kale, almonds and spinach. It is also one of the richest sources of phosphorous. Sesame has 18.6% protein, 52% fat and 47 calories per tablespoon. Butter in comparison, has only 20 mg calcium, less than 1% protein, is 80.6% fat and has 102 calories per tablespoon.

Hulled Vs. Unhulled: Which form of the sesame seed should we use—hulled or unhulled? The hull is the branish jacket that encloses the seed. It contains relatively high amounts of oxalic acid—an acid which, among other things, binds calcium. More popular is the hulled variety which is the source for our halvah. The hulled seed eliminates concern about oxalic acid. Although, the issue may remain in debate for a long time, the immediate answer, for all practical purposes, must involve the total amount of oxalic acid consumed on a regular basis from all dietary sources. As with many things, excessive use has the potential to cause harm. Still, if in doubt, hulled sesame is the safest choice.

Once you've decided to have your sesame with their jackets off (hulled), the method of removing all those tiny skins becomes the next question—mechanical or chemical? Of course, everyone prefers mechanical hulling, but it is not as common and is more expensive. The consumer can be drawn down the path of distrust not knowing whether the product is really mechanically hulled despite the claims on the label. How do they get those tiny jackets off? All is hushed under the cloak of patent secrecy, but we know it is Lilliputians with sharp fingernails. *(For more on sesame seeds, see Natural Halvah under snacks.)*

Sesame Oil, Dark

Dark sesame oil is the oil pressed from toasted sesame seeds. It has a very rich flavor. Light sesame oil is made by pressing sesame seeds. When these seeds are toasted and pressed, dark sesame oil results. It is analogous to toasting bread. The toasting darkens the color and adds a "toasted" flavor.

Sunflower Seeds

These extremely nourishing seeds are high in zinc, phosphorus, potassium and linoleic acid and are a rare plant source of vitamin D and protein. Like any oil bearing seeds, it is important that they be properly stored so as to protect the nutritional integrity of their oil. Nature protects the seeds for nearly a year while they are in their shells. But once the protective covers are removed, the seeds are more readily exposed to air, light and temperature. In addition, the mechanical hullers break a percentage of the seed during the shelling process. The broken seeds turn rancid faster than the others. Rancid seeds are recognizable by their foul smell. Most broken seeds also discolor. Be careful to select seeds that are good tasting, pure steel gray in color and free of any rancid odors. A mixture of grays and browns in the seed indicates rancidity in the fractionated seed. Rancid oils are notorious for creating free radicals in the body like peroxides and aldehydes. These chemicals can create chain reactions that have carcinogenic results. Your clue to testing for good seed is good taste, good odor and good color. These three criteria will result in successful recipes and the most positive of health benefits from this highly nutritious seed.

— T —

Tahini

Tahini is an essential ingredient for hummus and the kind you use can make a real difference in the success of your recipe. Tahini, or tahina, is the nut butter made from ground, hulled sesame seeds. Some tahinas are tastier than others. Some have added oil. Most tahini is made from roasted sesame seeds, but the best is raw tahini, made from raw, hulled sesame seeds. Raw tahini is thicker and has true sesame flavor. Regular tahini is made from toasted sesame seeds. It is darker and has a toasted flavor. If you like that flavor, you can get it by adding a teaspoon of toasted (dark) sesame oil to the raw tahini. This is the rich, flavorful oil, popular in Chinese cuisine, that is extracted from roasted sesame seeds. This way you can have the flavor without eating roasted seeds. Heated oils, whether they be from fried foods like tempura, natural potato chips or roasted nuts, should be avoided. Raw tahini is available in better natural food stores.

Tamari

Tamari is the excess liquid resulting from making miso, a fermented soybean paste. That is why tamari is known, generically, as "soy sauce." Good tamari should have no preservatives. Wheat is a common ingredient in the process, but wheat-free varieties are available. It should be low in salt, dark in color and rich in flavor and aroma. Good tasting tamari makes a difference. Try different brands until, like a fine wine, you find the one you like the best. An alternative to tamari would be the popular *"Dr. Bronner's Soya Bouillon."* This dark, salty liquid has no added salt, but is made with salty ingredients like sea vegetables.

Tomatoes—How To Pick

Getting good tomatoes can be a fine art. At certain times of the year, corrugated cardboard can be tastier than a trans-continentally transported tomato. Ripe tomatoes are rich in color, soft to the touch, plump and . . .they even smell like tomatoes! Often farmers are forced to dump ripe tomatoes because consumers refuse to buy them when they get soft. If you time it right, you can buy perfectly ripe tomatoes at half price. Use the overripe and squashed ones to make tomato leather. *(See recipe for Tomato Sun Cheese, p.166 and Ode to a Tomato, p 154.)*

— U —

Umeboshi Paste

A sour paste made from fermented plums. Used in Japanese cuisine for generations. It is not sweet but sour. It has the kind of tartness that makes your lips pucker. As a fermented food, it belongs in the category of sauerkraut, pickles and miso and is a good source of friendly bacteria and B-vitamins.

— V —

Vanilla Bean and Extract

Vanilla beans are the pods of a rare tropical vine-like orchid from the vanilla genus. In nature, hummingbirds are the most frequent pollinators, but only one day per year! Commercially, pollination is performed by hand. Each orchid produces one pod that can take as much as 9 months to ripen. The beans must be picked during a brief two-day window when they are in their prime. Of every ten pounds harvested, only two pounds make it to market after fermenting and drying. During a 6 to 9 month curing process, the beans are dried in the sun, wrapped in fabric until their pods wrinkle. For this elaborate and labor intensive process, vanilla beans are rare and expensive, but their flavor and aroma are unsurpassed. They are available from natural and specialty food stores.

The vanilla bean can easily be used with excellent results. Just chop it into pieces and blend it with maple syrup. Blending creates lots of brown bean speckles and a few larger pieces that have a pleasant, crunchy taste. If you choose to buy vanilla extract, try to find one with a low alcohol content, preferably less than 35%. Some varieties are made by curing the beans in a glycerin (non-alcohol) base. Avoid buying "vanillin," which is an artificial flavor. You can make your own vanilla without alcohol. Just blend fresh vanilla beans with water and strain.

Vinegars

Vinegar comes in several varieties. There are many herbal vinegars that use tarragon, thyme, basil and other herbs. The standard is apple cider vinegar.

— W —

Wheat, Kamut

Kamut is the Egyptian word for "wheat." It is a long grain wheat that has a higher protein content than conventional wheat. The Egyptian name is partly fanciful. The story goes that this ancient wheat was rediscovered in the tombs in Egypt. It was subsequently clarified that it was brought there by an American. In any event, it is an ancient strain rediscovered. The high protein content is made of a different gluten making it less of an allergen to wheat sensitive persons.

Wheat, Hard Red

Hard red wheat is the most common variety of wheat in America. It may be labeled "Spring" or "Winter" signifying the season in which it was planted. Any variety of hard wheat is suitable for sprouting and is the preferred variety when making sprout bread, pizzas, bagels, etc.

Wheat, Soft White

Soft wheat is the lower gluten cousin of hard wheat. It is used by bakers to make pastries and is, in fact, often called "pastry" wheat. It is ideal for making cookies, crackers and croissants, and is used for making the sprouted versions of these treats as well.

Wheat Germ

Wheat may be considered a miracle food when one considers its versatility and nourishment. Most of that nourishment comes from the germ. The wheat kernel consists of 3 parts: the outer skin or "bran," the germ, and the filling or "gluten." The germ is the seat of the grain's vitality. If the germ is damaged in hulling, for example, it will not grow (germinate). So it is not surprising to find most of the nutrition there. It is an excellent source of B-vitamins, minerals and essential fatty acids. In fact, it has such a wonderful reputation that the germ is removed and sold as a separate food. Wheat germ is very popular as a cereal or snack. Wheat germ oil, extracted from the germ, is considered one of the finest of the "health" oils.

— Y —

Yeast, Nutritional

Can you believe it? This yellow, flaky dried powder has a relationship to sprouts. Its connection? It comes from a live source. At the risk of making this valuable food sound unpalatable, the truth is that yeast is a living micro-organism that is grown on a food source such as molasses. Molasses grown yeast has a nutty flavor. The flavor can vary quite dramatically depending on the growing medium. Most yeasts, especially the kind used in baking, are very bitter. Seek out 'good tasting yeast' or 'molasses grown' yeast both of which would be indicated on the label. Yeast can also be used as a thickener, a topping for salads, and a flavoring agent for soups.

Broccoli Sprouts Prevent Cancer

   In a 1997 study by John Hopkins University scientists, broccoli contains glucoraphanin, a chemical that, when eaten, is converted by the body into sulforaphane—the strongest natural inducer of the body's own enzymes against carcinogens. According to Paul Talalay, Ph.D. the Hopkins pharmacologist: "In animals and human cells, we have demonstrated, unequivocally, that this compound can substantially reduce the incidence, rate of development and size of tumors." The scientists found that broccoli sprouts contain a concentration of glucoraphanin that is up to 50 times greater than the mature broccoli we buy at the grocer. The sprouts raise the levels of protective enzymes that seem to work on many kinds of precancerous cells, although statistics link broccoli mainly to a lowered risk for colon cancer. The National Cancer Institute has funded several human studies of the sprouts.

Final Words from the Food Guru

SWAMI SPROUTANANDA

The following was received by wireless transmission from the famous Swami at his retreat center on the top of Mount Germarest in the Herralayas.

Food. So much talk about food. Your excessive concentration on food is because you derive much of your pleasure from it. Food can be pleasurable, it is true. But real pleasure comes first from a pure heart. If your day is empty, you strive to fill that emptiness. As you add pleasure to your palate and warmth to your stomach, you are giving yourself the enjoyment you lack in your life. Let us be frank, food is one of the great temptations of this world and of the body. But too much of a good thing makes us sick. Yes? A belly ache is not pleasurable. Even if your belly was made of steel and you could put all the wonderful tasting foods of the world inside it, it would not solve your loneliness. Food will not supplant your search for love.

Really, humankind needs to eat very little. When you are fulfilled, you do not need to fill up! Now you are learning to eat wonderful, healthy foods. That is good because your body is the only "house" you have to live in for this life's journey. Keep it pure. But even the purest of foods can pollute when you overdo them. Eat like a mouse. One half of what you eat today is still much more than is necessary to nourish you. Lasting enjoyment does not come from food. Your troubles do not go away after a good meal. Happiness is not the absence of pain; it is the presence of love.

APPENDIX

Sprouting Beans & Grains
The Sprout Bag Method

a. Soak Your Seeds in a jar of Pure Water Overnight.
b. Pour Soaked Seeds into Moistened Sprout Bag.
c. Rinse and Hang Bag on Hook or Knob. Rinse Bag Simply by Immersing it in Water.
d. Rinse Twice per Day, No More Than 12 Hours Apart, for a Minimum of 30 Seconds.

SEED VARIETIES & NUMBER OF DAYS TO MATURE			
Easy for Beginners	*Days*	*Intermediate - Advanced*	*Days*
Lentil	4–5	Soybean	4
Red Pea or Adzuki	4–5	Hulled Sunflower	2
Mung	4–5	Peanut	7
Green Pea	4–5	Garbanzo	4
Hard Wheat	2–3	Chia	12
Soft Wheat	2–3	Spelt	3
Kamut	3–4	Rye	3

Sprout bags can germinate almost any kind of seed, but they are best suited for the grains and beans listed above. The left column consists of easy-to-grow varieties; the right is more difficult.

Avoid large beans such as lima, navy, kidney and black beans. They have low yields and spoil quickly. Oats, barley, rice and millet are commonly dehusked and will not sprout. Some packaged beans are sterilized. Roasted, salted and processed seeds will not sprout.

Alfalfa, radish, clover, fenugreek and other vegetable seeds can grow in a Sprout Bag, but because they are chlorophyll–developing plants, better results will be obtained using a vertical growing method in which the roots are anchored and the leaves climb straight up. *(See basket method, this chapter.)*

Preparation

Always examine your seeds for foreign debris and rinse them in cold water prior to soaking. Soak your new bag thoroughly in warm water prior to placing the pre-soaked seeds inside.

Soaking the Seeds

Soak your grains or beans in a quart jar or other container for 8–12 hours or overnight. Fill the jar nearly to the top with pure water. Add a few drops of liquid kelp for extra nutrition (optional). Then, pour the soaked seeds into the sprout bag. (Don't soak the seeds in the bag. Natural dye from the seed can stain the bag.) Rinse the seeds by immersing the bag in pure water.

Rinsing

Rinse your sprouts twice daily by immersing the bag in a pot or basin or just fill up your sink with pure water. Let it set for at least 30 seconds. You may use the same rinse water if you are working with more than one bag, but change the water as soon as it is discolored or dirty. Two rinsings per day is all you need, but a third is beneficial in hot weather or when working with large beans such as soybean and chick pea. Thorough washing prevents mold and fungus growth. Be faithful to your sprouts. Don't miss a rinsing. If you cannot be home, refrigerate them in the bag until you return or...take them with you!

As the sprouts grow, they may sink their roots into the weave of the sprout bag. The solution: *A Sprout Massage.* Grab the bag by the ends while under water and swish it around for a moment allowing the seeds to move freely inside the bag.

Draining

Hang your sprout bag to drain on a hook or knob. Small hooks are easy to install and the sprout bag stops dripping after only 1–2 minutes. If you prefer, you may lay the bag on a clean dish rack, dishwasher machine or oven rack. Always keep your bag in a medium-to-warm spot (70°–85°F) and away from drafts.

Nature Does the Rest

Now, the sprouts are tucked away in their comfortable natural fiber home. In just 3 to 6 days, they will be ready to eat *(see chart maturation times).* But don't skip out on your sprouts! Remember to rinse them twice per day.

How Much Seed?

A sprout bag sprouts 1–2½ cups of dry grains or beans depending on the size of the seed. Generally, sprouted grains and beans multiply 3 times their volume. As a rule, fill your bag to ¼–½ capacity with soaked seed, thus leaving room for expansion.

Merry Mixtures

Do sprouts sleep together? Is there a secret life of sprouts? Yes! Most seeds will readily co-habitate especially if they are from the same tribe and have the same maturation times. Try these proven combinations: *(Red pea can be substituted for adzuki.)*

COMBO I	COMBO II	COMBO III
½ cup Green Pea	½ cup Adzuki	¼ cup Mung
1 cup Lentil	½ cup Mung	1 cup Lentil
	½ cup Green Pea	¼ cup Adzuki

Light

Neither grains nor beans require darkness to grow indoors. Keep them in a neutral spot that is convenient for you. If you choose to grow fenugreek, alfalfa or other chlorophyll developing sprouts in your sprout bag, spread the top of the bag open during the final sprouting days for exposure to light.

Storage

Once mature, store your sprouts in the refrigerator right in the sprout bag. Rinse once every second or third day or often enough to keep the bag moist. If you need your sprout bag for starting the next batch, pour the sprouts into a glass or tupperware container with a lid. Plastic bags suffocate. Sprout bags breathe. They're great for storing vegetables, too. Generally, sprouts will keep for 7–14 days after maturity depending on variety and season. Refrigerate early in the hot summertime.

About Flax

The *Flax Sprout Bag* is so named because the material is made from the fibers of the flax plant. Flax also gives us linen. This special plant is today processed for fabric in only a few parts of the world. Flax is the strongest of all the vegetable fibers and is known for its high moisture absorbency. In fact, it has the unique quality of being 20% stronger when wet than dry. These characteristics make it superior to other fibers like cotton which shrinks, burlap which rots, or nylon which dries out. The flax fibers maintain their porosity for perfect drainage and aeration, and their strength for years of service.

Cleaning and Maintenance

It's easy. Empty your sprout bag and turn it inside out. Simple rinsing by hand with good water pressure is all that is necessary. Please do not use soap, bleach, hydrogen peroxide or a scrub brush on this material. If a batch goes sour, sterilize the bag in a pot of boiling water for 3–4 minutes. Then straighten the sterilized bag and let it hang dry. It is a good policy to sterilize if your sprouts smell sour or your water gets cloudy when rinsing. Boiling does not hurt the bag and avoids the transfer of bacteria from one crop to another.

Advanced Bean Sprouting

Peanuts, soybeans and chick peas (garbanzos) are all sproutable but require quality seed and conscientious rinsing. Cooking is recommended for these sprouted beans to sterilize any bad seed and increase their overall digestibility. Shelled sunflowers are easily sproutable but require a maximum growth of only two days. After that, seed that was damaged during the shelling process will commence to decay. Popcorn is the most sproutable variety of corn. However, it is extremely hard and as such has few uses. Chia, psyllium and cress are gelatinous seeds that require special handling.

For more information about sprouting, read *Sprouts the Miracle Food* by this author.

Sprouting Salad Greens

The Home-Made Basket Sprouter

Developed by Sproutman in 1977

Variety	# of TBSP	# of Days	Basket Size	Skill Req'd	General Description
Alfalfa	4–5	7	6 or 8 in	Beg.	Mild, all purpose
Clover	4–5	6–7	6 or 8 in	Beg.	Spicer cousin of alfalfa
Radish	2–3	5–6	6 inch	Beg.	Very radishy & hot
Garlic	2–3	12	6 inch	Adv.	Powerful garlic flavor
Onion	2–3	12	6 inch	Adv.	Rich onion flavor
Blk Sunflower	5–6	9–10	9 inch	Int.	Hearty texture & flavor
Red Pea	5–6	8–9	9 inch	Int.	Mild, big tall leaves
Buckwheat	5	10	9 inch	Adv.	Mild flavor, big leaf
Fenugreek	4–5	7–8	6 or 8 in	Beg.	Tall, healthy bitter herb
Cabbage	2–3	5–6	6 inch	Int.	Small size, rich flavor

Soaking

First, examine your seeds and remove any foreign matter. Wash your basket with soap and water and a vegetable brush. The recommended beginning varieties are Clover or Radish *(see chart above)*. Pour the seeds into a clean jar and add 1–2 cups of pure, cold water. Soak overnight (7–9 hours).

Rinsing — Your Most Important Task

Next, pour the seeds, water and all, into the appropriate size basket *(see chart)*. Rinse the seeds with cold water using the flexible spray hose attachment on your sink. If you do not have a built in sprayer, purchase a faucet spray adapter from your local hardware store.  It easily connects to the end of your faucet.

Shower your seeds and your baskets with good water pressure for approximately 10 seconds. Good rinsing with strong water pressure washes away fungi-mold and mildew. Do not rinse with a regular faucet. Their insufficient coverage will help create mold. Leave the bed of seeds even and level after rinsing.

Draining

Baskets need to be held at an angle in order to properly drain. Hold the basket by the rim for 5–10 seconds or until it stops dripping. A slight swinging motion sheds excess moisture. (Don't swing away your seeds!) Or drain your baskets in a dishrack or dishwasher rack.

Life is a Greenhouse...for a Sprout

If you're a sprout, nothing could be finer than growing up in a warm, moist greenhouse. The greenhouse envelops the basket like a tent with the open end tucked  underneath. (It does not have to be 100% airtight.)

The tent can be a heavy duty plastic bag or other enclosure tall enough to allow 4–8 inches of air space above the growing sprouts. Without a greenhouse, part of your crop may dehydrate or decay.

Harvest Time

These special leafy green sprouts are at their nutritional peak when the leaf develops a clef (divides in two) and drops its shell or hull. Harvest time is when 90% of the crop is hull-free. Grab your mini-vegetables by the tops and wiggle them out, roots and all. Rinse to remove any remaining hulls. (Hulls are not harmful, but can detract from the taste.) With sprouts, you can eat the whole plant including the roots which have never touched soil!

Advanced Immersion Rinsing

This method is fast and easy but is only possible when the roots are securely anchored into the basket (approximately 4 days for alfalfa and clover). First, check that lots of rootlets show through the underside of the basket. Then, fill your sink, bowl or pot with pure water. Dip the entire basket in for a total bath. Once the sprouts are securely anchored, you can even turn the basket upside down and nothing will fall out except...the fallen seed jackets. This is the best method for the cleaning and removing seed hulls. Hulls are dead matter that can decay and cause root rot and mildew. Cleaning the hulls keeps your sprouts healthy and beautiful. Fresh hulls, however, are simply vegetable fiber similar to bran, and although they can detract from the flavor of the sprouts, they are not harmful to eat. The inversion method is the fastest and most thorough method for rinsing away the hulls. Leave your sprouts under for about 10 seconds, then drain and set in the greenhouse.

Storage

Store your mature sprouts in the refrigerator for up to two weeks (depending on variety). Remove the mature sprouts from the basket, wash and set them in a glass or plastic container with a lid. Do not store in plastic bags. They suffocate live sprouts. Or, you may refrigerate the sprouts in the basket enveloped in the greenhouse. Store your dry seeds in a jar with a moisture proof lid. If kept cool and dry, most seeds will last several years.

About Water and Light

Use pure water whenever possible, especially during the soaking stage. While washing and bathing your sprouts, always change the water if it gets cloudy or dirty. Normal daylight is all you need to develop green-looking sprouts. Caution: too much direct sunlight may overheat your crop in a small greenhouse, especially in hot weather.

Cleaning Your Basket

Wash your baskets with plain water using a natural bristle vegetable brush. Let your basket and brush dry out completely, then brush out any remaining rootlets. They flake off easily. Sterilize your baskets periodically by boiling them in water for 2–3 minutes. Use diluted Clorox bleach or bleach alternatives such as hydrogen peroxide (environmentally superior) to brighten baskets that have become stained from age, seed dye or mildew.

Advanced Seeds

Buckwheat sprouts are delicious but require lots of labor to removed the seed jackets from the delicate leaves. They grow best in soil and sunshine. Sunflower is much easier to grow hydroponically. The shells fall off automatically when using the black sprouting grade seed. Good seed is imperative for successful garlic and onion sprouting. Store in a cool, dry place. They take a long 12–14 days to mature and are more perishable than the others.

For more information about sprouting, read *Sprouts the Miracle Food* by this author.

SPROUT CHART

Variety	Cups TBSP	# of Days	Method	Skill Req.	Comments
Alfalfa	4–5T	7	Vertical	Beg.	Mild, all purpose salad
Clover	4–5T	6–7	Vertical	Beg.	Spicer cousin of alfalfa
Broccoli	2–3T	6	Vertical	Beg.	Rich broccoli flavor, potent
Radish	2–3T	5–6	Vertical	Beg.	Very radish
Garlic chives	2–3T	12	Vertical	Adv.	Powerful garlic flavor
Onion	2–3T	12	Vertical	Adv.	Very onion
Blk Sunflower	5–6T	9–10	Vertical	Int.	Popular texture hearty flavor
Stripe Sunflwr	5–6T	9–10	Vertical	Int.	Bigger but lots of shells
Red Pea	5–6T	8–9	Vertical	Int.	Mild, 8-10" tall, big leaves
Buckwheat	5T	10	Vertical	Adv.	Succulent, big leaf, lots shells
Fenugreek	4–5T	7–8	Vertical	Beg.	Tall green healthy bitter herb
Cabbage	2–3T	5–6	Vertical	Int.	Small, very cabbage taste
Lentil	1 cup	4–5	Bag/Jar	Beg.	Salads or steamed veggie
Adzuki	1 cup	4–5	Bag/Jar	Int.	Cousin of mung & red pea
Mung	1 cup	4–5	Bag/Jar	Int.	Salads or steamed veggie
Green Pea	1+cup	4–5	Bag/Jar	Beg.	Very popular & easy
Pea Shoots	5–6T	8–9	Vertical	Int.	Mild, 8" tall and leafy
Hard Wheat	2 cup	2–3	Bag/Jar	Beg.	Wheatgrass or sprout bread
Soft Wheat	2 cup	2–3	Bag/Jar	Beg.	Rejuvelac or sprout cookies
Kamut	2 cup	3–4	Bag/Jar	Beg.	Wheatgrass or sprout bread
Soybean	2 cup	4	Bag	Adv.	For cooking, casseroles
Hull'd Sunflwr	1 cup	2	Bag/Jar	Int.	Delicious snack, perishable
Peanut	2 cup	7	Bag	Adv.	Fabulous dry roasted snack
Garbanzo	2 cup	4	Bag/Jar	Adv.	Cook for dips and spreads
Chia	3–5T	12	Vertical	Adv.	Gelatinous. Grow with alfalfa
Spelt or Rye	1 cup	3	Bag/Jar	Beg.	Sprout bread

Personality Traits

of Common Foods

Food is more than its nutrition. Scientists are now finding that what you eat can affect your disposition. Nature endows food with many qualities other than vitamins. For example, sprouts make you laugh. They are adorable, wiggly and tickle your insides. Stone fruit, on the other hand, weighs you down. Horseradish is electrifying. The prudent choice is to be fully informed The following chart is designed to help you watch what you eat in order to avoid unexpected results.

Angel Hair	*Saintly*	Prunes	*Gushy*
Cucumber	*Cool*	Succotash	*Mushy*
Crépe	*Sophisticated*	Half and Half	*Uncertain*
Jelly	*Nervous*	Maize	*Corny*
Curry	*Impatient*	Fudge	*Deceitful*
Mexican Beans	*Restless*	Pepper	*Irritable*
Sausage	*Obnoxious*	Gum	*Stickler*
Cottage Cheese	*Homey*	Flapjack	*Unflappable*
Bologna	*Unbelievable*	Cinnamon	*Sinful*
Shish Kebab	*Punctual*	Gooseberries	*Ticklish*
Lard	*Galling*	Cayenne	*Fiery*
Buttermilk	*Two-timer*	Tomato	*Sexy*
Eggplant	*Confused*	Margarine	*Impostor*
Breadfruit	*Ambidexterous*	Wine	*Cordial*
Shellfish	*Evasive*	Espresso	*Fidgety*
Cheddar	*Untrustworthy*	Elderberry	*Wise*
Ham	*Clownish*	Bagels	*Holy*
Dandelion	*Ferocious*	Gorgonzola	*Scary*
Tabasco	*Zesty*	Pine Nut	*Sorrowful*

A Sample Daily Diet for the
SPROUTARIAN

BEFORE BREAKFAST
Water

BREAKFAST
Fruit, Juice or Green Smoothie

LUNCH
Salad, nuts/seeds,
or just Liquids

DINNER
Salad, Grain
Juices, Liquids

AFTER DINNER
Fruit
Liquids

ALL DAY
Fresh Air & Pure Water

NUTRIENTS IN SPROUTS					
Mineral Content of Fresh Sprouted Beans vs. Other Vegetarian Foods					
Milligrams per 100 grams edible portion [19]					
	CALC	IRON	MAG	PHOS	POT
ALFALFA	32	0.96	27	70	79
RADISH	51	0.86	44	113	86
MUNG	13	0.91	21	54	149
LENTIL	25	3.1	37	173	322
GREEN PEA	36	2.26	65	165	381
SOYBEAN	67	2.1	72	164	484
NAVY PEA	15	1.93	101	100	307
POTATOES	5	0.35	25	50	391
SPINACH	58	0.8	39	28	130
MILK	119	0.05	13	93	152
EGGS	56	2.09	12	180	130
LETTUCE	36	1.1	6	45	290
Values represent fresh sprouted beans with 70%-95% water content. Milk is whole with 3.5% fat. New Zealand spinach. Calc=calcium, Mag=magnesium, Phos=phosphorus, Pot=potassium.					

Protein: Comparison Of Lettuce & Sprouts			
Nutrients in sprouts: Protein in grams per 100 gram portion.[19]			
COMMON LETTUCE		SPROUTS	
0.9	Iceberg	4	Alfalfa Sprouts
1.3	Cos, Looseleaf	4	Sunflower Sprouts
1.6	Romaine Lettuce	3.8	Radish Sprouts
1.7	New Zeal Spinach	3.1	Mung Sprouts
All values are for fresh produce and fresh sprouts.			

Selected Nutrient Comparison of
Alfalfa & Radish Sprouts vs. Whole Milk & Raw Egg

Milligrams per 100 grams edible portion [19]
Values are for fresh sprouts, whole milk with 3.3% fat and raw egg. Calories=kilocalories.

NUTRIENTS		ALFALFA	RADISH	MILK	EGG
Water	grams	91.14	90.07	87.99	74.57
Calories	kcal	29	41	61	158
Protein	grams	3.99	3.81	3.29	12.14
Fat	grams	0.69	2.53	3.34	11.15
Carbohydrate	grams	3.78	3.06	4.66	1.2
Fiber	grams	1.64	0.53	0	0
MINERALS					
Calcium	mg	32	51	119	56
Iron	mg	0.96	0.86	0.05	2.09
Magnesium	mg	27	44	1.3	12
Phosphorus	mg	70	113	93	180
Potassium	mg	79	86	152	130
Sodium	mg	6	6	49	138
Zinc	mg	0.92	0.56	0.38	1.44
Copper	mg	0.16	0.12	-.-	-.-
Manganese	mg	0.19	0.26	-.-	-.-
VITAMINS					
Ascorbic Acid	mg	8.2	28.9	0.94	0
Thiamin	mg	0.08	0.1	0.04	0.09
Riboflavin	mg	0.13	0.1	0.16	0.3
Niacin	mg	0.48	2.85	0.08	0.06
Pantothenic	mg	0.56	0.73	0.31	1.73
Vitamin B6	mg	0.03	0.29	0.04	0.12
Folacin	mcg	36	94.7	5	65
Vitamin A	IU	155	391	126	520

SPROUT HISTORY LESSON

The Dark Ages	*The Modern Age*
## THE JAR	## THE SPROUT BAG

Never designed for sprouting. Cumbersome. Requires cheesecloth, rubber bands, screens or lids.

Made for sprouting. Convenient. Made from durable flax fibers. Discovered by Sproutman circa 1979.

Difficult to transport. Breakage accidents ruin crop. Takes up space.

Great for traveling, camping, boating. Lightweight, unbreakable. Holds 3/4 gallon of sprouts.

Won't sprout many vegetables, large beans and gelatinous seeds (like chia).

Sprouts everything. All grains, beans and gelatinous seeds.

Poor air circulation. Narrow opening limits air.

All sprouts get air. Good circulation prevents mold.

Incomplete drainage. Mold develops in stagnant water.

100% drainage without tilting or waiting. Never collects water.

Stagnant air & water promote mold. Cheesecloth top collects bacteria.

Flax won't shrink or mold like cotton, burlap or cheesecloth.

Time consuming. 3 steps. Fill up, pour out, tilt at an angle, drain.

Convenient. 2 steps. Dip in water, hang on hook or knob or lay in dish rack.

Takes up precious shelf and refrigerator space. Fixed size. Difficult to get hands in and out.

Saves counter and refrigerator space. Bags expand or contract with volume. Wide opening.

Day 1

Rinse your pre-soaked seeds twice daily with a spray faucet. Good water pressure helps cleanse seeds in addition to moistening them.

Day 2

In only 1–2 days, these red peas start to send out roots. Their greenhouse home stands in the background.

Day 5

The growing tray lives in the greenhouse from the very first day. Greenhouses maintain the warmth and moisture the seedlings require for healthy growth.

Day 8

Mature 'pea lettuce' grows up to 10 inches tall. You can eat the whole plant—roots and all, or just eat the tops. Harvested sprouts can store for 1–2 weeks in the refrigerator.

FOOTNOTES

[1] *Vegetarianism—A Way of Life*, by Dudley Giehl. Barnes and Noble (Harper & Row) 1981.

[2] *Handbook of Livestock Management Techniques*, by Battaglia and Mayrose, Burgiss Publishers, 1981.

[3] *Radical Vegetarianism* – by Mark Mathew Braunstein. P.O. Box 474, Quaker Hill, CT 06375

[4] *The Effects on Human Health of Subtherapeutic Use of Anti–microbials in Animal Feeds.* National Academy of Sciences, 1980, p.8.

[5] *The New Vegetarian*, by Gary Null. Dell, New York, 1979. *The Science of Providing Milk for Man*, by J.R. Campbell and R.T. Marshall. McGraw–Hill, New York. 1975, p.137.

[6] *On Raising All–Natural Beef*, by Bill Keller. The New York Times, Wednesday October 31, 1984.

[7] *Sprout For The Love Of Everybody, Nutritional Evaluation of Sprouts and Grasses*, by Victor Kulvinskas, M.S. 21st Century Publications, Fairfield, IA. 1978.

[8] *Nutrient Content of Germinated Seeds.* Dr. Jeffrey Bland, Ph.D and Barbara Berquist. Chemistry Department, University of Puget Sound, Tacoma, WA. Journal of The John Bastyr College of Naturopathic Medicine, Vol.2, No.1, June 1980.

[9]   *Natural Living Newsletter*, Box 849, Madison Square Station, New York, NY 10159. Volume I, Number 7, page 4.

[10] *Effects on Human Health of Sub–therapeutic Antimicrobials in Animal Feeds.* National Academy of Sciences, 1980, p.22.

[11] *Fact Sheet Issue No. 24.* Food Animal Concerns Trust, Box 14599, Chicago, IL 60614.

[12] *The Pesticide Jungle*, by Laura Tallian, El Cajon, California.

[13] Food and Drug Administration, News Release, Febuary 22, 1956. *The New Vegetarian*, by Gary Null. Dell, New York, 1979.

[14] *Nutrient Content of Foods*, By H.B.U. Inc. Box 363, Hermosa Beach, CA 90254.

      Composition and Facts about Foods, by Ford Heritage. Health Research, 70 Lafayette Street, Mokelumne Hill, CA 95245

      Nutritive Value of Foods, Bulletin #72. U.S. Dept of Agriculture. Supt. of Documents. U.S. Gov't Printing Office, Wash. D.C. 20402

[15] *Dr. Ann Wigmore's Complete Live Food Program*, by Dr. Ann Wigmore. Hippocrates Press, 25 Exeter St., Boston, MA 02116

[16] *Naturama Living Textbook*, by Dr. Ann Wigmore. Ann Wigmore Foundation, 26 Exeter St., Boston, MA 02116. 617–267–9525.

[17] *Science and Culture*, 1958. Nandi, D.S., "Studies on the changes of free amino acids and B–vitamin content of some leguminous seeds during germination." p. 23, 659.

[18] *Journal of American Medical Association*, by Maurizio Trevisa, M.D. Univeristy of Buffalo Medical School, NY. Feb. 2, 1990.

[19] *Composition of Foods, Handbook #8*, 1963. by B.K. Watt, A.L. Merrill, & *Handbook #8–20 Cereal Grains*, rev. 1989, D.L. Drake, S.E. Gebhardt, R.H. Matthews. U.S. Dept. of Agriculture, Human Nutrition Information Service.

RESOURCES

Where to Go to Get More Information

For additional sources, visit www.Sproutman.com

Seed Sources

Natural Food Stores. Packaged seeds are superior to bulk seeds because the latter lose germination from exposure to the elements. Better still are brands that specify their devotion to sprouting or include a germination count on the label. If you see a packaged seed that is not on *Sproutman's 'turn-the-dial' Sprout Chart* or the chart in the appendix of this book, it is probably not dependable for sprouting.

The author tests a full line of sprouting grade seeds called *Sproutman's Organic Sprouting Seeds.* They can be found in health food stores or via mail order 800-695-2241 or at www.Sproutman.com

Johnny's Selected Seeds. 207-437-4357, fax 800-437-4290. RR 1, Box 2580, Foss Hill Rd, Albion, ME 04910. Large selection of organic garden and sprouting seeds. www.Johnnyseeds.com

The Sprout House. 718-544-6858, fax 718-575-8570. East Meredith, NY. Organic sprouting seeds. Originally founded by Sproutman in 1980. Now independently owned and operated. www.SproutHouse.com.

Sproutpeople. 877-777-6887, 608-637-6500, fax 608-637-6520. 311 South Main Street, Viroqua, WI 54665. Full line of organic sprouting seeds. www.sproutpeople.com

Sun Organic Farm. 888-269-9888, fax 760-751-1141. PO Box 2429, Valley Center, CA 92082. Organic foods, seeds. www.sunorganic.com

Organic Provisions. 800-490-0044. fax 215-443-7087. PO Box 756, Richboro, PA 18954. Mail order & internet supplier of natural foods including sprouting seeds. www.Goodeats.com

Handy Pantry. 800-735-0630, 480-967-4338, fax 480-921-4232. 2226 S. Coconino Drive, Apache Junction, AZ 85220. Organic sprouting seeds and health products. www.handypantry.com

Optimum Health Institute. 619-464-3346. See *Healing Retreats.*

Walton Feed. 800-847-0465. P.O. Box 307, Montpelier, ID 83254. Food storage specialist. Sprouting seeds. www.waltonfeed.com

Healing Retreats for Sprouts & Raw Foods

Optimum Health Institute - San Diego. 800-993-4325 reservations. Tel. 619-464-3346, Fax 619-589-4098. 6970 Central Avenue, Lemon Grove, CA 91945-2198. www.optimumhealth.org

Optimum Health Institute - Austin, Texas. 800-993-4325, Reservations. Tel. 512-303-4817, Fax: 512-332-0106. Rt. 1, Box 339-J Cedar Lane, Cedar Creek, TX 78612

Tree of Life Center. Gabriel Cousens, MD. PO Box 1080, Patagonia, AZ 85624. 520-394-2520, fax 520-394-2099. Spiritual, eco-retreat center with organic Kosher live-food cuisine, plenty of sprouts and wheatgrass. Private consultations with renowned medical doctor and author. Also juice fasting retreats. www.treeoflife.nu

Ann Wigmore Institute - Puerto Rico. PO Box 429, Rincon, PR 00677. 787-868-6307, fax 787-868-2430. www.AnnWigmore.org

Ann Wigmore Foundation. PO Box 399, San Fidel, NM 87049. 505-552-0595, fax 505-552-0595. www.wigmore.org

Hippocrates Health Centre of Australia. Elaine Ave, Mudgeeraba 4213, Gold Coast, Queensland, Australia, for brochure. Tel (07) 5530-2860. Ann Wigmore inspired live-in training program for fasting, wheatgrass, juices and raw foods

Hippocrates Health Institute. 561-471-8876, fax 561-471-9464. 1443 Palmdale Ct., West Palm Beach, FL 33411. www.hippocratesinst.com

All Life Sanctuary. 800-927-2527 ext 00205, fax 501-760-1492. PO Box 2853, Hot Springs, AR 71914. Hosted by wheatgrass pioneer Rev. Viktoras Kulvinskas, MS. www.naturalUSA.com/viktor/sanctuary.html

General

Sproutman. The author gives private consultations on health, healing, diet and fasting. Tel. 413-528- 5200, fax 413-528-5201. E-mail: Sproutman@Sproutman.com Website: www.Sproutman.com

Loreta's Living Foods. Consultations on living foods and wheatgrass therapy by an experienced teacher who worked with Dr. Ann Wigmore. Tel. 610-648-0241

Rhio's Raw Energy Hotline. 212-343-1152. A raw/live foods help line and resource directory of classes and events in the New York metro area and beyond. Ask for Rhio's new raw foods cookbook.

San Francisco Live Food Enthusiasts. The *Sproutline* 415-751-2806. San Francisco, CA. Telephone help line and listing of live foods potlucks, lectures and outings in the San Francisco area.

RawTimes. An excellent website resource for testimonials, e-mail forums, recipes, restaurant reviews, networking, events and book reviews on living foods diet. www.rawtimes.com

Food Grade Hydrogen Peroxide [H_2O_2] in non-hazardous 6% concentrated form but made from original 35% concentrate. Contact: *The Family News.* 800-284-6263. 305-759-9500. 9845 NE Second Ave, Miami, FL 33138. www.familyhealthnews.com

International Sprout Growers Association. Professional trade association for commercial sprout and grass growers worldwide. 800-572-3015, fax 206-367-8777. www.ISGA-Sprouts.org

Manufacturers

Tribest, Inc. 888-254-7336, fax 562-623-7160. Manufacturers of the Freshlife Automatic Sprouter. www.Freshlife.com

Seed & Grain Technologies. 113 Alvarado Drive NE, Albuquerque, NM 87108. 702-869-4662, fax 702-920-8717. www.easygreen.com Manufacturers of hydroponic wheatgrass and sprout growers.

International Specialty Supply (ISS). 820 East 20 Street, Cookeville, TN 38501. 800-277-7688. fax 615-526-8338. Manufacturer of large scale commercial sprout farming equipment. Line of non-organic sprouting seeds. For professionals only. www.sproutnet.com

Miracle Exclusives, Inc. PO Box 8, Port Washington, NY 11050. 800-645-6360, fax 516-621-1997. Makers of a full line of electric and manual wheatgrass juicers. www.MiracleExclusives.com

Omega Juicers. 800-633-3401, fax 717-561-1298. PO Box 4523, Harrisburg, PA 17111. www.omegajuicers.com

The Green Power Juicer. 888-254-7336. Downey, CA 90241. Also Green Life Juicer. www.greenpower.com

L'Equip. 555 Bolser Ave., Harrisburg, PA 17043. 800-816-6811. 717-730-7100, fax 717-730-7200. www.lequip.com

Other Books

Living in the Raw. Recipes for a Healthy Lifestyle by Rose Lee Calabro. www.rawlivingfoods.com tel. 831-768-7400

Warming Up to Living Foods by Elysa Markowitz. $15.95. Raw foods, vegan recipes. ISBN 1-57067-065x

The Sprout Garden by Mark Braunstein. Includes sprouting information and recipes. $12.95. ISBN 1-57067-073-0.

Survival Into the 21st Century. by Rev. Viktoras Kulvinskas, MS. PO Box 2853 Hot Springs, AR 71914. Also **Sprout for the Love of Every Body** by Viktoras. Both available through *Twenty First Century Press*, Fairfield, IA 52556. Tel. 515-472-5105, fax 515-472-8443.

The Hippocrates Diet. by Ann Wigmore. Published by Avery Publishing Group, Garden City Park, NY 11040. 800-548-5757.

RECIPE LIST

Cheeses, Yoghurts, Ice Creams

Recipes From The Food Dehydrator

Salads & Salad Dressings

Dressings & Sauces

Soup, Juice, Soda Pop, Beverages

Low Cooking

LIST OF CHARTS

GLOSSARY OF FOODS

Who Is This Sproutman?

Steve Meyerowitz began his journey to better health in 1975 to correct a lifelong chronic condition of severe allergies and asthma. After two months of eating a raw foods–vegetarian diet, his symptoms disappeared. Steve endured 20 years of disappointment with conventional medicine before he restored his health through his own program of purification, lifestyle adjustment, exercise, fasting, juicing and living foods.

Over the years, he has lived on and experimented with many so called 'extreme' diet/lifestyles including raw foods, fruitarianism, sprouts, dairy and flourless vegetarianism and fasting. In 1977, he was pronounced "Sproutman" by *Vegetarian Times Magazine* in a feature article that explored his innovative sprouting ideas and recipes.

After 10 years as a music and comedy entertainer, he made a complete lifestyle change for his health. In 1980, he opened *The Sprout House*, a "no-cooking school" in New York City. There, he began a formal program of teaching kitchen gardening and the preparation of gourmet sprouted and vegetarian foods. Steve has invented two home sprouters, the *Flax Sprout Bag* and the *Kitchen Garden Salad Grower*. He founded the Sprout House, a company supplying home growing kits and organic sprouting seeds.

Steve has been featured on the *Home Shopping Network, TV Food Network,* in *Prevention, Organic Gardening* and *Flower & Garden Magazines.* In 3 minutes on QVC, 953 people ordered his Cookbook and Salad Grower.

Steve and his family, including three little sprouts, now live and breathe the fresher air of the Berkshire mountains.

Other Books

by Steve Meyerowitz

**Sproutman's
Sprout Chart**

**Wheatgrass
Nature's Finest Medicine**

**Food Combining
& Digestion**

**Juice Fasting
& Detoxification**

**Sprouts
The Miracle Food**